The Poetry of George Herbert

The Elixir, from the Williams manuscript,
with revisions in Herbert's hand

THE POETRY OF

George Herbert

HELEN VENDLER

HARVARD UNIVERSITY PRESS

*Cambridge, Massachusetts
and
London, England*

1975

To Morton Berman

> *Literae hoc debent tibi*
> *Queîs me educasti.*

Acknowledgments

Douglas Bush and the late Rosemond Tuve were, among my teachers, those whose attachment to Herbert reassured my own.

I am grateful to the American Philosophical Society, the Boston University Graduate School, the American Council of Learned Societies, and the Guggenheim Foundation for grants aiding in the composition of this book; and to Professors Morton Berman, Harold Bloom, Marie Borroff, Reuben Brower, and Douglas Bush for sponsoring me for those grants.

The frontispiece appears by the kind permission of the Librarian of Dr. Williams's Library, London, and of the Renaissance English Text Society, which will reproduce the Williams manuscript in facsimile.

Chapters 1 and 2 have been previously published, in *Ariel* 1 (April 1970), pp. 54–70, and in *Forms of Lyric,* ed. Reuben Brower (New York: Columbia University Press, 1970). Permission to reprint is gratefully acknowledged.

Contents

The Poetry of George Herbert

Introduction

George Herbert's poems, praised in his own time and resurrected in the nineteenth century after general neglect, have been valued during three centuries chiefly for their piety, a piety thought to be exemplary and therefore, by an excusable logic, necessarily unremarkable in thought and sentiment, however finely structured and however charming or precise in phrasing. Herbert's subjects are such traditional ones that it might seem idle to inquire into what he actually says, the repertory of proper devotional responses being thought so limited. And so it has been to Herbert's Christian sources, or to his debts of style, or to his inventiveness in fertile variation on a known theme that his commentators have tended to turn.

The enthusiasm for Donne at the beginning of this century worked to Herbert's disadvantage. Paul Elmer More, for instance, in 1906 relegated Herbert to the status of a humble imitator: "There is nothing of the eagle in Herbert, nothing of the soaring quality which lifted Donne out of the common sphere . . . nothing of that originality which makes of Donne one of the few real turning-points in our literature. Herbert was content to look up at that dizzy height and follow with humbler wing."[1]

Later, in his influential anthology of metaphysical poetry, Herbert Grierson offered somewhat complacently a comparable view of Herbert: "If not a greatly imaginative, Herbert is a sincere and sensitive poet, and an accomplished artist elaborating his argumentative strain or little allegories and conceits with felicitous completeness, and managing his variously patterned stanzas . . . with a finished and delicate harmony."[2]

Grierson added, rather gratuitously, that Herbert stood to Vaughan as fancy ("the sensitive and happy discovery of analogies") to imagination. Even Herbert's devoted editor, George Herbert Palmer, who knew Herbert's verse more intimately than Grierson or More, felt he must apologize for his "minor poet": "Whoever . . . values literary history will be glad to seek out the gentle and incomplete poet, be willing for a while to dwell dispassionately in his narrow surroundings."[3]

The "originality" Palmer conceded to Herbert is chiefly metrical and structural, and assuming the orthodoxy of Herbert's sentiments, Palmer chose to dwell rather on Herbert's aptness in suiting form to matter. These critics, whatever their modesty of claim, are among those few who attempted to judge Herbert as an artist rather than as a guide for the Anglican perplexed. Though their sobriety is welcome after the undiscriminating praise given Herbert in nineteenth-century ecclesiastical journals, still their uncertainty about his worth, especially by comparison with that of Donne, suggests that they were unaware of many of Herbert's poetic virtues.

It was probably the praise of T. S. Eliot that won for Herbert a serious reading from later twentieth-century critics. Yet Eliot's advocacy, like that of other recent commentators (Joseph Summers, Rosemond Tuve, and W. H. Auden among them), seemed prompted as much by religious sympathy as by aesthetic motives, and in spite of Eliot's remark that Herbert's poetry "is definitely an *oeuvre, to be studied entire,*"[4] that study has not yet been made. An unawareness of the variety within Herbert's apparently narrow range may account for the general unwillingness among critics to enter into detail about more than a few poems. Because these are several books and many articles devoted to Herbert, scattered remarks on his art are not wanting, nor are special studies of technical aspects of that art—his prosody, his puns, his titles, his fondness for certain grammatical constructions, his adaptation of hymn forms. But in such special studies of technical topics the wholeness of single poems is disregarded and Herbert's larger arts of construction and disposition and invention are ignored.

The aim of this book is to treat nearly all of Herbert's lyrics, and the poems that receive no commentary here are those that may be understood in the light of other poems treated or, in some cases, poems before which I found myself at a loss for words. I take for granted the work of earlier critics—the annotations of Canon Hutchinson, the contexts described by Summers, the iconographical allusions pointed out by Tuve, the puns and over verbal idiosyncrasies identified by Mary Ellen Rickey, the poetic strategies recounted by Stanley Fish. My hope is to establish, in the case of each poem discussed, what Herbert is saying (in all the complexity so rarely granted him) and the order and purpose of his utterance. Besides a number of readings, I include comparisons of Herbert with certain imitators and adapters of his verse, in order to point out what he possesses above and beyond devotional feelings, metrical invention, and emblematic interests. I also suggest which lyrical genres Herbert found most congenial, marking out his range within a given genre as well as his individual use of its conventions.

Although Herbert has too often been read superficially, it is reassuring to find that those most attached to his poetry have recently seemed to be protesting this superficiality in concert. The entire critical effort devoted to Herbert's work in the last two decades may be seen as a cooperative venture in learning to read him with greater attention. Nevertheless, in spite of their separate restorations of value, the studies by Summers, Tuve, Rickey, Fish and Arnold Stein discuss relatively few poems in aesthetic as well as moral terms, and only Stein's book aims at comprehensiveness of description.[5] I begin this book polemically with a deliberately detailed reading of one of Herbert's shortest and most famous poems, *Vertue* (I could as easily have begun with the readings of *Love* (III) or *Heaven* or *The Flower* that occur later in the book; it is only the principle of Herbert's depth that I wish to assert). To read Herbert less attentively is to miss many of his dimensions. Though it is impossible to continue throughout a whole book in such detail, I wish at least to establish as a principle that Herbert's apparent simplicity is deceptive.

The second chapter is also a polemic one, asserting that Herbert's poems, even those which seem most serene, often do not proceed tranquilly on their way but suffer abrupt changes of direction—changes differing from similar ones in other poets by being relatively invisible, since they bear no signals like "nevertheless" or "but" or "yet" which usually mark an alteration in perspective. Herbert's method in these poems is one of tacit accretion of successive (and often conflicting) points of view, with the principle of accretion often masking the conflicts, making these poems

3

sometimes seem blander than they are.[6] I wish to show that Herbert also provides inventive transformations of the original *donnée* of a poem, whether it be a passage of Scripture, a liturgical prayer, a feast, a ritual, or a hymn.

Subsequent chapters take up Herbert's use of characteristic genres: allegorical and emblematic poems, liturgical and homiletic poems, discursive and speculative poems, and finally the famous poems of personal experience. These genres of course overlap. Sometimes there is a developmental point to be made, and when possible, I have pointed out changes of attitude or emphasis between earlier and later poems, but my chief emphasis is not on development but on the remarkable consistency of Herbert's work. I have wished to show his entire range, his failures as well as his successes.

Herbert's poetry is as valuable to those who share none of his religious beliefs as to those who share them all. In saying this, I differ with Coleridge and with Eliot, both of whom believed that Christians made the best readers of Herbert. "You will not get much satisfaction from George Herbert unless you can take seriously the things which he took seriously himself and which made him what he was," said Eliot.[7] Coleridge's formulation is even more categorical: "To appreciate this volume, it is not enough that the reader possesses a cultivated judgment, classical taste, or even poetic sensibility, unless he be likewise a *Christian,* and both a zealous and an orthodox, both a devout and a *devotional,* Christian. But even this will not quite suffice. He must be an affectionate and dutiful child of the Church . . . religion is the element in which he lives, and the region in which he moves."[8]

Coleridge has been disproved, if only by time, but in offering a reading of Herbert which sees as the primary subject of his poems the workings of his own mind and heart rather than the expression of certain religious beliefs, I hope not to falsify his work, which though it uses a range of ideas and symbols peculiar to the Christian religion, is not thereby limited in meaning to any dogmatic content, nor dependent for its aesthetic success on a reader's assent to any of the religious premises it embodies. I even hope that Herbert may be better served when he is studied by one not sharing his beliefs, resting that hope on Housman's remark that "good religious poetry, whether in Keble or Dante or Job, is likely to be most justly appreciated and most discriminately relished by the undevout."⁹

The implicit views of poetry and poetic procedures underlying this book arise from reflection on Herbert's work. In my emphasis on coherence, order, and resolution in the poetry I am following Herbert himself, whose own sense of structure was, as Palmer noted, exceptionally strong. In inquiring closely into Herbert's language, I am only recalling that Herbert, as a student of classical languages and rhetoric, probably had a consciousness of his own desired effects far more acute than that which appears even in my most detailed reconstructions. It is scarcely credible that anyone could attribute to him more subtlety than he possessed. An expressive theory of poetry suits *The Temple* best: no matter how exquisitely written a poem by Herbert is in its final form, it seems usually to have begun in experience, and aims at recreating or recalling that experience. To approach such private poetry as an exercise in public communication with an audience is to misconstrue its emphasis. If the gist of Walton's report in his *Life* of Herbert is correct (and it accords with the development of Herbert's verse), to give "a picture of . . . many spiritual conflicts" was Herbert's essential intent, and the notion of a "dejected poor soul['s]" deriving comfort from the poems arose only subsequent to composition. My care in examining Herbert's art will, I hope, prevent my appearing to take poetry as the equivalent of life, but I do not think that there is significant help to be had in understanding Herbert by invoking theories of poetry that detach artifact, as a system of formal signs, from lived experience recreated in a mimetic form of speech.

No new generalizations about Herbert are proposed in this book. History has established the canon of his best poems (though I suggest a few new inclusions), and history has, at least since Coleridge, given him his due as one of the purest and most ravishing of English poets. He has yet to be ranked, as I believe he deserves to be ranked, higher than Donne; but such rankings are always disputable, as extension is measured against intensity, or intellectuality against feeling, or historical precedence over finish.¹⁰ History has praised in Herbert many of the aspects I praise in these papers: his extraordinarily complete perception of his own moods, his felicity in describing the most tenuous feelings, his freshness in religious discourse, even what Empson calls his "saintly impertinence."[11] These are all central qualities, and everyone who has read *The Temple* will recognize them. What I am more concerned to show, as one can do only in meditating on single cases, is the depth of poetic resource discovered by Herbert, his resolute unwillingness to take the world for granted, his fixed intention to plumb every appearance for its significant and original reality, his willingness, as he put it, to thrust his mind into whatever nourished it in order to find out the ingredients of that nourishment. Though such an intention implies intellectual work of a high order, I cannot agree with Palmer (who linked Herbert rather too strongly with Donne) that the poetry of Herbert is strongly and even overly intellectual. Herbert is quick to reject his own tendency to intellectualize life, as poems like *The Elixir* show, and though he was capable of unparalleled intellectual elegance, he rarely forgot, in his poetry, the advice he gave to the parson preaching: "He is not witty, or learned, or eloquent, but Holy. [This] Character . . . is gained, first, by choosing texts of Devotion, not Controversie, moving and ravishing texts, whereof the Scriptures are full. Secondly, by dipping, and seasoning all our words and sentences in our hearts, before they come into our mouths."[12]

Although the advice to season sentences first in the heart is here directed outward, we may guess, since Herbert was himself a preacher, that it was advice Herbert had himself first taken. Intellectuality alone, as in texts of controversy, was of no interest to Herbert: rather, as we can tell from *Divinitie* and other poems, he thought it positively dangerous insofar as it was likely to distract from feeling. No sentiment is more unequivocally expressed and more constantly affirmed in his work than the absolute primacy of lived experience over abstraction.

Helen Gardner, more than most other critics of Herbert, has seen the result of this strictness in Herbert's legacy of poetry: "Feelings and thoughts have been refined and controlled by the effort to give them their aptest expression . . . but feeling and thought had been refined, strengthened, and purified of extravagance before they received the discipline of poetic expression, by being brought to the test of their conformity with the truth by which Herbert lived."[13]

That interior work of seeing life accurately which must, at least in logical priority, precede accurate expression is particularly evident in

Herbert, and is sometimes not even complete before the poem begins; the refining and purifying continue even as the poem is actually being constructed. Before the notion or experience is written down, much has happened in the way of analysis, scrutiny, refusal, comparison, and testing. Yet "intellectual" is the wrong word for this process, since it aims not at a speculative truth but at a fidelity to experience. Herbert thought of God as someone equipped with a touchstone which could distinguish authentic gold, and over and over Herbert himself applies to his work the single indispensable touchstone of undeceived and undeceiving experience: Is that what I feel? Is that what I mean? Am I permitting illusions? Am I writing for my own applause for my elevating sentiments? Then, with a sigh, half pleasure and half pain, the adequate and truthful formulation, so much more unwilling to reveal itself than the handsomer or more self-justifying alternatives, is reached, and the poem can be begun, or ended, as the case may be. It is this fidelity to truth that Eliot singled out in Herbert for particular praise:

> All poetry is difficult, almost impossible, to write: and one of the great permanent causes of error in writing poetry is the difficulty of distinguishing between what one really feels and what one would like to feel. . . . [It is] extremely difficult not to confuse accomplishment with intention, a condition at which one merely aims with the condition in which one actually lives . . . and verse which represents only good intentions is worthless—on that plane, indeed, a betrayal. The greater the elevation, the finer becomes the difference between sincerity and insincerity, between the reality and the unattained aspiration. And in this George Herbert seems to me to be as secure, as habitually sure, as any poet who has written in English.[14]

From the rebuking yet forgiving irony which Herbert felt for his own lapses from candor springs his conception of Christ, always his better self commenting on his more specious moments, as in *Love unknown, The Collar, Dialogue,* or *Love* (III). When a divine dialogue is not articulated, a self-critical dialogue of the mind with itself still underlies the surface of the poems; but Herbert's interior dialogue, unlike Arnold's, is one where suffering does find vent in action, where endurance does lead

7

to something to be done: life is rethought, a text is reinterpreted, and a poem, begun in something less than perfect clarity, emerges possessing the strength of tempered metal and the lightness of silk twist.[15] In reconstructing, or conjecturing, the choices and self-criticisms implied by the conduct of these poems, I hope I have engaged in no misrepresentation of *The Temple,* one of the most beautiful and finished books in our language.

1

A Reading of *Vertue*

Sweet day, so cool, so calm, so bright,
The bridall of the earth and skie:
The dew shall weep thy fall tonight,
      For thou must die.

Sweet rose, whose hue, angrie and brave,
Bids the rash gazer wipe his eye:
Thy root is ever in its grave,
      And thou must die.

Sweet spring, full of sweet dayes and roses,
A box where sweets compacted lie;
My musick shows ye have your closes,
      And all must die.

Onely a sweet and vertuous soul,
Like season'd timber, never gives;
But though the whole world turn to coal,
      Then chiefly lives.[1]

For at least one of Herbert's critics, the poem *Vertue* is the touchstone by which one enters into Herbert's feelings and truly senses his poetry;[2] anthologists (following Coleridge's taste) have felt the poem to be peculiarly expressive of Herbert's spirit; John Wesley adapted it for the common Christian worshipper to sing at services.[3] Though it seems an "easy" poem, I do not find it easy to reconstruct Herbert's process of thought in writing it. Almost every line surprises expectation, though few poems in

English seem to unfold themselves with more impersonality, simplicity, and plainness.

When a reader attempts to imagine himself composing the poem, suddenly he finds his confidence in its simplicity quite gone. What, he wonders, led the poet to see the day as a bridal, and call the rose's hue an angry one; why did the poety gratuitously introduce a rash gazer; why should the music of the poet himself (since he has so far maintained anonymity) provide conclusive proof of the necessary ending of spring; and finally (a problem reluctantly taken on by every critic of the poem) how did the seasoned timber make its appearance? There are other difficulites, but these perhaps first strike a reader trying to reconstruct the creation of the poem.

Critics have reached two extremes in accounting for the surprising elements in conceits. One is expressed by Dr. Johnson's suspicion that metaphysical poets were simply striving for effect, while the sympathetic extreme, in Rosemond Tuve for instance, finds conceit often appropriate, granted special canons of decorum (the grotesque, for example, can be in certain contexts "decorous").[4] But both solutions seem inapplicable here. The startling conceits of *Vertue* do not disturb its harmonies of tone; and since the established decorum of the poem is one of praise—(of the limited sweetness of nature and the unlimited sweetness and virtue of the soul)—that decorum supports with difficulty either the angry hue of the rose or the timber-like quality of the soul, the latter seeming especially awkward in its modification of something "sweet" as well as virtuous.

There have been various rationalizations of the presence of the seasoned timber. Arnold Stein insisted on the formal nature of the simile, *"like season'd timber,"* by which, he argues, the quality compared in soul and wood is strictly limited to a fugitive resemblance;[5] and Joseph Summers makes somewhat the same point in speaking of the "limitation" of conceits: " 'Season'd timber' is limited to its one point of resemblance of the 'vertuous soul' that it 'never gives.' "[6] This seems a weak acquiescence to the famous stanza. The real question is not what accommodations we can make *post hoc* to the image but what made Herbert think of seasoned timber in the first place, and what effect this note, sounded at this point in the poem, has on the poem as a whole. I believe that Herbert is not arbitrary or willful in his comparisons, that on the contrary they tend to arise from a motive appearing perhaps *sotto voce* in the development of the poem, but which helps to guide the poem from the beginning.

Mary Ellen Rickey has remarked that *Vertue* is a *carpe diem* poem in reverse,[7] quoting the precedent that A. Davenport cited from Ovid for a conclusion in praise of virtue rather than in praise of seizing the day.[8] However, the difference in tone between this poem and its erotic predecessors (a difference occurring not only at the end) seems to remove the poem almost entirely from its parent genre. That is, we would, if we were sufficiently responsive, sense from the beginning that this poem could not possibly end with a call to gather the roses of today, any more than it could end, as the passage in the *Ars Amatoria* does, with a total rejection of all natural solace.

The high resignation of the first stanza of *Vertue* sets the initial theme, which, though it is ostensibly the death of a day, seems rather, metaphorically speaking, to be the immortal theme of the death of a maiden, etherealized into a virginal day. Herbert is struck, not by the sunny, earthly beauty of the day, but by its remoteness, its spiritual stillness; it is so cool, so calm, that it seems more heavenly than earthly, an appearance which engenders Herbert's metaphor of the bridal making the day a bridge between earth and sky; it is, in short, the most innocent and celestial of earthly beauties.[9] We can scarcely doubt that "bright" suggested "bride": the Spenserian adjectives—"so cool, so calm, so bright" —suggest a bride, but the suggestion is abstracted into a bridal, presumably to avoid confusion of the fall of night with the marriage bed. The weeping dew (it is of course the falling dew, or nightfall, which led to Herbert's invention of day-fall) reminds us of what is usually meant by the "fall" of something innocent, to which we respond by weeping —a fall into corruption, which is a premonition of the fall to death. A stanza, then, which is apparently about time's destruction of a day becomes, by virtue of its metaphors, a stanza about the fall of bridal innocence. This fall has not very much to do with time but everything to do with intrinsic corruptibility or, to use theological terms, with sin. Herbert has seen this day-fall before, and so his verb is prophetic, not factual (a tone later imitated by Hopkins in *Spring and Fall*), with a sister-recognition of the intrinsic (rather than time-caused) nature of the "fall" we weep for. The dew is the elegist of the day, the witness and mourner of its fall in an unmixed sympathy, and therefore stands as Herbert's representative in the stanza, a helpless and grieving spectator, dwelling "a weeping Hermit, there." The emotions in this stanza are pure and unalloyed, since the apparently "natural" character of the day-fall clears the day of any logical "guilt" in its descent into night.

If Herbert's representative in the first stanza feels only grief at vanished innocence, his representative in the second stanza is suffering from the smart of the sensual world. The hue of the rose, on which he has so rashly gazed (not glanced), irritates his tender senses (in the fanciful world of the poem) and brings involuntary tears to his eyes. The beauty of the rose (as Herbert will say explicitly in his poem of that name) is accompanied by qualities that make the flower physically harmful and therefore, in the emblematic universe of this poem, morally inimical to man. Whereas the weeping dew is more probably a female figure, appropriate attendant to the bridal day, the rash gazer is clearly masculine, and so is the rose, angry in hue. It is a small duel they engage in, in which the rose pricks the eye of the one so rash as to approach him. The mutually symmetrical relations between nature and the spectator in the first stanza (the falling day, the falling dew, the clear day, the clear dew) thus become mutually antagonistic ones after a seductive beginning in the gazer's rash love; and though on the surface the hostility is quickly passed by, it is nevertheless present in the little drama of the flaunting rose, the gazer's love, and the rose's retort. Herbert immediately takes revenge on the rose in a chilling statement, not of prophecy, as with the day, but of fact, in which he insists, in an image which has nothing temporal about it at all, on the simultaneous death-in-life of the rose, which is, in a sense, as much dead as alive, since its root is "ever" in its grave.

If we recall *The Book of Thel* and *The Sick Rose*, Blakean parallels to the first and second stanzas of *Vertue*, we may say that Herbert's feelings are considerably more mixed with respect to aggressive passion than with respect to necessarily-vanished innocence. Or it may be that he prefers the more feminine manifestations of nature (including his own nature) to the more thorny masculine ones. There was no need to endow the rose with masculine adjectives and properties (its Romance predecessors having been by gender feminine) except to insist on the principle of aggression and unexpected harm in the encounter with passion. In fact, the real question raised by the second stanza is why the rose is called "sweet" at all. If a reader, unacquainted with the poem, were to be shown the stanza with the first word missing ("————rose, whose hue, angry and brave . . .") and were asked to supply a plausible first word, the last adjective to come to mind, I presume, would be "sweet." Nothing else in the stanza supports the initial epithet, a fact especially striking because the sweetness of the "sweet day" is so wholly borne out by the succeeding adjectives. Is, in fact, Herbert's rose sweet at all? Not, certainly, by its angry hue, which is only a superior (because mobile) sort of thorn; and not, certainly, by its entombed root; by its bravery, perhaps? But "sweetness," in the conventional sense established by earlier poems on the sweet rose, and by the "sweet" day and the "sweet" spring in this poem, is almost antithetical to "bravery" in Herbert's sense. We are left with the deliberately unmentioned sweetness of the rose's perfume or nectar, what Herbert calls in another poem "hony of roses." No doubt this aspect of the rose is included in the next stanza with its "chest of sweets," but all mention of perfume, the only thing that could make the epithet "sweet" seem plausible, is suppressed in the second stanza.[10] The rose, in short, is not praised as the day was.

Let me, in an apologetic experiment, rewrite the second stanza so that it becomes a "praise" like the first, expanding its first epithet logically:

> Sweet rose, whose hue, so gently brave,
> Delights the gazer's tender eye,
> Thy root, alas, is in the grave,
>   And thou must die.

The first thing necessary, in such a rewriting, is to change Herbert's bold rhythm (so noticeable after the placid sweetness in the rhythmic conduct of the first stanza, with its perfect partition of stress among all the words of its first line, and its subsequent iambic regularity). The markedly irregular rhythm of Herbert's first two lines about the rose mimics the encounter of rose and rash gazer, with two head-on shocks ("hue"—"angry" and "brave"—"bids") and one slighter one ("rash"—"gazer"): the subsidence of this stanza into iambic rhythm can occur only after the duel of hue and eye has ceased.

The third stanza, with its feminine rhymes, breaks into a dance meter, and here there is no difficulty at all about the initial epithet. Spring is indeed not only sweet but the quintessence of sweetness, at once its expansion and contraction,[11] and Herbert's rush of responsive feeling betrays the passion underlying the poem, hitherto kept at an impersonal distance. For the first time Herbert himself enters the poem, and again he denies, as he had in the stanza on the rose, that dissolution is basically a temporal event. With the rose, death was cotemporal with life; with the spring, we discover that ending is, on this earth, of one essence with existing. It is not because music exists in time that it "has its closes," but rather because the beginning seeks the end, and makes no sense without it. All unities are also separations from other things; therefore all earthly essences, whether in life or in art, have limits.

Because *Vertue* has been seen so often as a poem contrasting the corruptibility of the natural order with the incorruptibility of the soul and, consequently, as a poem about nature's subjection to time, it is worth remarking on the fate attending each of Herbert's instances. The fall of the lovely day is almost a gravitational matter, coinciding with the setting of the sun, and implying no real change in the essence of the day itself; the passionate rose lives in its own grave and comes closest, though certainly not by a time-process, to "death" in the usual sense; the spring, like music, comes to a close in a "horizontal" ending that implies neither a burial nor a fall from a height. In fact, "death" is thrice defined in the poem, and the only grisly death (like the only equivocal "sweetness") belongs to the rose. The day dies intact, as effortlessly as it has lived; spring, like music, has a dying fall; but these declensions are sweet ones. The poem is occupied chiefly not with the *corruption* of nature by time, but rather with the eventual (and philosophically necessary) *cessation* of nature.

Similarly, though the temporal question can hardly be excluded from the poem (given the presence of temporal words like "tonight" or "spring"—I except the words "ever" and "never" as being eternal rather than temporal), the subject of each stanza, as it appears in the two initial lines, is conceived of not temporally but solely in spatial or visual terms. The day is a span between earth and sky; the rose sends forth its pricking hue to the gazer through the ether; the spring is a box full of days and roses. The word "day," itself, normally a temporal one, is transformed into a spatial unit by its alliance with the word "roses" in the phrase, "Spring, full of . . . days and roses." The oddity of the link becomes clear by comparison with a similar pair, say, "full of weeks and oranges." In a grouping of dissimilar things, one of the pair often tends to be assimilated to the other, and here "day" is clearly assimilated to "rose," since both are, in the poem, things that can be put into a box of compacted sweets. We might say, recognizing Herbert's stress on the visual, that these are objects which vanish rather than events which end; the poem, once again, is concerned not with time but with cessation.

When we reach the final stanza, we realize that there has been an abrupt revision of format. The principle of inertial movement, transferred to poetry, suggests that Herbert might have continued the poem in the strict framework of its repeated construction: "Sweet ————, thou must (or shalt) ————."[12] The frame is one of direct address, coupled with prophetic statement about the future destiny of the thing addressed. If I may be forgiven another rewriting, a fourth stanza resembling the first three in syntactic form would give us something like:

> Sweet soul, thy vertue cannot rust,
> Like timber aged thou dost not give,
> And when the world will turn to dust,
> Thou'lt chiefly live.

The question I want to raise by this affront to the poem is not one of worth but one of procedure. Why did Herbert depart from his "Sweet *X*" format and direct address? And why did he not put the future of the soul in the future tense? But I defer the answers in order to put another question.

If Herbert wanted to show that the soul was better than natural things, why did he not say that, though natural things were sweet, the soul was still sweeter? I again rewrite the final stanza:

> Only the sweet and vertuous soul,
> A honey'd spring perpetual gives,
> And when the whole world turns to coal,
> Then chiefly lives.

It is clear at once that the rewritten "sweet" last stanza, like the rewritten "sweet" stanza on the rose earlier, is insipid in conception, and we must conclude that the smarting gazer, the angry-hued rose, and the seasoned timber have some common stiffening function in the poem. That stiffening function lies behind the pun present in the title of the poem: the rose has "vertue" in the sense of power, and the soul must be given at least as much resistance as the world has power. The poem, then, centers on both power and sweetness.[13]

The customary Christian view is that to the seducing sweetness of the world must be opposed a stern and resistant power of the soul. Herbert is not unwilling to see the truth of this view, but he does not wish to adopt it at the cost of placing the order of nature and the order of spirit in radical opposition to each other. He wants to attribute to the soul a sweetness too. But as we might have asked what justification exists in the poem for the epithet "sweet" applied to the armed rose, so we may well ask what justification appears for calling the soul sweet. The only things we are told about it are that it "never gives" and that it lives now but "chiefly lives" after the Last Day.[14] These are colorless phrases. Are we to conclude that Herbert is illegitimately counting on our extra-poetic assent to the soul's sweetness because we are good Anglicans? The sweetness of the rose, after all, is at least justified later in the poem by its implicit inclusion in the "chest of sweets" of the elegiac third stanza, a ceremonial farewell to beauty paralleling the lines in *The Forerunners:*

> Lovely enchanting language, sugar cane,
> Hony of roses, whither wilt thou fly?

The soul, we might imagine, needs its sweetness defined even more desperately, because it seems in so many ways opposed to the previous sweetness—of day, rose, and spring—found in the poem.

The soul, linked to the other self-evidently sweet things by the epithet it shares with them, seems to be included as one member of the class of "sweets." However, it would be fatal to describe it, as I have done in rewriting the stanza, in terms of the sweetness of nectar, light, or perfume: it would then be in a natural subclass together with the day, the rose, and spring. George Herbert Palmer, in his beautiful but sometimes misleading edition of Herbert, represents the subject of *Vertue* as "the perpetuity of goodness," adding that goodness is "bright as the day, sweet as the rose, lovely as the spring, but excels them all in never fading."[15] Yet surely the emphasis of this paraphrase is mistaken. Herbert's poem is not one that says: "O Vertue, thou art beautiful as the day" in the first stanza; "O Vertue, thou art lovely as the rose" in the second stanza; and then "O Vertue, thou art sweet as the spring" in the third stanza. If the poem had spoken so, we should have no trouble in believing in the sweetness of the soul; it would have been demonstrated for us thrice over. Herbert, on the contrary, establishes first the absolute priority (in the development of the poem) of the sweetness of nature, allowing for the bitter-sweetness of the rose, and only then begins to talk of the soul. We cannot presume, as Palmer seems to do, a knowledge of the end of the poem in reading the first stanza.

The sweetness of the soul, then, is not precisely the sweetness of air, of perfume, or of nectar. What, then, is it? It is not the experienced sweetness of the felt ecstasy of the soul. That, for Herbert, is represented in *The Banquet,* where indeed the soul, to express its ecstasy, resorts to metaphors of melted sugar, sweetened wine, and the fragrance of "flowers, and gummes, and powders," but with the qualification:

> Doubtless, neither starre nor flower
> Hath the power
> Such a sweetness to impart;
> Only God, who gives perfumes,
> Flesh assumes,
> And with it perfumes my heart.

In *Vertue* the sweetness of the soul is not immediate or felt, but only remembered or inferred, and this memory or inference creates the pathos of the poem. It is a poem of faith, not of love. Therefore, Herbert cannot say anything sweet *about* the soul (as Palmer implies he does); he can only say that it *is* sweet, and trust us to believe that he knows whereof he speaks, having so elaborately presented in the first three stanzas his credentials as a connoisseur of sweetness. He then, without any elaboration of the adjective "sweet," immediately begins to illustrate the virtue of the soul—its unyieldingness, its staunch endurance. Some might argue that while the poem succeeds very well in realizing the beauties of spring, it succeeds less well in realizing their brother and antithesis, the staunch soul.

The answer to this problem lies partially in the second stanza, where a type of sweetness is shown to give a sudden smart in the "tasting." Our relish of the day and the spring is impeded only philosophically by our reflection on their brevity, but the relish of the rose is physically impeded by the after-smart—it "biteth in the close," either visually in *Vertue* or physiologically, as we see it do in *The Rose*. If things which seem sweet are not, then things which seem not may be. If the soul is sweet, it is with a hidden sweetness rather resembling the hidden smart in the rose, an "aftertaste" in the soul which comes on the Last Day.

In most *carpe diem* poems, the direct address is made by the lover to his mistress; (or he may address himself and her together, as Marvell and Herrick do in *To His Coy Mistress* and *Corinna's Going A-Maying*). If instances of natural brevity are given as proof of mortality, they are given in the third person. This convention is so strong that in a poem reminding us, as *Vertue* does, of the *carpe diem* genre, the thing addressed unconsciously becomes, whatever its logical function, the poet's "mistress" and by extension himself, since *carpe diem* poems addressed to a mistress are likewise, as Marvell and Herrick saw, addressed to onself; the poet wants his mistress to seize the day because, without her compliance, he cannot seize it himself. (In the special case of an elder poet counseling a younger, the elder is regretting his own lost opportunities and therefore symbolically and *a posteriori* addressing himself.) In a *carpe diem* poem, in short, the poet might say, "O Rose, thou shalt die," but he would be including himself or his mistress (his other self) implicitly in the statement: "Since *we* are but decaying," says Herrick.[16] The profound object of commiseration is always really the poet himself.

The day, the rose, and the spring, then are all figures by means of which, to the extent to which he uses the tradition of direct address, Herbert implicitly represents himself. This seemingly impersonal poem is in fact a miniature autobiography, which witnesses to the necessary cessation, in the order of nature, of Herbert's original innocence, "brave" passion, and rapturous youth. However, from the very beginning of the poem, the poet is also implicitly set against nature, not identifying himself with it *in toto,* though he certainly identifies elements of himself with it—his youth, his aggression, his passion. The pathos of the poem comes as a result of this partial identification of himself with nature, but the strength of the poem comes from the means by which Herbert distinguishes other elements of himself from mortal nature. The day dies—but the dew of tears remains behind (with Herbert) to mourn its fall; the rose's root is in the grave even while it sends forth an angry dart—but the rash gazer, wiping his eye, remains behind (with Herbert), the wiser perhaps for his experience, to moralize on the eventual powerlessness of the rose's power; the spring dies—but Herbert's music remains behind (with Herbert) to exemplify the years that bring the philosophic mind. In each stanza, then, someone or something—the weeping dew, the rash gazer wiping his eye, a strain of music—stands outside the pictured death of nature, just as Herbert's voice, tender but stern in its prophecies, stands outside the events it foretells. This is a voice which "never gives." Though it yields to its own passion of regret in the rush of sensibility betrayed in "Sweet spring, full of sweet dayes and roses,/A box where sweets compacted lie," it checks itself, recovers its equilibrium, and reverts, with the gravity of the seasoned soul, to the undeniable necessity for musical closes.

It is truly the voice of the sweet and virtuous soul which has been speaking to us all through the poem—sweet in its instant emotion of kinship toward all other sweet things, even to the point of being hurt by its own precipitancy, and virtuous in its response to the encounters with sweetness. It loves other beings of innocent sweetness and weeps for their disappearance; it chastises itself for rashness after an encounter with the bitter-sweetness of passion; and it acknowledges the philosophical necessity for all sweetness' coming to an end. The sweetness of the soul, however, is rather baffled by the end of the poem. It has watched the day die, the rose wound, and the spring disappear, and has reacted virtuously; but what to do with its sweetness when the whole world turns to coal? There is nothing left for the natural sweetness of the soul to turn to congenially. Springs, days, and roses are gone, so it is time for it to call on its other qualities: to be staunch, to be stoic, to be seasoned timber. No image of sweetness would do in this all-consuming end. There can be no natural appeal to sweetness in the fire which, in the words of the *Dies Irae,* "solvent saeclum in favilla," turns the world to a cinder.

Why this energetic holocaust at the end? Herbert may seem cavalier, in his over-severe "punishment" of the beautiful, in burning up, in his penultimate line, the "whole world" of his poem. It is his day and his rose and his spring that he burns to coal, deliberately. His conflagration raises the very old question of the possibility of "natural" virtue. Is unreflecting virtue—"innate" virtue, we might say—virtue at all? As Newman later put it, what has gentlemanliness, or sweetness, to do with holiness? What is the relation between natural virtue and "real" virtue? Is it possible to do good without the intention of doing good? Such is the "virtue," for instance, that goes forth from herbs. Shakespeare thought a flower could be said to be, in this sense, all unconsciously "virtuous":

> The summer's flower is to the summer sweet,
> Though to itself it only live and die.

The notorious ambiguity and bitterness that surround this statement in the *Sonnets* betray the difficulties of founding an ethic on beauty or sweetness or "virtue" of the natural sort.

A possible stiffening, Shakespeare thought, can be added to sweetness by way of truth:

> O how much more doth beauty beauteous seem
> By that sweet ornament which truth doth give!

Herbert hints at the deceptiveness of beauty in the "untruth" of the rose, with its root hidden in death (though it is uninvaded by Shakespeare's canker or Blake's worm). But it is not deceptiveness in worldly beauty that is Herbert's main difficulty. The day he gives us is pure truth (unlike Shakespeare's "glorious morning" which turns false under the "basest cloud"), and Herbert's spring is a quintessence of pure sweetness with no lilies that fester in it. For Herbert, then, beauty does not necessarily require the complement of truth, since it is so often of itself "true." Rather, it needs two other things: strength and usefulness. Beauty, for all Herbert's passionate sensibility, seemed frail to him; its action was no stronger than a flower, a "momentarie bloom." It needed some admixture of the masculine. When God first poured out his blessings on man, according to *The Pulley*, "Strength *first* made a way; /*Then* beautie flow'd, then wisdom, honor, pleasure." Perhaps this list represents Herbert's own scale of worth.

Are we convinced, then, by the end of *Vertue,* of the necessity of adding strength to sweetness, and if so, how? Herbert has regretted, in the poem, the perishing of his innocence and his passion, the passing of his springtime. If the selves of spring—the innocent self, the importunate self, the self full of "compacted" potential—are gone, who is the Herbert who is left, and does he have any continuity with these vanished selves? The problem is one generally thought of as Wordsworthian, but it is first of all a human problem, and certainly antedated Wordsworth. Is there a natural piety binding together the past and present selves of Herbert?

The word "sweet," applied to the soul, is the only verbal sign of identity between the later and the earlier selves. That identity is partly submerged by the dominant duties or possibilities of middle age: to be staunch, not to give in, to be useful. In youth one is beautiful, innocent, energetic, ravishing; in middle age one is to be a pillar, a piece of seasoned timber supporting the fabric of the world, like the just Sundays in Herbert's poem of that name:

> Sundaies the pillars are,
> On which heav'ns palace arched lies;
> The other dayes fill up the spare
> And hollow room with vanities.
> They [Sundays] are the fruitfull beds and borders
> In Gods rich garden: that is bare
> Which parts their ranks and orders.

Pillars are here identified with the fruit that follows the springtime of blossoms; to be useful or fruitful is the function of the seasoned soul.

But as it would be presumptuous to attribute fruit to oneself, Herbert forbears to attribute to himself in *Vertue* anything but staunchness.

Two things survive Herbert's holocaust of his blossoms and his spring days: the "vertuous soul," of course, exemplified not only in the last stanza but in the voice that speaks the entire poem and expresses its final attitudes toward day, rose, and spring; but also the order of music, which Herbert distinctly separates from the perishing order of natural decay. Its logical function is superior to the function of natural order, and its harmony allows it a spirituality near to the soul's own. "My music"—this is all that the speaker of the poem tells about his present self, that he has music. Each purely natural element in the poem is characterized by one deathlike attributed noun: the day by "thy fall"; the rose by "thy root . . . in its grave"; the spring by "your closes." The poet alone has a "living" attributed noun: "my music." That music is part of the continuity of sweetness, contributing its sweetness to the virtuous soul, linking age and youth, and binding each to each.

If we now return to the earlier question of direct address, we realize that Herbert's delicacy forbids his making a blunt apostrophe to the virtuous soul. "But thou, O sweet and vertuous soul"—such a line would seem to invoke his own soul, and though he can tell us he has music, he will not tell us that he has a virtuous soul. Yet neither will he use the usual form for abstract philosophical generalization, the definite article: he will not say, "Onely *the* sweet and vertuous soul . . . never gives." The use of the indefinite article in such a case points usually to the speaker's having a particular case potentially in mind: the indefinite article, in brief, attributes a superior reality-value to the illustration.[17] The reality-value of the soul is also increased by the reiteration of the epithet "sweet," which links it to those supremely real examples of sweetness already given in the poem, and which compares the soul, under that rubric, with the day, the rose, and the spring. It is true that the poem exists primarily to differentiate the soul from these, that the poem is as Rosemond Tuve remarked, a "definition by differences"— but the soul would not need differentiation unless at first blush it looked to belong to the same order as the day, the rose, and the spring.[18] What do we use *differentia* for if not to distinguish similar things? For this reason the soul must coexist with its companions. It may indeed "chiefly" live after the Last Day, but it certainly also lives a life of sweetness, like its companions, now.[19] When Wesley rewrote the poem into a hymn, he not only effaced Herbert's metaphor of timber, with its attributions of staunchness and usefulness, but also virtually effaced the soul from existence in natural life, as Elsie Leach has pointed out, quoting Wesley's final stanza:

> Only a sweet and virtuous soul,
>   When nature all in ruins lies,
> When earth and heaven a period find,
>   Begins a life that never dies.[20]

The firmness of the soul, which, though subjected to the hammer blows of life and death, never gives, is marked by Herbert's strong reversion to trochaic meter in his last stanza. If we cut the feet in iambs, the sense is badly served: "A sweet/and ver-/tuous soul/like sea-/son'd tim-/ber nev-/er gives." The more "natural" way to read these lines is in trochees, where the words fit easily into the feet: "Onely a/ sweet and/vertuous/soul like/season'd/timber/never/gives." The repeated strokes and lifts show the firmness of the staunch soul under attack. The tone in Herbert's last stanza, then, is not triumphant, as we might have expected, but rather grave and judicious, largely on account of the limiting word "chiefly." Wesley's version is a far more triumphant "religious" paean and shows us strongly, by its contrast with Herbert, how careful Herbert was to express dogma only insofar as he could make it real in his own feelings and therefore in a poem. The distinction between the hymn writer, versifying doctrine, and the poet, expressing feeling, is nowhere clearer than in Wesley's revisions of Herbert.

Vertue does not go on to the time when the intrinsic sweetness of the soul, borne company during life by the natural sweetness which it must see die around it, will find a correspondence in heavenly sweetness. We end in the deprivations of judgment, with the soul sternly more alive, but lonely in its solitary immunity to fire, its strength taking precedence, visibly, over its sweetness. We are accustomed to poems ending in stoicism; we know them well in Wordsworth. What Wordsworth could not write of was the recovered sweetness of the redeemed soul. Herbert could not write of it in this poem, either, but elsewhere he did, in *Love* (III), the most exquisite poem in English expressing the time when faith and hope, the necessary virtues of middle and old age, are dissolved, and pure sweetness returns forever: "Love bade me enter . . . So I did sit and eat." To write of the hoped-for future in the past tense, as Herbert does in *Love,* is only possible to a poet of a changeable temperament, who had already had the experience which he hopes to have again. If Herbert had not known so naturally the sweetness of the day, the rose, and the spring, and the different-but-similar sweetness of his own music and his own soul, he could not have imagined, in *Love,* the sweetness which, after the fire of the Last Day, should incorporate them all in a final banquet.

2

Alternatives: The Reinvented Poem

One of the particular virtues of Herbert's poetry is its provisional quality. His poems are ready at any moment to change direction or to modify attitudes. Even between the title and the first line, Herbert may rethink his position. There are lines in which the nominal experiences or subjects have suffered a sea-change, so that the poem we think we are reading turns into something quite other. The more extreme cases occur in Herbert's "surprise endings," in what Valentina Poggi calls his "final twist,"[1] in which Herbert "dismisses the structure, issues, and method" of the entire poem, "rejecting the established terms" on which the poem has been constructed.[2] A case in point is *Clasping of hands,* which ends, after playing for nineteen lines on the notions of "thine" and "mine," with the exclamation, "Or rather make no Thine and Mine!" In cases less abrupt, Herbert's fluid music lulls our questions: we scarcely see his oddities, or if we see them, they cease to seem odd, robed in the seamless garment of his cadence. When in *Vertue* he breathes, "Sweet rose," we echo, "Sweet rose," and never stop to think that nothing in the description he gives us of the rose—angry in hue, pricking the eye of the rash beholder, with its root ever in the grave—bears out the epithet "sweet." Is the stanza about a sweet rose, as the epithet would have us believe, or about a bitter rose? This is a minor example of Herbert's immediate critique of his own clichés (*The Collar* could serve as a major example) and poses, in little, the problem of this chapter: how to give an accurate description of Herbert's constantly self-critical poems, which so often reject premises as soon as they are established.

Herbert's willingness to abolish his primary terms of reference or his primary emotion at the last possible moment speaks for his continually provisional conduct of the poem. In *Grace*, after begging, for twenty lines, for God's grace to drop from above, Herbert suddenly reflects that there is, after all, another solution, equally good: if God will not descend to him, he may be brought to ascend to God:

> O come! for thou dost know the way:
> Or if to me thou wilt not move,
> Remove me, where I need not say,
> *Drop from above.*

In part, this change of terms is simply the cleverness of finding a way out of a dilemma; but more truly, in Herbert's case, the ever-present alternative springs from his conviction that God's ways are not his ways—"I cannot skill of these thy wayes." If man insists on one way—that his God, for instance, drop grace on him—it is almost self-evident that God may have a different way in store to grant the request, and Herbert bends his mind to imagining what it might be—in this case, that God, instead of moving himself, should remove Herbert. The pun in the "solution" shows verbally the pairing of alternatives to accomplish the same object.

Precision is all, and when Herbert catches himself in careless speech, he turns on himself with a vengeance. In *Giddinesse*, human beings are reproved for fickleness, and God is asked, first, to "mend" us; but no, we are beyond mending, and so Herbert must ask God to "make" us anew; but no, one creation will not suffice—God will have to "remake" us daily, since we sin daily:

> Lord, *mend*
> or rather *make* us; one creation/Will not suffice our turn;
> Except thou *make us dayly,* we shall spurn
> Our own salvation.

Equally, when Herbert finds himself lapsing into conventional pulpit oratory in the poem *Miserie*, he pulls himself up sharply from his clichés about "man" and in the last breath turns inward: "My God,

I mean myself." These second thoughts are everywhere in Herbert. The wanton lover, he says, can expend himself ceaselessly in praising his beloved; why does not the poet do the same for God? "Lord, cleare thy gift," he asks in *Dulnesse*, "that with a constant wit/I may—" May what? we ask, and if we continue the analogy, we would say, "That I may love and praise thee as lovers their mistresses." Something like this must have passed through Herbert's mind, and have been rejected as presumptuous, so that instead he writes:

> Lord, cleare thy gift, that with a constant wit
> I may but look towards thee:
> *Look* onely; for to *love* thee, who can be,
> What angel fit?

The italicized "look" and "love" show Herbert doing, as it were, the revision of his poem in public, substituting the tentative alternative for the complacent one. He takes into account our expectation, prompted by his analogy with lovers, of the word "love," and rebukes himself and us for daring to pre-empt such a divine gift. The proper reading of the poem must realize both the silent expectation and the tacit rebuke, as Herbert changes his mind at the last moment.

Some of Herbert's most marked and beautiful effects come from this constant reinvention of his way. One of the most spectacular occurs in *A true Hymne,* where Herbert has been praising the faithful heart over the instructed wit, and says:

> The fineness which a hymne or psalme affords,
> Is, when the soul unto the lines accords.
>
>   . . . If th'heart be moved,
> Although the verse be somewhat scant,
>   God doth supply the want.

He then gives an example of God's supplying the want:

> As, when th'heart sayes (sighing to be approved)
> *O, could I love!* and stops: God writeth—

27

Logically, what God should write to reassure the soul is, *"Thou dost love."* To wish to love is to love; but to love God, Herbert bethinks himself, is first to have been loved by God (as he tells us in *Affliction* [I]), and so God, instead of ratifying the soul's wish, *"O could I love!"* by changing it from the optative to the declarative, changes the soul from subject to object and writes *"Loved."*[3] If we do not intuit, as in *Dulnesse,* the "logical" ending (*"Thou dost love"*), we cannot see how Herbert has refused a banal logic in favor of a truer metaphysical illogic, conceived of at the last possible utterance of the poem. He stops in his course, veers round, writes *"Loved,"* and ends the poem in what is at once a better pride and a better humility.

What this means about Herbert's mind, this rethinking of the poem at every moment, is that he allows his moods free play and knows that logic is fallible: one may want one thing today and quite another on the Last Day, for instance. When, in *The Quip,* Herbert is tormented in turn by the jeering of worldly Beauty, Money, Glory, and Wit, he remains silent, but says in his heart that on the Last Day he will be revenged, when his God will answer his tormentors for him: *"But thou shalt answer, Lord, for me."* And yet, as soon as he truly thinks of that scene on the Last Day, he reinvents it. The last stanza of *The Quip* shows Herbert's God, not vindicating at large the now-triumphant soul, not administering an anathema to the defeated worldly glories, but engaging in an almost silent colloquy alone with the faithful soul:

> Yet when the houre of thy designe
> To answer these fine things shall come;
> Speak not at large; say, I am thine:
> And then they have their answer home.

When we hear, in *Love unknown,* of God's wishes for Herbert (which amount to Herbert's best wishes for himself), we learn that "Each day, each houre, each moment of the week,/[He] fain would have [him] be new, tender, quick." Nothing is to be taken for granted, nothing should be habitual, nothing should be predictable: every day, every hour, every moment things have to be thought through again, and the surface of the heart must be renewed, quickened, mended, suppled.

An accurate description of Herbert's work implies the locating of his true originality. A few years ago this was the subject of some debate between William Empson and Rosemond Tuve, when Empson claimed as "original" images that Tuve proved traditional in iconographic usage. Empson retorted that traditional images could nevertheless bear a significant unconscious meaning, and that choice of image in itself was indicative. Certainly "tradition" is used differently by different poets, and each poet decides what décor he will choose from the Christian storehouse in order to create his stanzas. Though every single image in a poem may be "traditional," the choice of emphasis and exclusion is individual and revealing. Herbert often begins poems with, or bases poems upon, a traditional image or scene or prayer or liturgical act or Biblical quotation; but a question crying out for answer is what he makes of the traditional base. A similar question would ask what he does with the experiential *donnée,* personal rather than "traditional," of an autobiographical poem. In short, what are some of Herbert's characteristic ways of "conducting" a poem? My answer, in general, appears in the title of this chapter, and in the examples I have so far offered: Herbert "reinvents" the poem afresh as he goes along. He is constantly criticizing what he has already written, and he often finds the original conception inadequate, whether the original conception be the Church's, the Bible's, or his own. Nothing is exempt from his critical eye, when he is at his best, and there is no cliché of religious expression or personal experience that he does not reject after being tempted into expressing it. A poem by Herbert is often "written" three times over, with several different, successive, and self-contradictory versions coexisting in the finished poem. A different sort of poet would have written one version, felt dissatisfied with the truth or accuracy of that account, written a second, more satisfactory version, then rethought that stage, and at last produced a "truthful" poem. Herbert prefers to let his successive "rethinkings" and reinventions follow one another, but without warning us of the discrepancies among his several accounts, just as he followed his original qualification of the rose as sweet with a description of the rose as bitter, without any of the usual "buts" or "yets" of semantic contradiction. I should add that the evidence of the Williams manuscript, which gives Herbert's revisions of some poems, supports these conjectures on Herbert's rethinking of his lines, but what I wish to emphasize is not his revisions before he reached a final version but rather the reinvention of the poem as it unfolds toward its final form.

Herbert's reinventing appears in any number of poems. One which combines the liturgical, the ethical, and the Biblical is *The Invitation,* a poem in which Herbert the priest is inviting sinners to the sacraments. He is probably remembering, in the beginning, St. Paul's statement (Rom. 14:21) that it is good neither to eat flesh nor to drink wine, and he begins his invitation with the Pauline view of sinners as prodigal gluttons and winebibbers, whose taste is their waste, and who are defined by wine:

> Come ye hither All, whose taste
> Is your waste;
> Save your cost, and mend your fare . . .
>
> Come ye hither All, whom wine
> Doth define,
> Naming you not to your good.

For Herbert, however, St. Paul's revulsion is not congenial; Herbert, who "knows the ways of pleasure" and knows as well the pains of remorse, begins to alter his portrait of swinish and sensual sinners in a remarkable way. In the third stanza, the invited sinners become "All, whom pain/Doth arraigne"; in the fourth stanza, they are people who are misled by their delight to graze outside their bounds; and by the astonishing fifth stanza the sinners are positively seraphic:[4]

> Come ye hither All, whose love
> Is your dove,
> And exalts you to the skie:
> Here is love, which having breath
> Ev'n in death,
> After death can never die.

Sinners, in fact, are finally seen in the poem as people with all the right instincts—they want joy, delight, exaltation, and love; and that, Herbert implies, is what the redeemed want too. The sinners, misled in their desires, seek the carnal and the temporary, Venus' doves instead of the Holy Spirit, sky instead of heaven. The equation of wants in saints and sinners permits Herbert's final startling stanza:

> Lord, I have invited all . . .
> For it seems but just and right
>   In my sight,
> Where is All, there All should be.

The liturgical "dignum et justum est" and the verbally indistinguishable "All's" (both capitalized) give the sinners a final redeemed and almost divine place at the banquet. The poem amounts, though implicitly, to a total critique of the usual scorn toward sinners, a scorn with which Herbert himself began, but which in the course of the poem he silently rejects. He makes no announcement of his rejection as he changes his view, and therefore we are likely to miss it, as we miss other changes of mind in his poems. Nevertheless, over and over, Herbert reinvents what he has received and embraced, correcting it to suit his own corrected notions of reality.[5]

Our received notion of Doomsday, for instance, is a severe one, the *Dies Irae* when the whole world, as Herbert says in *Vertue,* will turn to coal. That day is sometimes thought of from God's point of view, as when the Creed says, "He shall come to judge the living and the dead," or from the human point of view, as when St. Paul says, "We shall be changed, be raised incorruptible"; but Herbert chooses to think of it in *Dooms-day* via a fanciful construct of the emotions felt by the bodies already-dead-but-not-yet-raised, unhappy in their posthumous insensibility, imprisonment, noisomeness, fragmentation, and decay. The "fancy" behind the poem is that it is not so much God who awaits the Last Day, nor is it those on earth who wish to put on immortality, nor is it the disembodied souls in heaven, but rather it is those poor soulless corrupting bodies confined in their graves. It is they who really yearn after a lively and sociable Judgment Day, when they can at last each "jog the other/Each one whispring, *Live you, brother?*" A poem like this begins with a poet thinking not, "What are the traditions about Doomsday?" but rather, "I know what is usually said about Doomsday, but what would it *really* be like, and who *really* longs for it?" Herbert's poem is very different from Donne's more conventional "At the round earth's imagined corners, blow/Your trumpets, Angels, and arise, arise/From death, you numberless infinities/Of souls"—a poem in which we at once recognize the Doomsday conventions at work.

Herbert "reinvents" not only Doomsday but also, in *The Pulley,* Genesis. To many of Herbert's modern readers it must seem utterly natural that God should speak and act as he does in *The Pulley,* since Herbert's easy way with speech in verse is designed to make just that impression.[6] However, to a reader accustomed to the usual limitations of decorum in representing God in verse, Herbert seems here to be adopting an extreme in fancifulness. Herbert's God, it has often been said, is "humanized" or "domesticated," and this anthropomorphic presentation of God is usually mentioned as one of Herbert's "homely" additions to the body of religious poetry. Yet, Herbert's God is not ever and always the same in all his appearances. Only in certain poems, especially those in which God speaks, do we recognize this "humanized" deity. *The Pulley* is one of these poems, and logically speaking, it is somewhat bizarre, since it shows God in the process (common in the Old Testament) of changing his mind. The poem uses elements from both the account in Genesis of the creation of man and from the story of Pandora, and simply the conjunction of these two sources—one solemn and the other fanciful, so incompatible in tone and intent—would make *The Pulley* an odd poem. But not only are the sources conjoined; they are rewritten. Genesis narrates the material creation of man, but Herbert in *The Pulley* imagines man's "psychological" creation. The story of Pandora tells how man is allowed to keep only one blessing, Hope; Herbert shows all blessings being granted to man and Rest only being withheld.

The Pulley is an explanation-poem, one that creates a myth to answer a riddle. There are comparable verses in earlier poetry,[7] but perhaps the

English example that comes closest to Herbert's poem is Shakespeare's Sonnet XX: "A woman's face with nature's own hand painted/Hast thou, the master mistress of my passion." The riddle with which Shakespeare begins asks how a creature with a woman's face can nonetheless possess a man's sexual organ. The "creation myth" which Shakespeare invents to explain the riddle says that Nature intended this creature to be a woman, but in creating "her," Nature fell a-doting, and so "prick'd out" the creature for woman's pleasure (that is, as a suitable beloved for herself), creating a man where she had planned to create a woman. This "myth," as well as others of the same sort, including the story of Pandora, are deliberately frivolous inventions; they do not aspire to the gravity of religious myth, which nevertheless begins, perhaps, with the same wish to solve a riddle. The charm of such explanatory myths, which lies in their very improbability, is self-sustaining, and in a story like Pandora's, the images of girl and box remain more strongly in our minds than does the riddle ("Why, in the wretchedness of his lot, does man still possess hope?") which they were invented to explain. Such is not always the case, however: Shakespeare's riddling master-mistress is more memorable than the explanatory story of Nature's doting. Theoretically, the literary emphasis in such myths can rest either in the riddle, the explanation, or both.

Herbert's practice in *The Pulley* resembles Shakespeare's in Sonnet XX: though God's speeches and action, forming the explanatory myth, take up most of the lines of the poem, Herbert's chief interest, and best lines, lie in his riddle. The riddle reads: "Why is man full of ennui, though rich in blessings?" or "Why, in spite of his riches, is man weary, restless, and repining?" St. Augustine, as Palmer noted in his gloss on the poem, is visibly in Herbert's mind: "Our heart is restless until it finds rest in Thee." The most complex portions of the poem have to do with the paradox of man's wealth and deprivation, expressed in God's successive invented fiats. The first fiat is brimming with generosity, as my italics emphasize:

> Let us (said he) poure on him *all we can:*
> Let *the worlds riches,* which dispersed lie,
> Contract into a span.

Had the poem ended there, we could have added Herbert's exclamation of praise in *Man:*

> Oh mightie love! Man is one world and hath
> Another to attend him.

God's fiat receives a cruel amendment, however, theologically defended but nevertheless catastrophic in view of the earlier unclouded benevolence. In this poem, the Fall occurs in the creation itself, as the world is made forever insufficient to man's desire. It is as though God wished at first, in creating a microcosm, to create a creature who, like God, would be his own end; but then God saw the fallacy of such a creation, since the result would be another self-sufficient god rather than a man. So God has second thoughts in the middle of his alchemical work and reserves the jewel Rest that remains in his "glass of blessings." Man is forever deprived of rest, and will be forever restless. The least convincing portion of the poem is the speech in which God changes his mind, for awkward reasons:

> He would adore my gifts in stead of me,
> And rest in Nature, not the God of Nature:
> So both should losers be.

God would be the loser of man's adoration, presumably, but "God doth not need/Either man's work or his own gifts"; as for man, he would lose the sight of God, but this is not a poem in which that state of beatitude can be expressed and made forcibly present to a reader. Vaughan's "great ring of pure and endless light" would aesthetically balance man's loss of rest, if only Herbert were the sort of poet capable of seeing such a vision and writing it down. But here, as in *Vertue,* faith is the evidence of things *un*seen: to "rest . . . in the God of Nature" is a fate dryly stated, not a destiny radiantly evoked.

Finally, with his myth and his rationale complete, Herbert can arrive at the fourth stanza which, with its rich and musical ornamentation, is the *raison d'être* of the whole poem:

> Yet let him keep the rest,
> But keep them with repining restlessness:
> Let him be rich and wearie, that at least,
> If goodnesse lead him not, yet wearinesse
> May tosse him to my breast.

Owning "the rest," man is nonetheless "restless." This pun, one of Herbert's most conspicuous, draws, in an almost demonic sense, on a fierce anti-etymology. One who has the "rest" should not be "rest"-less. "Rest" should mean "rest." In the poem *Heaven,* by contrast, words tally: "perserver" and "ever" chime in the celestial world, for all their humanly different etymologies, as do "light" and "delight." But here, the deceptive opposition between the two "rest" roots (the Latin *re-stare* and the Old High German *rasta*) is allowed to stand and confound the trusting soul. Such deception in language is deeply disharmonious to Herbert and seems to violate the "truth" of correspondence that ought to be established in words. By itself the uneasy "restlessness" of man is bad enough, given its tormenting overtones of sleeplessness provoked by the conjunction with "wearie"; yet the most painful stroke in the poem comes with the modifying of "restlessnesse" by "repining," chiefly because the disquiet implicit in the noun is intensified by the reiterative nature of *re*-pining and its embedded "pine" (in the two senses of "wither" and "yearn"). What repining restlessness, as a stage beyond restlessness *tout court,* can mean is almost inconceivable: but we are quickly led beyond this condition of mortal life to its exhausted end, that weariness which, even more than repining restlessness, disillusions man with the world, no matter what riches attend him.

The apparent inhumanity of God, his strict adherence to an absolute ideal of worship in the penultimate stanza, are suddenly and strikingly qualified in the last two lines of the poem. We might expect that the stern God of the third stanza, so unwilling to be a "loser," would care about what sort of a winner he might be, and would require that man cede to him from the highest and most absolute motives. Goodness, we might think, is the prerequisite for entrance into heaven. But God is willing to take man via any route: man may come upright, as Everyman led by Good Deeds, in his best passage; but if he does not come that way, God will welcome him as one shipwrecked upon the shore of salvation, "tossed" by that unquiet sea of restlessness succeeded by weariness onto his final refuge. In a more desperate poem, *Perseverance,* the man tossed by weariness cries,

> Onely my soule hangs on thy promisses
> With face and hands clinging unto thy brest,
> Clinging and crying, crying without cease,
>   Thou art my rock, thou art my rest.

The God who is willing to compromise, to grant salvation to weariness as well as goodness, is an example of that "care in heaven" somewhat more coldly asserted earlier in the rather unpleasantly reasoned deprivation of rest. Because of the narrative form of *The Pulley,* we may see these successive views of God (who first generously dispenses riches, then amends his fiats by logically deciding to withhold rest, and finally acquiesces in weariness as a substitute for goodness as a means of salvation) as redefinitions of an essence: the imagined God is perhaps all three, but the last takes precedence by position, followed by the first, with Herbert's least appealing view of God almost "lost" in the middle.

Though the moral import of the poem exacts some gravity in commentary, the poem is all the while correcting its mythical models. What would be really useful, the poem tells us, would be a Book of Genesis that explained to us not how man's body was made but how his paradoxical psychology came into being, and why God created him to feel persistent discontent in the midst of riches. Also, a story corresponding to man's state, according to Herbert, would ask not how it is that man has Hope (as in the story of Pandora) but rather how it is that man is depressed. To each his own riddle: Herbert is interested in mind, not matter, and in ennui, not hope. Nevertheless, there remains, for all the beautiful ending of the poem, an edge or frame of frivolity or entertainment about the whole, as about all such fanciful speculations. Though God's words are serious, the words of the narrator, in their storytelling "Once upon a time," establish a neutral medium, reassuring us that this is not a primary or solemn myth, but rather the secondary myth proper to the literary, not the religious, imagination. It is also the literary imagination that creates the stanza, unique in *The Temple,* used in *The Pulley,* with its small coda in the "unexpected" fifth line superadded to a quatrain already complete in its rhyme, *abab,* the kind of quatrain which is one of the most self-complete and final of literary forms. The additional line in *The Pulley* virtually visualizes the contraction of all riches into one span, the residue of rest at the end of the gift-giving, the conclusive vision of both God and man as losers, and the final repose on God's breast. In Herbert's echo of the conventional close of the Collect form in the concluding "that" clause, the calm serenity of the Collects (which never propose "if not this, then that," as God here does) is "humanized" by the presence of the concession to mortal weakness. We end by suspecting that for poetic purposes at least an arrangement of existence which can yield the complexities of the last stanza of *The Pulley* is preferable to one in which everything should have been absolute; in which nothing was left in the bottom of the glass; in which man was solely rich; in which the path of righteousness was placidly walked straight to heaven. Collects, in their earnest hope, make flawed poems: inconsistent and troubled inventions, however, make riches of restlessness.

Herbert's corrections extend to himself as well as to his liturgical or Biblical sources, and these self-corrections are his most interesting reinventions. Some of them do not at first seem personal, however, and since these are rather deceptive, I should like to begin with one of them —his self-correction in the sonnet *Prayer* (I). This impersonally phrased sonnet is a definition-poem, consisting of a chain of metaphors describing prayer. "Rethinking" is in fact most likely to occur in ordinary life in just this sort of attempt at definition, but whereas in life such rethinking and refining is generally an exercise in intellectual precision, in Herbert it is an exercise in the affections.

Herbert's images cannot be said to be ambiguous; though sometimes recondite, they are, in general perfectly clear. It is the whole which is complex, a something (prayer in this instance) which can be any number of things, not only at different times, but even at the same time. This tolerance of several notions at once appeals to us nowadays in Herbert, just as his profusion of images appeals. As Rosemond Tuve pointed out in *Elizabethan and Metaphysical Imagery,* an attempt to make clear the logical actions or passions of a subject will all by itself engender images, as in *Prayer* (I). These twenty-six or so images of prayer tell us several things. The easiest image, appearing in the second quatrain, concerns the sort of prayer which is an engine against the Almighty, reversing the Jovian thunderbolt and hurling it back at its source. It is not too much to call this the prayer of resentment uttered by the wounded soul; it is the sinner's tower (with overtones of Babel) raised against a seemingly unjust God. Any number of these "rebellious" prayers appear in the Herbert canon. To pray in this indignant warlike way is scarcely a sign of perfection; it is an emanation of the lowest possible state above the outright rebellion of sin. The next easiest group of images in the poem, by all odds, is the group toward the end—the Milkie Way, the Bird of Paradise, the Land of Spices. When prayer seems like this to the soul, the soul is clearly experiencing an unearthly level of feeling quite without aggressive elements. The poem, then, arrives at a state of joy from an earlier state of anger and rebellion; so much is clear as soon as we assume a single consciousness behind the metaphors of the poem.

But what, if we do assume that single meditating mind, are we to make of the beginning of the poem, which seems neither aggressive nor exalted?

> Prayer, the Churches banquet, Angels age,
>   God's breath in man returning to his birth,
>   The soul in paraphrase, heart in pilgrimage,
> The Christian plummet sounding heav'n and earth.

In what state is the soul when it speaks these lines? It must be a state that precedes the sudden rise of injured "virtue" in the use of engines and thunderbolts and spears against God; it is certainly not the heavenly state of the sestet. The lines that begin the sonnet are, in fact, without affect; they are the expression of the man who sets himself to pray frigidly, out of duty, drawing his metaphors not from feeling but from doctrine. What has he been taught, theologically, in dogma, about prayer? That it is the banquet of the Church, that the angels' age may be determined by how long they have been praying, that it engages both the heart and the soul, that it is "the Christian plummet" connecting the Church militant to the Church triumphant. When, from these received ideas, the speaker turns to his own feelings and takes stock of his own state and lapses into his own resentment, the poem takes on human reality: what, thinks Herbert, aside from these stock phrases, is prayer really? to me? now? A weapon, a spear, against the God who cripples my projects and cross-biasses me; and the aggressive images multiply. But that weapon (in the traditional image on which the entire poem hinges), by piercing Christ's side, initiates a countermovement, not of Jovian thunder this time but of grace, an infusion transforming the workaday world into the Sabbath—or rather, a transposing not a transforming, says Herbert with his usual precision, for we are not changed but glorified. Whereas earlier the man praying had been active, launching engines, building towers, piercing with spears, he now relaxes in an ecstasy of passivity; prayer becomes a constellation of experienced essences, "softnesse, and peace, and joy, and love, and blisse." But Herbert cannot rest in that passivity of sensation; with a remarkable energy he introduces, again just as the poem is about to end in its celestial geography, the hitherto neglected intellect. Prayer, he says, correcting his delighted relaxation, is in the last analysis not simply a *datum,* something given, but a *comprehensum,* "something understood." This phrase is at once the least and the most explicit in the poem. Finally the poet understands, and is no longer the frigid reciter of theological clichés, the resentful beggar, the aggressive hurler of thunderbolts, the grateful receiver of manna, nor the seeker of a Land of Spices. The final definition of prayer as "something understood" abolishes or expunges the need for explanatory metaphors. Metaphor, Herbert seems to say, is after all only an approximation: once something is understood, we can fall silent; once the successive rethinkings of the definition have been made, and the truth has been arrived at, the poem is over.

To arrive at that truth, to be able to end a poem, is often difficult. *The Temper* (I) has to try three different endings before it succeeds in ending itself satisfactorily, or at least to Herbert's satisfaction. He has complained that God is stretching him too hard, subjecting him to exaltations succeeded by depressions:

> O rack me not to such a vast extent!
> Those distances belong to thee.

God's stretching and then contracting him suggests to Herbert another image, not this time the rack but an image of equal tension, introduced with a characteristic concessive "yet":

> Yet take thy way; for sure thy way is best:
> Stretch or contract me, thy poore debter:
> This is but tuning of my breast,
> To make the musick better.

If Herbert had been content (as he sometimes could be) with resolution on an easy level, this would have been it. Herbert's pain does not diminish, but he has found a new vision of God to explain it by: God is no longer the inquisitor torturing his victim on the rack, but is rather the temperer, the tuner of Herbert's heartstrings. The ending seems adequate enough, and in fact Herbert's unknown adapter of 1697 stopped here, deleting Herbert's final stanza: to him the poem was finished, since Herbert had rediscovered the true "corrective" meaning of suffering, and had found a new image adequate to his discovery.[8] But for Herbert the poem was not finished. The image of tuning still adhered to the poem's original primitive and anthropocentric notion of being stretched, of being first lifted by God to heaven and then dashed to earth. From a more celestial point of view, however, heaven and earth are equally in God's presence and of his making, so Herbert repents of his shortsightedness and invents a brilliant coda to the poem, expunging all its former terms of spatial reference:

> Whether I flie with angels, fall with dust,
> Thy hands made both, and I am there.

The compact use of the one adverb, "there," to stand for two places, heaven and earth, because both were made by God's hands, seems yet another final resolution of the distances in the poem. Still, Herbert is not satisfied. He continues with what seems at first to be a reiteration: we expect him to say that God's power makes everywhere, heaven and earth alike, one place. Instead, he says the reverse:

> Thy power and love, my love and trust,
> Make one place everywhere.

In short, Herbert first rewrites racking as tuning, then rewrites distance as unity ("there"), and finally rewrites unity ("one place") as immensity ("everywhere"). We should not forget that he is at the same time rewriting the cause of this transformation: at first everything was his God's doing, but at the penultimate line the change becomes a cooperative act in which two loves intersect, and God's power is conjoined with man's trust.

In addition to correcting himself, whether in the impersonal terms of *Prayer* (I) or in the terms of repeated experience in *The Temper* (I), Herbert corrects his autobiography too, but as usual without flaunting his reinventions. They are for us often the discoveries of a second reading, since at first we take them wholly for granted. The blandness of most critical paraphrase of Herbert indicates that readers have been misled by the perfect grace of the finished poems and have concluded that an uninterrupted cadence means an uninterrupted ripple of thought. Herbert knew better: he said his thoughts were all a case of knives. The wounds of those knives are clearest in the three greatest autobiographical poems, *Affliction* (I), *The Flower,* and *The Forerunners.*

In *The Forerunners,* the simplest of the three, Herbert complains that in age he is losing his poetic powers, and in explaining the loss he offers several alternative explanations which a more anxious poet would be at pains to reconcile with each other. Herbert simply lets them stand: truth, not coherence, is his object. First, the harbingers of age come and evict his "sparkling notions," who are of course guiltless since they are forcibly "disparked." They and Herbert suffer together. Next, the "sweet phrases, lovely metaphors" are apparently not being evicted but are leaving of their own free will. Echoing Wyatt, Herbert asks reproachfully, "But will ye leave me thus?" accusing them of ingratitude after all his care of them. Next, they are no longer ungrateful children leaving home but are fully of age, seduced virgins: "Has some fond lover tic'd thee to thy bane?" Finally, they are debased, willingly prostituting themselves in the service of the lover who loves dung. In Herbert's last bitterness, even their essence and power are denied them: they are no longer creative "enchanting" forces but only "embellishments" of meaning. There is no resolution to these successive metaphors of loss—no comprehensive view is taken at the end, and we suffer with Herbert the final defensive repudiation of those servants who have in fact deserted him. His powerful love of his "beauteous words" has its own independent force within the poem, but so does his gloomy denial of value to those words at the end. The only true critical description of poems such as this must be a successive one; a global description is bound to be misleading.

Affliction (I), like *The Forerunners,* depends on a series of inconsistent metaphors for a single phenomenon, God's treatment of his creature. Herbert's ingenuity is matched only by his frankness: his God is at first a seducer, "enticing" Herbert's heart; next he is a sovereign, distributing "gracious benefits"; then an enchanter, "bewitching" Herbert into his family. He is an honest wage-paying master, a king dispensing hope of high pleasure, and a mother, indulgent:

> At first thou gav'st me milk and sweetnesses;
> I had my wish and way.

But then God becomes one who inflicts sickness, and the poet groans with the psalmist, "Sicknesses cleave my bones." Worse, God becomes a murderer—"Thou took'st away my life"—and an unfair murderer at that, leaving his creature with no means of suitably vengeful retaliation—"A blunted knife/Was of more use than I." God sends famine, and Herbert becomes one of Pharaoh's lean kine: "Thus thinne and lean without a fence or friend,/I was blown through with ev'ry storm and winde." In two lines of sinister genius, God is said to "betray" Herbert to paralysis (a "lingring" book) and death (he "wraps" Herbert in a gown made unmistakably shroudlike by the sequence of verbs). Next, God becomes a physician, deluding Herbert with his "sweetned pill," but then cruelly undoes his own healing when he "throws" Herbert into more sicknesses. God's last action seems his wickedest, surpassing all his previous enticements and tortures: he "clean forgets" his poet, and the abandonment is worse than the attention. These indictments of God are only one strain in this complaint, with its personal hesitations, accusations, self-justifications, and remorse, but they show Herbert's care and accuracy in describing his own notions of God as they changed from episode to episode. There is a remarkable lack of censorship; even with the Psalms as precedent, Herbert shows his absolute willingness to say how things are, to choose the accurate verb, to follow the truth of feeling. We can only guess at Herbert's inconsistencies of self-esteem underlying the inconsistencies in this portrait of God. This God, changeable as the skies—first lightning, then love, and then lightning again—is reflected from a self first proud and then craven and then proud again, a self which does not know whether it is a child or a victim or a dupe, a self for whom all self-assertion provoked a backwash of guilt.

The inconsistent God addressed in *Affliction* may at first cause us some dismay. Yet I believe that Herbert had a reason for choosing each of his metaphors, and though his "underthought" may not emerge as explicit accusation, the metaphors he chooses to employ (in respect to God and God's actions) are on the whole accusatory. While the tradition of religious poetry does not forbid the reproaching of God, it scarcely ever refuses, as Herbert does here, to allow God a response, and the confounding of Job shows the usual course of such divine responses, imitated by Herbert in *Dialogue.*,

In *Affliction* the metaphors representing God's inflictions and Herbert's afflictions are the vehicles of the narrative, but the length of the narrative and the cumulative addition of metaphors are themselves metaphors for the cruellest infliction of all—duration, repetition, inventively varied torture in which respites only intensify recurrences. Yet all the retrospective narration, though painful, memorializes only the suffering possible to receptivity: Herbert is passive in both torment and delight. There are tempests raining all night here, as in *The Flower,* but *The Flower* postulates a personal sin of presumption, which justifies God's wrath, and by so doing assumes an intelligible universe in which anyone can read his proper state:

> These are thy wonders, Lord of love,
> To make us see we are but flowers that glide . . .
> Who would be more,
> Swelling through store,
> Forfeit their Paradise by their pride.

In *Affliction,* however, there is no such assumption of personal guilt, and God seems capricious and arbitrary. Only his first "enticing" actions are explicable, used as they are for seductive purposes; after that, there is no predicting what cordials or corrosives are to follow, nor in what sequence, nor for what cause. "Now I am here," says Herbert, "What thou wilt do with me/None of my books will show." This is the central affliction of the poem, the utter unintelligibility of the universe, a universe which, seeming patternless, was an especial torment to a poet whose nature bent everything to form, neatness, order, and music, to whom randomness was the ultimate temperamental antithesis.

Herbert asks for nothing less than a law to encompass God, a law by which God's actions can be brought into the range of a reasonable hypothesis like that in *The Flower,* where God's chastisements always mean that one has sinned. In *Affliction,* as in many of Herbert's strongest lines, simplicity encompasses former meanings in its resonance. "Now I am here" means, at this point in the poem, "Now I am here enticed, bewitched, wrapped in a gown, betrayed to a book, thrown into sicknesses, bereft of friends, without fruit or profit"; and "What thou wilt do with me" reads, "What—after enticing me, making me ill, murdering me, killing my friends, giving me false medicine, cross-biassing me —thou wilt do with me/None of my books will show." It is as though Herbert had drawn an elaborate map of a journey as well as the history of his life, so that he can say "Now" and "Here" and "What" to an audience who can fill in the data of "Before" and "Then" and other "Whats."

We might expect, in this Job-like case, a reply from a voice out of the whirlwind. But Herbert's situation is worse than Job's: he is answered only by silence. God has forgotten him, and Herbert's cries are, as Hopkins was to say later, "Cries like dead letters sent/To dearest him that lives alas! away." But Herbert's response is neither to curse God and die nor to announce that he is gall and heartburn; with less vital force to spare, he withdraws dangerously into abstraction, apathy, and loss of ego: "I reade, and sigh, and wish I were a tree." God visits no afflictions on trees: they flourish in due season, they bear fruit, and they house birds. Their "justice" inheres in mere being, not doing. In what lies man's justice?

> I say more: the just man justices;
> Keep grace; that keeps all his goings graces.

So said Hopkins, confronting the same problem of being and doing: all natural things—and a just man is a natural thing—radiate themselves in their actions. But for Herbert, choice is meant to reign over instinct or physical laws, and in the case of man the problem of will intersects obliquely with the effortlessness of being. Herbert does not see any possible parallel between himself and the tree: he lacked Hopkins' confidence in the fundamentally just nature of mere being.

God, says Herbert, arrogates to himself all the right to change, but expects Herbert to be steadfast—stout in weakness, meek in trouble, ever the faithful servant. "Well, I will change the service," Herbert retorts, "and go seek/Some other master out." The defiance sounds plausible until we remember that Herbert had earlier told us that he had come to a place where he could neither go away nor persevere. If he could do neither of these, it is hardly more likely that he could swerve sharply away from his lifelong path. It is also true that the mere summoning of the notion of another master would make Herbert recall that there are only two: God and Mammon, in one formulation; God and the Devil, in another. The alternative of another master is terrifying even in the naming of it and accounts for Herbert's frightened "Ah my deare God!"

Although the Christian pilgrimage, in its usual appearance, is beset with dangers and difficulties, these are normally attributed either to the pilgrim's weakness or to the intervention of wicked tempters, not to the agency of God himself. Even in *Job*, it is not God who *causes* evil to befall his servant. Herbert's boldness in attributing direct agency to

45

God in respect not only to joy but also to trouble is imitated by Hopkins:

> How wouldst thou worse, I wonder, than thou dost
> Defeat, thwart me?[9]

The morass into which *Affliction* has led us is not easily quitted, and perhaps Herbert has not so much resolved as ended his poem. A satisfactory ending would in some way exculpate God, reconcile Herbert to remaining in God's service, and offer him the renewal of energy he needs to persevere or to advance, extinguishing his helpless exhaustion. Terrified by his own threat to abandon his master, Herbert recoils with his first epithet of affection, "Ah my deare God!" In the beginning of the poem Herbert's heart was brought into God's service (by whatever seductive means) and he must deal, as he has not yet done, with that primal fact. His own emotions are, in short, the missing factor in the poem up to this point. His life investment—his only life investment—has been in God, and should he leave God, his heart would be entirely empty. Love that has been placed in one hope alone is not so soon transferred. Whether or not we consider the object of that love a chimera makes no difference: the absence of love, Herbert realizes, is worse, as a suffering, than the loss of health, life, or friends; it would be the worst of afflictions to be prevented from loving. And so his final paradox hastily reaffirms his love and swears that if he fails to love, God may punish him by preventing him from loving. In this way, God is re-established as the source of value—value being love—and Herbert's love, his motive for perseverance, is renewed.

It is impossible to know to what extent Herbert was conscious of the many uneasy phrasings in *Affliction*. Paralleling the irreconcilable metaphors for divinity are the equally unsettling versions of the self. One way to look at the poem is to say that the poet is engaged in constructing an ideal self and is experiencing the psychological stages of that construction. The ideal self is modeled on expectations putatively coming from God, but from a psychological point of view one may equally well see the expectations as issuing from the self. The construction of a "better self" seems at first inspection a task bringing only the delights of self-approbation. The self identifies itself wholly with God and becomes quasi-divine in sharing God's benefits, God's furniture, God's stars, God's pleasures. The natural self, in this phase of construction, seems only a happy base to the celestial self: besides his "natural delights" Herbert will have God's "gracious benefits." This harmonious supposition seems mostly of Herbert's own making, as the phrases I have italicized reveal:

> *I thought* the service brave:
> So many joyes *I writ down* for my part . . .
>
> I looked on thy furniture so fine
> And *made it fine to me* . . .
> Such starres *I counted mine* . . .
>
> What pleasures could I want, whose King I served?

None of these appropriations and conjectures is of God's doing. The leap into identity with God makes the self intensely happy with its new superimposed construct, and in a burst of confidence the soul entirely forgets its moral nature:

> Thus argu'd into hopes, my thoughts reserved
> No place for grief or fear.

There is a childlike pleasure in the apparent reconciliation of the natural and supernatural selves; and the integral harmony of childhood, the loss of which drove the soul to the construction of a second self, is regained in "milk and sweetnesses," "flow'res and happinesse."

Sorrow and sickness, woe and pain are so closely intertwined in the fourth and fifth stanzas that psyche and soma become one. The terrible influx of this sorrow (which seems to have caused Herbert's physical sickness, rather than the reverse) is unexplained: "With my yeares sorrow did twist and grow." Later, some causes for Herbert's sorrow are suggested—his loss of health, the death of friends, his dissatisfaction with academic life. But it is truer to the poem to believe that after Herbert's complacent construction of an easy spiritual life, the inevitable war broke out between instinct and conscience. Herbert's demands on himself were never other than extreme, so much so that even he himself was conscious of the eventual severity of his conscience, scratching at him tooth and nail, as he says in *Conscience,* carping and catching at all his actions. This cruelty of the self to the self continues throughout the rest of *Affliction,* and though the attacks of the self against itself are projected onto God, they are, to speak psychologically, Herbert's own doing. Moved by aspiration, conscience, and the ideal, he chose academic life over the worldly inclinations of both birth and spirit, as he tells us, thinking thereby to approve more of himself. Instead, he found himself in a rage. The rage, an advance in psychological truth over his earlier sorrow, plunges him into more sicknesses. In wishing to forgo his mortal nature by becoming a tree, Herbert is retreating from the siege of one self by the other, just as by reading and sighing he retreats from his former rage. His boast that he will seek out "some other master" is, in this interpretation, meaningless: he has no other internalized self to serve. The principle of annihilation lurking in the final paradox (since not to love is not to be) reflects this quandary. To seek another master is equivalent to extinguishing a self long-constructed, and this recognition, though not explicit, acts as a temporary resolution to the problem of the two selves. Rage solves nothing; only the love of one self for the other can restore inner harmony. But a constant guilt resurfaces and causes the many phases of Herbert's autobiography.

With guilt comes a sense of God's absence, and that experience, habitual with Herbert, is the central topic of the third of these autobiographical poems, *The Flower.* Just as the sonnet *Prayer* redefines over and over, with increasing approximation to the truth, what prayer is, so *The Flower* redefines over and over, with increasing approximation to the truth, what has in fact been happening to Herbert. We are told that he has suffered a period of God's disfavor, during which he drooped, but that God has now returned to him, making him flourish once again. This simple two-stage event could have been told, presumably, in a plain chronological account; but instead, we are given several versions of the experience undergone. It is this repetitiveness, incidentally, here and elsewhere in Herbert, which caused Palmer to class this poem with others as redundant, lacking that fineness of structure he saw in Herbert's simpler two-part and three-part poems.[10] The redundancy is apparent, but not real; each time the experience is rede-scribed, it is altered, and each retelling is a critique of the one before.

The first version of Herbert's experience is a syntactically impersonal one, told without the "I." Herbert could be meditating on some uni-versally known phenomenon:

> How fresh, O Lord, how sweet and clean
> Are thy returns! ev'n as the flowers in spring;
>   To which, besides their own demean,
> The late-past frosts tributes of pleasure bring.
>   Grief melts away
>   Like snow in May
> As if there were no such cold thing.

Now these last three lines say something not strictly true. We do keep a memory of grief. But in the first flush of reconciliation, Herbert gen-erously says that God has obliterated all past grief in the soul. This version of the incident also says that God has been absent and has now returned, just as spring absents itself and then returns, in a natural cyclical process. We, and Herbert, shall discover in the course of the poem how untrue these statements—about the cyclical absence of God and the obliteration of grief—are.

The second stanza gives us yet another, and almost equally rosy, view of Herbert's experience, this time in the first person:

> Who would have thought my shrivel'd heart
> Could have recover'd greennesse? It was gone
>   Quite under ground; as flowers depart
> To see their mother-root, when they have blown;
>   Where they together,
>   All the hard weather
> Dead to the world, keep house unknown.

Here the period of grief is represented as, after all, not so difficult: it was not really God who went away, but rather Herbert; and his absence was on the whole cosy, like the winter hibernation of bulbs, where the flowers, in comfortable company, visiting their mother the root, keep house together with her, while the weather is harsh aboveground. This certainly does not sound like a description of grief, but like a situation of sociable comfort. The only ominous word, keeping us in touch with the truth, is "shrivel'd," which sorts very ill with the familial underground housekeeping.

So far, a cloak of palliation lies over the truth. But when Herbert has to summarize what this experience of grief followed by joy has taught him, he admits that he finds the God who lies behind such alternations of emotion an arbitrary and incomprehensible one, who one day kills (a far cry from absenting himself) and another day quickens, all by a word, an absolute fiat. We are helpless to predict God's actions or to describe his intent; we await, defenseless, his unintelligible decisions, his arbitrary power:

> These are thy wonders, Lord of power,
> Killing and quickning, bringing down to hell
> And up to heaven in an houre;
> Making a chiming of a passing-bell.
> We say amisse,
> This or that is:
> Thy word is all, if we could spell.

An early anthologist of Herbert cut off the poem here;[11] for him, and probably for Palmer, too, the poem might just as well have ended with this summarizing stanza. For Herbert, however, it cannot: he has presented us with too many contradictions. Does God absent himself cyclically, like the spring, or arbitrarily and unpredictably? Is God benevolent only, or in a fact a malevolent killer as well? Was it he who was absent, or Herbert? Was the absence a period of hellish grief or of sociable retirement? The poem had begun in earthly joy, but now, with the admission that we cannot spell and that God's word is arbitrary and incomprehensible, Herbert's resentment of his earthly condition has gained the ascendancy, and he repudiates wholly the endless emotional cycles of mortal life:

> O that I once past changing were,
> Fast in thy Paradise, where no flower can wither!

Not God's changeableness, but his own, is now the issue; the "withering" and "shriveling" are now uppermost in his mind, as once again his past grief, tenacious in memory and not at all melted away, comes to his mind.

Yet once more, for the fourth time, he recapitulates his experience. This time he does it in the habitual mode, the present tense of habit, emphasizing its deadly repetitiveness:

> Many a spring I shoot up fair,
> Offring at heav'n, growing and groning thither . . .
>
> But while I grow in a straight line,
> Still upwards bent, as if heav'n were mine own,
> Thy anger comes, and I decline.

This habitual recapitulation leads Herbert to realize that his God's actions are in fact not arbitrary, as he had earlier proposed, but that punishments come for a reason: Herbert has been presumptuous in growing upwards as if heaven were his own, and therefore he has drawn God's terrible cold wrath upon himself.

We must stop to ask whether this confession of guilt on Herbert's part is a realization or an invention. The intolerable notion of an arbitrary and occasionally malevolent God almost necessitates the invention of a human fault to explain such punishments. That is Herbert's dilemma: either he is guilty, and therefore deservedly punished, or he is innocent, and his God is arbitrary. Faced with such a choice, he decides for his own guilt. We cannot miss the tentative sexuality of his "budding" and "shooting up" and later "swelling"—one question the poem puts is whether such self-assertion can ever be guiltless, or whether every swelling is followed by a punitive shriveling. The answer of the poem is equivocal: his present "budding" seems innocent enough, but the inevitable alternation of spring and winter in the poem, of spring showers and icy frowns, tells us that we may always expect God's wrath. When that wrath directs itself upon the sinner,

> What frost to that? What pole is not the zone
> Where all things burn,
> When thou dost turn,
> And the least frown of thine is shown?

There is no more talk about keeping house snugly underground through all the hard weather. Herbert, on the contrary, has been nakedly exposed to the hard weather, has felt the freezing cold—the tempests of God. The truth is out; he *has* suffered, and he still remembers his grief. Oddly, once the truth is out, Herbert has no more wish to reproach his God; he feels happier considering himself as guilty than indicting God. It is not God, he says, who is arbitrary and capricious, but we; God's actions only follow ours; he is changeless, and we are the changeable ones. Herbert, having put off the old man, scarcely recognizes the new man he has become:

> And now in age I bud again;
> After so many deaths I live and write;
> I once more smell the dew and rain,
> And relish versing: O my only light,
> It cannot be
> That I am he
> On whom thy tempests fell all night.

In the unearthly relief of this stanza, Herbert returns to the human norm. His two constant temptations are to be an angel or a plant, but the second half of *The Flower,* like the second half of *Prayer,* discovers human truth after the self-deception of the first half. With the unforced expression of relief, Herbert can acknowledge that in truth he was not comfortably visiting underground, but was being beaten by tempests. The paradisal experience of "budding again," like any paradisal experience in life, is forfeit if the reality of past grief is denied: the sharpened senses that once more smell the dew and rain are those of a Lazarus newly emerged from the sepulcher; to deny the cerements is to deny the resurrection. At this point, Herbert can engage in genuine "wonder." The previous "These are thy wonders, Lord of power" may be translated "These are thy tyrannies"; but now that Herbert has assuaged his anxiety by deciding that power is not arbitrary and perverse but rather solicitous and redemptive, he can say, "These are thy wonders, Lord of love." The poem is one of perfect symmetry, marked by the two poles of "wonder." It is redundant, if one wishes to call it that, in circling back again and again to the same experience, but each time it puts that experience differently.

The end of the poem embodies yet another self-reproof on Herbert's part, put this time as a warning to all who, like himself, may have been presumptuous in thinking heaven their own:

> These are thy wonders, Lord of love,
> To make us see we are but flowers that glide:
> Which, when we once can finde and prove,
> Thou hast a garden for us, where to bide.
> Who would be more,
> Swelling through store,
> Forfeit their Paradise by their pride.

This homiletic neatness is probably a flaw in the poem, and the harsh judgment that Herbert passes, in so impersonal and universal a way, on his earlier presumption makes this one of his comparatively rare poems with an "unhappy" ending. Since the fundamental experience of the poem is one of resurrection, and since the best lines of the poem express that sense of renewal, we may reasonably ask why the last lines are so grim. They are, I think, because of the two truths of experience at war in the poem. One is the immediate truth of renewal and rebirth; the other is the remoter, but larger, truth of repeated self-assertion, repeated guilt, repeated punishment. Until we are "fast in Paradise," the poem tells us, we are caught in the variability of mortal life, in which, however intense renewal may be when it comes, it comes uncertainly and not for long. Intellectually, the prospect is depressing, with innocence and relish spoiled by guilt and punishment. The hell of life may continue into a hell after life. But this, since it is an intellectual conclusion, cannot fundamentally damage the wonderful sense of restored life that has made the poem famous. It speaks, however, for Herbert's pained fidelity to fact that he will not forget the gloomy truth in the springlike experience.

The inveterate human tendency to misrepresent what has happened is nowhere more strongly criticized than in Herbert. Under his repetitive and unsparing review, the whole truth finally becomes clear. Herbert knows that to appear pious is not to be pious; to pay formal tribute is not to love; servilely to acknowledge power is not to wonder; to utter grievances is not to pray. His readers, often mistaking the language of piety for the thing itself, are hampered by dealing with an unfamiliar discourse. We have a rich sense of social deception in human society and can detect a note of social falseness in a novel almost before it appears; but it sometimes does not occur to us that the same equivocations, falseness, self-justifications, evasions, and defensive reactions can occur in a poet's colloquies with his God. We recognize defiance when it is overt, as in *The Collar* or *Affliction* (I), but other poems where the presentation is more subtle elicit assenting readings and token nods to Herbert's sweetness or humility. Herbert spoke of himself in *Affliction* (IV) as "a wonder tortur'd," and his own estimate of himself can be a guide in reading his poems.

Even in that last-placed and most quietly worded poem, *Love* (III), which is spoken in retrospect by the regenerate soul from the vantage point of the something understood, the old false modesty lingers. There is, as Herbert says in *Artillerie,* no articling with God, but in this poem the soul is still refusing to give up the assertion of the private self. When Herbert catches glimpses of God's order, which may be termed the best order he can imagine for himself, he finds it almost unnatural, odd, even comic. His impulse is to deny that he has any connection with such a disturbing reordering of the universe, to feel a sense of strain in attempting to accommodate himself to it. Often, he prays that his God will remake him to fit in with a divine scheme: "Lord, mend or rather make us." But sometimes Herbert rejects this claim on God's indulgence. At his best, and at our best, says Herbert, God refuses to accept the view we like to take of ourselves as hopelessly and irremediably marred and ignorant creatures. Herbert's protests that he is not capable of glory are not catered to; expecting a gentle solicitude from God, he is confronted by an equally gentle but irreducible immobility. Each of his claims to imperfection is firmly, lovingly, and even wittily put aside, and he is forced to accept God's image of him as a guest worthy of his table. What Herbert wants is to linger in the antechambers, to serve, to adopt any guise except the demanding glory of the wedding garment, but Love is inflexible, and the initial "humility" of the guest is revealed as a delusive fond clinging to his mortal dust and sin.

Herbert's God asks that he be more than what he conceives himself to be. Herbert may have invented this sort of God to embody the demands that his own conscience put upon him, a conscience formed by that "severa parens," his mother. But even in such a brief poem as *Love* (III), Herbert's originality in transforming his sources, in reinventing his topic, strikes us forcibly. We know that the poem depends on St. Luke's description of Jesus' making his disciples sit while he served them; and on the words of the centurion transferred to the Anglican communion service, "Lord, I am not worthy that thou shouldst enter under my roof"; and on Southwell's *S. Peter's Complaint,* in which St. Peter knocks on sorrow's door and announces himself as "one, unworthy to be knowne." We also know, as Summers first made clear, that Herbert's actual topic is the entrance of the redeemed soul into Paradise.[12] Now, so far as I know, this entrance has always been thought of as an unhesitating and joyful passage, from "Come, ye blessed of my father" to "The Saints go marching in." The link between St. Peter knocking at a door and a soul knocking at St. Peter's door is clear, but it is Herbert's brilliance to have the soul give St. Peter's abject response, while standing hesitant and guilty on the threshold, just as it is a mark of his genius to have the soul be, instead of the unworthy host at communion, the unworthy guest in heaven. When we first read *Love,* it strikes us as exquisitely natural and humanly plausible; it is only later that the originality of conception takes us aback. As in *Dooms-day,* Herbert looks at the event as it really would be, not as tradition has always told us it would be. If the redeemed soul could speak posthumously and tell us what its entrance into heaven was actually like, what would it say? And so the process of reinvention begins.

Herbert's restless criticizing tendency coexists with an extreme readiness to begin with the cliché—roses are sweet, redeemed souls flock willingly to a heavenly banquet, sinners are swinish, Doomsday is awesome, past grief was not so painful. Over the cliché is appliquéd the critique—roses are bitter and smarting, the soul would in reality draw back from Love's table, sinners are, in desire, indistinguishable from saints, Doomsday would in fact be agreeably social, past grief was, if truth be told, intolerable. It makes little difference to Herbert where he finds his *donnée*—in the images of courtly poetry, in the Bible, in his personal experience. The artless borrowed beginning soon becomes the scrutinized personal statement. The anxiety that must have made Herbert want to begin with the safe, the bland, the familiar, and the taken-for-granted coexists permanently with the aggression that impelled him almost immediately to criticize the received idea. He seems to have existed in a permanent reversible equilibrium between the two extremes of tradition and originality, diffidence and protest, the filial and the egotistic. His poems do not "resolve" these extremes into one attitude; rather, they permit successive and often mutually contradictory expressions of the self as it explores the truth of feeling. At any moment, a poem by Herbert can repudiate itself, correct itself, rephrase itself, rethink its experience, reinvent its topic. In this free play of ideas lies at least part of Herbert's true originality.[13]

3

Beauty in Discovery:
Emblems and Allegories

Many of Herbert's lyrics use emblematic and allegorical materials, and these poems, considered together, define one aspect of his attachment to traditional materials, on the one hand, and one the other, his inventive departures from those traditions. I see no useful reason, in speaking of Herbert, not to use the two adjectives emblematic and allegorical almost interchangeably, since by his time the impetus to write long narrative allegories was on the wane, and the allegorical method, learned from those works, had become detachable from narrative proper. Rosemond Tuve connected allegory to emblem in *Allegorical Imagery*:

> That [mediaeval Catholic devotional figures] were fully comprehended [in the seventeenth century] is one observation to be made, and that they were deemed worthy of keeping and transmitting is another . . . It may be that we should recognize certain reasonable affinities responsible for the likenesses, drop our preoccupation with chronology and the baroque tensions, and observe how the methods and the subjects of religious allegory—and the traces left by exegetical theory pushing figures beyond didacticism to mystical truth—produce *at any time* imagery with the qualities we had thought were those of the seventeenth century. The phenomenon may be literary instead of psychological.[1]

Among Herbert's lyrics are "allegorical" poems of a strict sort (for example, *The British Church* and *Humilitie*), some containing narrative material, some not; there are as well poems in which a subject (usually abstract, such as Love or Sin or Hope) is presented "allegorically," that is, engaged in certain actions which define its character; in other poems Herbert uses visual material statically presented in emblematic form (a man in agony, a scale), which is then "read" or "interpreted" allegorically; he also takes pleasure in finding hidden "meanings" in common words or initials, or even in his own poems (*Coloss.* 3.3); and finally, he retells spiritual experience as parable (*Love unknown* and *Redemption*). In each of these cases, the "fiction" of the poem points beyond its own scope, and such a form, whether we call it "allegorical" or not, is clearly rich in possibilities for the poetic generalization of experience. Yet the more we read Herbert's allegorical or emblematic poems, the more we realize how elusively he uses the form, how willing he is to embrace it or drop it at will (especially in the later poems), and how inventively he modifies it in the direction of personal inner experience.[2]

The most famous example of Herbert's verse allegory is *Love* (III), the beautiful concluding poem of *The Temple*:

> Love bade me welcome: yet my soul drew back,
>   Guiltie of dust and sinne.
> But quick-ey'd Love, observing me grow slack
>   From my first entrance in,
> Drew nearer to me, sweetly questioning,
>   If I lack'd anything.
>
> A guest, I answer'd, worthy to be here:
>   Love said, You shall be he.
> I the unkind, ungratefull? Ah my deare,
>   I cannot look on thee.
> Love took my hand, and smiling did reply,
>   Who made the eyes but I?
>
> Truth Lord, but I have marr'd them: let my shame
>   Go where it doth deserve.
> And know you not, sayes Love, who bore the blame?
>   My deare, then I will serve.
> You must sit down, sayes Love, and taste my meat:
>   So I did sit and eat.

These are two "stories" here. In the first, a "secular" story, a guest arrives at a feast but feels himself unworthy to sup with his host because he is dusty from the road. Pressed to enter, he remains reluctant, then finally consents on condition that he be allowed to serve at table rather than sitting and being served. His host gently refuses this condition, and vanquished by courtesy, the unworthy guest sits and eats. This story sounds rather like one of Jesus' parables, and we would expect it to have some kind of preface or postlude, like "Who is my neighbor?" or "I am the living Bread." But in Herbert's poem we are given neither. Instead, mixed with the secular story is another story in process. In this story, the soul arrives at heaven and is greeted by its Lord; the soul, guilty of sin, draws back in shame. Pressed to enter, he avows his unkindness and ungratefulness, saying he cannot look on his God and live. God reminds him that he made those eyes; the soul retorts that what God made he has marred. His Lord responds that he has borne the blame for that sin. The soul, still overcome with shame, says that in heaven he will take a subservient place. God refuses, and insists that the soul participate fully in the pleasures of heaven. The soul acquiesces and joins his Lord.

We might think that by conflating these two stories, we could arrive at Herbert's poem. But even that is not true. A parabolic poet would have told the first story, and let us guess the application; an emblematic poet would have told the first story, and added the second by way of a gloss to his text. But Herbert, neither parabolic nor allegorical in any "pure" way, has mixed text and gloss, and has added as well a third and perhaps even a fourth element. The third element, part neither of the host-guest-dust story nor of the Lord-soul-sin story, appears in scattered words throughout the poem: *"Love* bade me welcome," *"quick-eyed Love," "sweetly* questioning," "Ah *my deare," "smiling* did reply," *"my deare."* Something in these words is extrinsic both to a story of Lord-soul-sin and to a story of host-guest-dust. The other incongruous ingredient, which may be thought of as a fourth element, is the rhetoric of debate, of gentle irony, and of competition pervading the poem, making it one of those contests of "gentilesse" typical of medieval literature. Though this "contest in courtesy" may in some sense seem to belong to the host-guest story, normally the parabolic form would exclude such gentle frivolity on God's part, since in a gospel parable God may be a neutral, a stern, or a generous figure, but never a witty one.[3] Therefore, when we read the poem *Love,* we slide, so to speak, from genre to genre, from love poem to allegory to homily to *débat.* Herbert is cavalier with his allegory: no writer who wanted to maintain an illusion of allegory would feel free to "give away" his "sentence" as Herbert does in "guiltie of dust and *sinne.*" The two attributes, dust and sin, would be kept on two different planes, and the one (dust) would "stand for" the other (sin). In Herbert's consciousness, however, they are simultaneous and coterminous, so that we can scarcely decide where the locus of "reality" lies in the poem.

Even in a far more sustained "parable," *Redemption,* Herbert immediately gives his "meaning" away (italics mine):

> Having been tenant long to a rich Lord,
> Not thriving, I resolved to be bold,
> And make a suit unto him, to afford
> A new small-rented lease, and cancell th'old.
> In *heaven* at his manour I him sought.

There was no need to let vehicle give way to tenor in this fashion unless Herbert wanted that effect: the title itself gives the key to the parable, and we scarcely need another clue to the identity of the "rich Lord," especially since we are to see him dying at the end. We can only conclude that Herbert meant what he said in *Jordan* (I) when he criticized poets whom one reads "catching the sense at two removes." Mystification is no part of Herbert's allegories; like many other allegories, they exist to be deciphered easily, but they are not concerned to keep up a consistent fictional existence. Even structural figures are, as soon as established, abolished. In the *Superliminare,* for which the central image is the instrument used for sprinkling holy water, Herbert addresses his reader:

> Thou, whom the former precepts have
> Sprinkled and taught, how to behave
> Thy self in church; approach, and taste
> The churches mysticall repast.

"Sprinkled and taught" is like "dust and sinne" in joining two orders of significance, and a shadowy version of the same intermingling appears in the invitation to "taste" a "mysticall" repast. It begins to be idle to speak of the literal level and the figurative level, since they coexist so visibly on the same plane in Herbert.

In fact, Herbert is often plaintively explicit in elucidating his figures, not once but often. In *The Altar,* he considerately explains his metaphor to God:

> A broken Altar, Lord, thy servant reares,
> Made of a heart, and cemented with teares:
>   Whose parts are as thy hand did frame;
>   No workmans tool hath touch'd the same.
>   A Heart alone
>   Is such a stone,
>   As nothing but
>   Thy pow'r doth cut.
>   Wherefore each part
>   Of my hard heart
>   Meets in this frame
>   To praise thy Name:
>   That, if I chance to hold my peace,
>   These stones to praise thee may not cease.
> O let thy blessed Sacrifice be mine,
> And sanctifie this Altar to be thine.

Though this is not, I think, one of Herbert's better poems,[4] it is immediately recognizable as his by its peculiar mixture of apparent naïveté with genuine obscurity. The "allegory" seems too simple at first glance, as Herbert takes such pains to elucidate it: the altar is a heart, the cement is tears, God is the stonemason, the altar is a place for sacrifice. But as soon as we begin to examine the terms in their interrelations, mysteries arise. A hard heart is one not likely to spend its time praising God; neither is a hard heart one normally associated with tears. We decide that perhaps the heart *used* to be hard: after all, it is now "broken," presumably by God's "cutting," and God has used the tools of suffering, provoking tears, to re-establish the heart, not in its natural heart-shape, but in the shape of an altar. The heart, we then conclude, has been converted. But Herbert tells us in a paradoxical quatrain that even though it is in pieces, his heart is *still* hard (italics mine):

> Wherefore each part
> Of my *hard* heart
> Meets in this frame,
> To praise thy Name.

The praise seems to be almost involuntary. Has Herbert, God's "servant," reared this altar, or has God forcibly rearranged the pieces of Herbert's heart into a shape which by itself alone praises its creator? The most peculiar dissociation of self takes place in the distinction between "I" and "my heart" ("These stones"), as if to say, "If *I* am silent, at least these stones will praise thee." (In *Sailing to Byzantium*, Yeats makes a similar dissociation: "Consume *my heart* away . . ./ and gather *me*/Into the artifice of eternity.") The tears in Herbert's poem, then, seem to be tears of suffering, not tears of contrition, since he is still capable of holding his peace and not praising God. But is it truly possible to have one's heart converted into an altar by God and still remain hostile to him? There is one final step, apparently, which God, having constructed the altar out of the recalcitrant heart, has yet to take: he has to sacrifice something (and that something will be himself) on the altar, put it to use. For this he needs a priest, to repeat on the altar his own original sacrifice in offering himself on the Cross. Only by becoming that priest will Herbert "activate" the hard heart, make it functional, let it do more than utter praises by its mere shape. So Herbert prays that God's sacrifice may be his, and that the altar may finally be sanctified to God's use. The unification of the previously "split" personality into the harmonious image of the priest at the altar provides appropriate closure for the poem.

Nevertheless, something is wrong with this schema. No "hard heart" spoke the first two lines of this poem, the most touching of the whole (perhaps the only touching ones in the poem):

> A broken Altar, Lord, thy servant reares,
> Made of a heart, and cemented with teares.

No one can read these lines without being reminded of the Psalmist (51:17): "A broken and a contrite heart, O God, thou wilt not despise." The conceits, and even some of the phrases, of the poem were determined by Herbert's Biblical sources (Exod. 20:25 and Luke 19:40), and though normally Herbert took sparks from Scripture and fanned them into a flame rather more idiosyncratic than traditional, here the Biblical references acted to constrict rather than to stimulate poetry. From a genuine metaphorical insight (God's quarrying the heart by suffering to make an instrument of his praise) and from an affecting echo of the Psalms, Herbert passes into elaborations that confuse his original intent. A true allegorist would have attached himself more closely to his emblem and allowed himself fewer distractions. Herbert's essential indifference to the strict maintenance of emblematic or allegorical fictions is once again manifest even in so brief a poem. The self is far more genuinely unified in the opening lines than it is by the closing conceit of sacrifice; no coherent personal development can be conjectured to underlie the progress of the poem. Like *Antiphon* (II), though for different reasons, *The Altar* is a piece of "false wit."[5]

Quite different is the case of *Hope,* a poem often anthologized but rarely commented on except by Herbert's editors. It is almost disarmingly simple, consisting of three bare exchanges and one brief comment:

> I gave to Hope a watch of mine: but he
>   An anchor gave to me.
> Then an old prayer-book I did present:
>   And he an optick sent.
> With that I gave a viall full of tears:
>   But he a few green eares.
> Ah Loyterer! I'le no more, no more I'le bring:
>   I did expect a ring.

Herbert's editors have been anxious to define the emblematic meaning of his nouns. Canon Hutchinson is scrupulous on the subject: "The *watch* given to Hope suggests the giver's notion that the time for fulfilment of hopes is nearly due, but the *anchor,* given in return, shows that the soul will need to hold on for some time yet; the *old prayer-*

book tells of prayers long used, but the *optick,* or telescope, shows that their fulfilment can only be described afar off; *tears* receive in return only *a few green eares,* which will need time to ripen for harvest; and then the donor's patience gives out."[6] While all these significances are plausible, and the anchor has scriptural authority as well, Herbert takes no care to ensure their coherence (*Q:* "What is it that owns an anchor, a telescope, and ears of corn?" *A:* "Hope") nor to attach explanatory verses. Instead, the poem depends on the oddness of the story it tells.

The poet gives a love-token, the watch—and receives in return, absurdly, something much too large to be given house-room, an anchor. He tries once more, again with a treasured private possession and plausible gift; this time he gets back an impersonal scientific instrument, also too large to be conceived of as a trinket. Finally, he sends the most intimate and smallest gift, a vial of tears (but analogous to a vial of perfume or unguent); he receives back the green ears, uncooked and inedible as well as impersonal (a strange variety of bouquet). Until the last couplet, Hope has been discussed in his presumed absence; now, by a sudden vocative, we are made aware that he has been present all the time. We expect a reproof to this ungentle giver of preposterous gifts, but we hear instead a bantering reproach: not "Why do you give me such ridiculous and unsuitable tokens?" but "Why do you so delay in giving me what I have been wanting, a ring?" The "marriage" emblem is not consistent with the earlier exchanges (a girl, expecting a ring, would be unlikely to send love-tokens of a watch, an old prayer-book, and a vial full of tears); only the literal meaning has coherence (I expected commitment, and all I kept receiving was postponement). Even when the speaker rebels at the end of the poem, after having naïvely continued to send gifts in the confidence that Hope would finally yield the expected ring, he "turns" in familiar raillery (with a lilting prosody and mock-serious repetition), assuring us that the rupture with the gently-named "Loyterer" is more apparent than real. Tomorrow he will be presenting yet one more token, and hoping again that the Loiterer will speed his betrothal ("I'll no more, no more I'll bring" is hardly a serious vow). The rueful self-knowledge in the close takes the poem out of the realm of the emblematic and puts it into the realm of intro-spective lyric; though emblemata remain its forms, they are not its substance.

The most heavy-handed of Herbert's allegorical poems are surely *The British Church* and *Humilitie*. Three female figures form the emblematic subject of *The British Church;* they represent the Church of England, the Church of Rome, and the Church of Geneva, and the poem exists to praise, by contrast with the other churches, the Church of England. There is scarcely a redeeming line in the entire poem, except for the Herbertian version of the golden mean:

> A fine aspect in fit array,
> Neither too mean, not yet too gay,
> Shows who is best.

The air of gallantry in the metrical verve and alliteration of this generalization shows that the subject of the mean is an attractive one, as we might expect, to Herbert: it suits well with his native delight in neatness and order. So we may conclude that the subject of the poem is itself suitable to Herbert, since his affection for the British Church, as the entire *Temple* shows, was deep, confident, and exclusive. What then could have played him so false in this poem? The poem, in its description of the two rejected damsels, is both simplistic and grotesque—and not with an imitative grotesquerie, but with simple ineptness:

> She on the hills, which wantonly
> Allureth all in hope to be
> By her preferred,
> Hath kissed so long her painted shrines,
> That ev'n her face by kissing shines,
> For her reward.

> She in the valley is so shy
> Of dressing, that her hair doth lie
> About her ears:
> While she avoids her neighbour's pride,
> She wholly goes on th'other side,
> And nothing wears.

The British Church by contrast is said to have "perfect lineaments and hue/Both sweet and bright," but this is not in itself a compelling description. What is wrong with these allegorical figures, poetically speaking? Several answers might be hazarded, all of them with some claim to truth. Herbert perhaps does not understand fully here the difference between visual and verbal emblems. Although visual figures are often identified iconographically by one or two significant features (wanton stance, shiny face = Rome; naked body, hair uncoiffed = Geneva), we expect more from personages suggesting powerful abstractions—at least since Spenser we do. The simple conventional emblem (anchor = Hope) has pure iconographical significance and stands in a closed relation with its signification. In the visual arts, personifications are often similarly rendered in minimal ways, but in the verbal arts they are normally (if successful) far more vividly presented, either by decorative ornament or by developed narrative function. These poor figures are relatively unadorned and are given nothing much to do; they are almost painfully underdeveloped, considering the powerful entities they represent. No true verbal allegorist would let pass such skimpy figures; he would be more interested in their adequate representation. Herbert is concerned here with a schematic opposition after the manner of the emblem books rather than with a full representation in the Spenserian manner.

A second conjecture about the weakness of the poem may come closer to the truth. Herbert's kind of poetry was not particularly well suited to describing damsels: he did not have the relish in delineating female figures, whether good or bad, that is such a characteristic feature in Spenser. It appears that Herbert never really "saw" his allegorical personages in any sense, nor felt compelled to make his readers perceive them first as visual objects and only later as emblems. In fact, Herbert's poetry lacks any well-developed descriptive sense of the outside world. All his descriptive powers seem to have been turned inward and focused on the fluctuations of the soul.

A third speculation about this poetic lapse requires reconsidering the subject of the poem: three rival churches. While it is true that Herbert loved the British Church, he loved it, as *The Temple* shows, in its rituals, its calendar, its sacramental consolations, and its Scripture. He shows no particular interest in it as a corporate body. A solitary soul himself, he rose, in a way we still find humanly moving, to the communal duties of the priesthood; but nothing in *The Country Parson* betrays a true congeniality to the pastoral office in its social and corporate aspects. Herbert found in the Church a daily means of mediation between himself and his God, but he shrank from ecclesiastical rivalries and theological controversies. So he could not, apparently, vivify the corporate churches, rivalrously different, in a series of emblems: the damsels were not real enough to him to enliven the churches, and the churches were not real enough to enliven the damsels.

Humilitie is another explicitly "allegorical" poem, and like *The British Church*, it is so schematic and algebraic in its story (in which four virtues receive from four submissive beasts tokens representing the beasts' vices) that its predictable end (in which all the virtues except Humility fall to wrangling over the token of Pride, a peacock's plume), though scarcely continuing the virtuousness of the virtues, at least shows that pride can undo them all, and only humility is a final safeguard. One thing that distinguishes this poem is the Aesopian irony that enlivens the action:

> At length the Crow bringing the Peacocks plume,
> (For he would not) as they beheld the grace
> Of that brave gift, each one began to fume,
> And challenge it as proper to his place,
> Till they fell out: which when the beasts espied,
>   They leapt upon the throne.

The other, more Herbertian aspect is the self-abnegating presence of Humility:

> Humilitie, who held the plume, at this
> Did weep so fast, that the tears trickling down
> Spoil'd all the train: then saying *Here it is*
> *For which ye wrangle,* made them turn their frown
>   Against the beasts.

But the simple conduct of the foreordained narrative, with a beginning, middle, and end, has a complacency of recounting foreign to Herbert's temperament (the same problem is visible in a comparable poem, *The World*). Ordinary narrative was usually not a suitable medium for Herbert simply because of its internal, ongoing placidity; he liked doubling-back, self-correction, revision, repentance, enlightenment, complication. If he were to use emblems, they had to be emblems capable of these eddies of avowal and recognition, repudiation and enlargement, and could not be such external and static representations as those of the three churches, nor such simple fabular constructions as those in *Humilitie*.

Two more successful emblem-poems which may at first seem to occupy a middle ground between the memorable and the unimpressive, and which almost demand comparison with each other, are *Love-joy* and *Jesu*. Devotees of Herbert will remember these poems because they are so indubitably his, but they are not likely to make their way into anthologies as among his greater triumphs. In them, Herbert resorts to a congenial form of emblem—the verbal riddle or puzzle (*Ana-*$\begin{Bmatrix} \text{MARY} \\ \text{ARMY} \end{Bmatrix}$ *gram* and *Coloss. 3.3* are other instances of the type in Herbert).[7] There are other similarities: in both *Love-joy* and *Jesu*, one word means two things; a "secular" identity for Jesus is proposed; and the name of Jesus is shown to hide another significance. In each, nature and divinity coincide; in each, it is shown that by linguistic manipulation (pronouncing sounds in one case, interpreting initials in the other) the speaker may come to wisdom. It becomes a challenge, given these correspondences, to attempt to discriminate between the two so-comparable uses of written emblems.

Jesu

Jesu is in my heart, his sacred name
Is deeply carved there: but th'other week
A great affliction broke the little frame,
Ev'n all to pieces: which I went to seek:
And first I found the corner, where was *J*,
After, where *E S*, and next where *U* was graved.

When I had got these parcels, instantly
I sat me down to spell them, and perceived
That to my broken heart he was *I ease you,*
And to my whole is J E S U.

Love-joy

As on a window late I cast mine eye,
I saw a vine drop grapes with *J* and *C*
Anneal'd on every bunch. One standing by
Ask'd what it meant. I, who am never loth
To spend my judgment, said, It seem'd to me
To be the bodie and the letters both
Of *Joy* and *Charitie.* Sir, you have not miss'd,
The man reply'd; It figures JESUS CHRIST.

It is hard to say which is the more bizarre of the situations imagined in these two poems. Not that each does not begin calmly enough: a broken heart is conventional material, and looking at a stained-glass window is a rational starting-point for a meditation of some sort. It is what happens after the tranquil openings that strikes us as so peculiar to Herbert. In *Love-joy* he inscribes initials on things that are normally not written on (grapes);[8] and in the other instance, though a name carved on a heart is quite common in poetry, the idea that a broken heart would also have a broken name—rather like a broken tombstone—seems original with Herbert. Although both poems record intellectual discoveries ("I perceived," "It seemed to me"), the manner in which these discoveries are made is strange. *Love-joy* is the simpler of the two poems, though Herbert's simplicity is here, as elsewhere, deceptive. The essential intellectual discovery in *Love-joy* is that moral virtue is only a mask, or a veil, hiding divine grace, that behind every exercise of joy or charity stands the figure making those virtues possible, the figure of Jesus. There is a faint hint of the Pharisee in the man who is "never loth to spend [his] judgement," and who can declare so confidently that of course wine-giving grapes stand for joy (in private consumption) and charity (in wedding feasts and such). It is, or could be, a purely naturalistic answer, and the speaker is somewhat complacently satisfied to have found two such suitable words to answer the "riddle" of the meaning of *J* and *C* inscribed on grapes. A secular pleasure in emblems is evident. The speaker's "answer" responds to the picture (the "bodie") and to the letters, too: his answer is quick to point out his knowledge that any "solving" of such an emblem has to make sense of both the picture and the inscription. The "man standing by" gives another interpretation of the emblem: he says, "It figures JESUS CHRIST."

Now with two interpretations on the board, so to speak, the poem ought to enunciate the impasse between them with something like, "Sir, you are wrong, the man reply'd." The "one standing by," like those other "friends" in Herbert, is Jesus himself, and he, more than any other, should have the right to correct mortal perception (as indeed he does in other poems). But here he is the courteous host in his own house. "Sir, you have not miss'd," he replies with gentle irony, concession concealing indulgence; and in defining the figure, he defines the religious life, where virtues like joy and charity have meaning only through participation in Jesus' redemptive grace. This may seem an unduly sectarian poem, but it really takes up once again Herbert's unceasing interest in the proper function of symbolism. The speaker here is, in the words of *The Elixir,* looking on glass, and on it staying his eye, seeking an explanation within the natural realm for the symbolism he sees ("Joy" and "Charity," though both can have theological meaning, begin as ordinary English words). If the bystander had said, "Sir, you are wrong," he would have been opposing the divine to the natural, and thus would have opened a chasm between them. By saying, "Sir, you have not miss'd," he implies that continuity by which one can espy heaven through the glass. The natural object (grapes), its pictorial representation in art (the window), its "moral" meaning (Joy and Charity), and its divine import (Jesus Christ) inhabit a continuum. Even if we insist on the theological interpretation of the two abstract nouns (they form the first two nouns in St. Paul's list of the fruits of the Spirit in Galatians 5:6), they appear as "fruits" of the holy life rather than as its source when so named. Their final meaning, Herbert would still have us understand, resides in their divine origin in Jesus Christ.

So what makes this poem "untrivial" is not the simple *presence* of a traditional Christian emblem, as Tuve seems to suggest. It is untrivial by its correction of a mistaken point of view about emblems, and by its irony directed at the complacent interpreter. It is poetic not by its employment of a Christian symbol, nor even by its enunciation of an intellectual discovery, but rather by its chastised selfhood and its perfect final alignment of its four orders of being—natural, aesthetic, moral, and divine.

A portion of the charm of *Love-joy* comes from its self-revelation; in *Jesu*, the self-revelation is more prolonged, and therefore even more charming. The voice that artlessly narrates the story of his broken heart reminds us, in its "I went to seek," of those other talkative speakers in *Redemption* and *Love unknown.* "Th'other week," this voice tells us plaintively, "A great affliction broke the little frame,/Ev'n all to pieces." This faintly querulous worrying care for his fragile heart reveals the speaker as no hero, but rather as a weak vessel. Stoicism, we think, might be what he needs. Or else a little self-blame, attributing that "great affliction" to some failing of his own (Herbert's characteristic response, more often than not, to affliction). But this is to be a poem about God's tempering the wind to the shorn lamb. The lamb, even in affliction, cooperates proleptically with God's oracular intent by going out to seek the pieces of his broken heart. With exemplary realism, Herbert takes us through the tiny search ("First I found the corner with *J* written on it, next, the piece inscribed *E S,* and last the one with *U*"). What we then expect is that he will rearrange the pieces in the right order and somehow glue them together: the line should read, "When I had got these parcels, instantly/I sat me down to unite them." But this childlike creature, alive to the possibility of sermons in stones, wants to see if there is sense in fragments (a broken heart) as well as in wholeness. The function of a whole heart is to utter praises ("My joy, my life, my crown," "My God and King," "Jesu"—those "private ejaculations" mentioned in the title of the 1633 *Temple*), and to the whole heart Jesus is *Jesu,* the vocative of those ejaculations. What is he to the broken heart? The frail searcher takes his primer and spells out, "I ease you." The vertical upward motion of prayer voiced by the heart in times of wholeness is replaced by the care and solace descending to the broken heart from Jesus. It is a great relief to perceive that one has a right to be comforted. Stoicism, fortitude, heroism are not expected of this shattered soul; he can sit and be consoled. If, however, he had not sat down to spell out the parcels of his broken heart, he would not have perceived the sacred message; the poem is a guide to the perplexed and suggests that brokenness has its own messages, consoling ones, to convey.

But moral advice, however virtuous, does not make a poem, any more than religious symbols do. Even the witty charade (my parts, my whole) does not of itself suffice. It is the winning sweetness of the speaking self, however naïve, that enhances the lines into poetry. Even in the suffering of a broken heart, the speaker sets himself staunchly to gather up the pieces, and all his appeal lies in his own adverb, "instantly." Which of us, holding the pieces of our broken heart in our arms, would not sit down to lament our condition? But such is the speaker's confidence in the absolute presence of meaning in all events, that he trustingly sits down not to weep but to spell out the new intelligibility of his state —he rearranges his psyche, and begins a new lesson. His faith is rewarded: the lesson, after all his sturdy and enterprising responses to disaster, is unexpectedly sweet. No exhortation to bear up; no reminders about the value of tears; only kindness—"I ease you." This solace restores the broken heart and enables the poem to end heart-whole, saying "Jesu" again as it did before its "great affliction." The speaker sees, in significant tenses, "That to my broken heart he *was* I ease you,/And to my whole *is* J E S U." These natural motions of the heart, together with the psychological truth of the great relief in abandoning stoicism, combine with the wit in tone and action to make this poem, too, far from trivial. It asserts a fluctuating, but entire, intelligibility in human experience, whether of joy or of crisis. Such small means to such great ends appear in Herbert's most loving uses of emblematic language, and it is no accident that these two successful emblematic poems, together with *Coloss. 3.3*, rest on a foundation of the intellectual manipulation of language, and, in the case of *Love-joy*, of linguistic signs.

If we look for instances of Herbert's emblematic presentation of visual spectacle, *The Agonie* and *Justice* (II) come to mind. There are not enough examples of this kind of poetry in Herbert to offer secure generalizations about his practice, but these poems do resemble each other in interesting ways. *The Agonie* declares that philosophers, instead of measuring natural things, like seas and fountains, should measure "two vast, spacious things" sounded by few—Sin and Love. The second and third stanzas of the poem give an emblem for each of these vast abstractions. Since no two concepts could seem less alike, we expect a horrifying picture for Sin, and a beautiful picture for Love. For Sin, we might be given a picture approximating the one suggested in *Sinne* (II), an earlier poem. There, Herbert says that "we paint the devil foul, yet he/Hath some good in him, all agree" (since he has being); but sin, "flat opposite to th' Almighty" and lacking all being, is more horrible even than the devil:

> If apparitions make us sad,
> By sight of sinne we should grow mad.
> Yet as in sleep we see foul death, and live:
> So devils are our sinnes in perspective.

So, for the emblem for Sin in *The Agonie,* we might choose a horned devil. And what for Love? Perhaps the Incarnation, perhaps the Resurrection—in any case, something appropriate to that seraphic word. However, Herbert has advanced considerably in subtlety since the crude approximations of *Sinne* (II). For Sin and Love he gives two pictures, one in each stanza, but they are *identical.* Each picture shows Christ shedding blood under torture. One, granted, is the agony in the garden of Mount Olivet; the other is the agony on the cross at Calvary; yet the details are comparable. The beholder can point to either and say, with equal truth, "This is Sin" or "This is Love." As Jesus is made to say of his passion in *The Sacrifice:*

> Ah! how they scourge me! yet my tendernesse
> Doubles each lash: and yet their bitternesse
> Windes up my grief to a mysteriousnesse.

The reciprocity of Sin and Love (the paradox of the fortunate fault) winds in Herbert's mind "to a mysteriousnesse" of which these identical emblems are the sign:

> Who would know Sinne, let him repair
> Unto Mount Olivet; there shall he see
> A man so wrung with pains, that all his hair,
> His skinne, his garments bloudie be.

> Sinne is that presse and vice, which forceth pain
> To hunt his cruell food through ev'ry vein.
>
> Who knows not Love, let him assay
> And taste that juice, which on the crosse a pike
> Did set again abroach; then let him say
> If ever he did taste the like.
> Love is that liquour sweet and most divine,
> Which my God feels as bloud; but I, as wine.

It is necessary to recognize that the *visual* portions of the emblems carry the identity: a picture of a man with blood being wrung out of him; a picture of a man with blood being "broached" out of him. The distinctions between the two pictures are made in the mind, not in the pictorial elements. Two distinct meditations are possible when one looks at a picture of Christ's passion: first, how Sin has caused this event; second, how Love has caused this event. Interestingly, only the first of Herbert's "two" emblems follows the emblematic manner, by first presenting the picture, then the explanation—"Sinne is that presse and vice." The second of the two stanzas introduces the "picture" almost casually, between two pauses ("which on the crosse a pike/Did set again abroach"), and the whole intent of the stanza is not to paint a scene, and then draw a moral, but rather to pass immediately beyond the pictorial, beyond even the intellectual definition ("Sin is X"), to the experiential: "Who knows not Love, let him assay/And taste that juice." The motivating moral reason to read an emblem is here given precedence, as it was in the earlier stanza, over the mere pictorial and intellectual pleasure of deciphering emblems; but where the first stanza said, "let him repair/Unto Mount Olivet; there shall he *see*," the second says, "let him assay/And taste . . ./then let him *say*." The involvement in the second emblem is participatory, while the relation to the first was visual (naturally Herbert does not want his bystander to "know" Sin experientially, as he "knows" Love). The second fashion is a more wholehearted way of entering into an emblem and silently corrects the first way, the way of the bystander.

In the second emblem, a double circulatory system is suggested, by which the same "liquour" that flows through the veins of Jesus flows also through the veins of Herbert. Herbert feels from it the elevation and well-being one feels after drinking wine, because being loved confers that same sensation of headiness; but as the "liquour" flows in Jesus, Jesus senses it as his own blood. Is there a common name (instead of the two names *wine* and *blood*) that we can give to this elixir? Herbert answers that in both cases it may properly be called "Love," the word *love* having the convenient property of being both active and passive, since he who loves is said to feel love, and he who is loved is said to experience love. "What do I feel?" asks Jesus, and the answer is "Love" (for man); "What do I feel?" asks Herbert, and the answer is again "Love" (from God). However, though this analysis is logically true, the poem emphasizes not the shared name but the different experience. We do not read, for example:

> What my God feels as blood, but I as wine,
> Is Love, that liquour sweet and most divine.

Because Herbert knows Sin and Love not from God's perspective but from a mortal one, he distinguishes between the divine and the human way of feeling love. The modes of perception differ, but the ontological reality is one. In short, the second emblem in *The Agonie* offers far more both for meditation and for participation than the first, which seems almost like a medieval woodcut in its factual exemplifying of every detail. The second emblem, as we would expect from Herbert, embodies a new, more mental and moral aspect of what began as a visual and spatial ("wide and spacious") conceit.

Justice (II), like *The Agonie,* consists of two emblems—in one sense similar, in another opposed. It draws on imagery representing the Old Law and the New:[9]

> O dreadfull Justice, what a fright and terrour
> Wast thou of old,
> When sinne and errour
> Did show and shape thy looks to me,
> And through their glasse discolour thee!
> He that did but look up, was proud and bold.

The dishes of thy ballance seem'd to gape,
    Like two great pits;
    The beam and scape
Did like some torturing engine show;
Thy hand above did burn and glow,
Danting the stoutest hearts, the proudest wits.

But now that Christs pure vail presents the sight,
    I see no fears:
    Thy hand is white,
Thy scales like buckets, which attend
And interchangeably descend,
Lifting to heaven from this well of tears.

For where before thou still didst call on me,
    Now I still touch
    And harp on thee.
Gods promises have made thee mine;
Why should I justice now decline?
Against me there is none, but for me much.

Once more, through its two emblems, this poem takes up Herbert's concern with epistemology. It presupposes a few axioms: that although God (and his attributes) cannot change, God seems to us to change; and while the "God of justice" of the Old Law seems to become the "God of mercy" in the New Law, since God is unchanging, it is actually our "angle of vision" that makes us see now one aspect, now another. Though the poem employs religious imagery, it is not for that reason any less in touch with what we might call "reality." Since allegory and emblems by their nature generalize, a disagreement (two emblems purporting to represent the same "reality") is unnerving. Which is the "true" picture and which the "false"? Or is there some sense in which these two contradictory emblems, each one bearing the label "Justice," can be reconciled with each other?

    The poet has a number of choices in the presentation of his dilemma: the conflicting emblems may be simultaneously present (the most difficult case); the poet may experience first one, then the other; or he may only experience one, but know of the existence of the other. Herbert chooses the second way, less immediate and less problematic than the first, but more convincing than the third. Had he followed the third choice, the poem would have been a poem of the New Law contrasted with the Old (as in *Decay*) and would have read, "Of old, Justice was terrifying; men saw it as a frightful balance. But now since Jesus has intervened, we (I) can see Justice as a force lifting us to heaven." Had Herbert taken up the first option, the poem would have been like *The Temper* (I), oscillating on "sometimes"—"Sometimes I see Justice as terrifying; sometimes I see it as intercessory." But Herbert avoided both these options and wrote a strange poem of the second choice: "Once I saw Justice thus; now I see it differently." The underlying text is St. Paul's: "For now we see through a glass, darkly; but then face to face." Herbert "rewrites" it to read: "For then I saw through a glass, darkly; but now through a pure veil fearlessly." *Justice* seems thus a conversion poem, telling how once Herbert saw Justice misshaped and discolored through the glass of sin and error, but how he now sees it fearlessly through "Christ's pure veil." Hutchinson cites St. Paul (Heb. 10:17–20) who, after invoking God's promise, "And their sins and iniquities will I remember no more," concludes that we may now "enter into the holiest by the blood of Jesus, by a new and living way, which he hath consecrated for us, through the veil, that is to say, his flesh." The passage from the Old Law to the New seems to parallel the individual passage from sin to grace. But though Herbert attributes his dark vision to his own sin and error, he does not count himself the cause of his conversion, or tell of a change of *heart*. He is, perhaps, as full of sin and error as before, but he now chooses to look not on his deserts (who should 'scape whipping?) but rather on God's love. Everything personal has therefore remained the same: Herbert is a sinner, God is just. The true moral import of the poem is that self-regard yields a mistaken perception of reality. When Herbert saw himself at the center of his vision and pondered his own sin and error, the universe (to him, as later to Carlyle) seemed a torture-house. When, however, he ceased looking at his own soul and looked instead at Christ, he saw through Christ another vision of the universe, where, from this well of tears, one could be lifted to heaven. Once again, it is a case of a man looking on a glass (here sin and error) and there staying his eye, or else choosing to look beyond it (here, to the figure of Christ) and then espying the heavens. The process of change from one vision to another is described by Herbert in *Faith*:

> That which before was darkned clean
> With bushie groves, pricking the lookers eie,
> Vanisht away, when Faith did change the scene:
> And then appear'd a glorious skie.

The "falsehood" of the first vision in *Justice* is shown by a number of locutions: the "looks" of Justice were shown and shaped by a "discolored" glass; the dishes of the balance "seem'd" to gape; the beam and scape "did *show like*" a torturing engine. There is, however, no uncertainty about the present vision. God's hand "is" white, and while a simile appears, its conflation with its tenor (so that one cannot tell whether it is the scales or the buckets which are attending and descending and lifting to heaven) precludes its giving cause for skepticism. By its two emblems, the poem denies the value of a self-centered view of "reality" and chooses rather an upward glance, that very glance forbidden (line 6) by the false humility of self-regard. The final recapitulation of "before" and "now" comes with extraordinary firmness of structure (italics mine):

> For where *before thou still* didst call on *me*
> *Now I still* touch
> And harp on *thee*.
> Gods promises have made *thee mine;*
> Why should *I justice* now decline?
> *Against* me there is *none,* but *for* me *much.*

The perfect reversal of relation exemplified in the first three lines prepares us for the compatibility of Herbert with justice in "thee [Justice] mine" and "I justice," making himself and justice verbal Siamese twins. The temptation with which the poem began—to decline justice—is a plausible response under the Old Law, as we know from the Psalmist: "If thou, Lord, shouldest mark iniquities, O Lord, who shall stand?" (130:3). That response is no longer needed under the New Law, and there is a confident ring to Herbert's "Why should I justice now de-cline?/Against me there is none, but for me much."[10] Blake would say of this poem, "The eye altering alters all," but Herbert would prefer to say that the medium altering alters all, since vision face-to-face is not to be expected in this world. However, by presenting two versions of a vision-through-a-glass—one self-regarding and the other God-directed —Herbert implies a third state, in which the medium will be dissolved and one will see without mediation. In that state, no names will be needed for attributes like "justice" and "mercy," since those names are only human inventions, each one partial, for aspects of divinity, as Herbert says in *The Glance:*

> If thy first glance so powerfull be,
> A mirth but open'd and seal'd up again;
> What wonders shall we feel, when we shall see
> Thy full-ey'd love!

I make so much of the epistemological self-correction in both *The Agonie* and *Justice* because the correction of the point of view in the latter and the enlargement of the possibilities of emblem-writing in the former seem to be the *raison d'être* of these poems. *The Agonie* and *Justice* do not exist simply to incarnate Christian symbols in verse. It is true, as Rosemond Tuve remarked with eloquence, that poems employ-ing traditional Biblical, patristic, or liturgical symbols cannot be under-stood if the reader does not "speak" that language; but to take in the meaning of the building-blocks (to give them a name no nobler than that) is not necessarily to take in the meaning of the poem or Herbert's reason for writing it. Tuve usually stops after explaining the significance of the imagery in Christian terms, but the poems require an additional explanation in personal terms, and an additional scrutiny of poetic (not religious) means.

Herbert's best poems in the emblematic mode repay such triple scrutiny. Two of them, besides *Love* (III), stand among his most beau-tiful and accomplished verses—*The Windows* and *The Rose,* neither of them in the Williams manuscript. The first is notable in being one of the few poems in *The Temple* having an "unhappy" ending.

Herbert is gloomy on the subject of "speech alone," speech not validated by a way of life, and this poetic, so uncompromisingly intertwining life and art, has made some of Herbert's critics uncomfortable. It is a poetic that might not succeed for a poet of lesser genius: "If I please [God]," says Herbert, "I write fine and wittie" (*The Forerunners*). For Herbert, pleasing God meant not playing himself false, and Herbert must have noticed that his best poems were the result of his more stringent moments with himself, those times in which he asked himself for the greatest clarity and the most unflinching self-examination. That honesty, so pleasing to God, seemed as well pleasing to the Muse; it is no wonder that Herbert thought the two one.

It is probable that Herbert set himself the same standards (or higher ones) for the composition of sermons as for the writing of poems—an intimidating standard for the preacher, as *The Windows* suggests. The poem presents three emblems. The first is the emblem for natural man: he is "a brittle crazie glasse." The second is the emblem for the preacher who has not lived his life in the imitation of Christ: his pale glass lets God's light through, but it shows "watrish, bleak, & thin." The third emblem represents the preacher in whom shines the life of Christ: he is a stained-glass window with Christ's "storie" "annealed" in it, which causes the "light and glorie" to grow yet "more rev'rend." All three appear in the first two stanzas, but the last lines desert the emblem:

> Lord, how can man preach thy eternall word?
>   He is a brittle crazie glasse:
> Yet in thy temple thou dost him afford
>   This glorious and transcendent place,
>   To be a window, through thy grace.
>
> But when thou dost anneal in glasse thy storie,
>   Making thy life to shine within
> The holy Preachers; then the light and glorie
>   More rev'rend grows, & more doth win:
>   Which else shows watrish, bleak, & thin.
>
> Doctrine and life, colours and light, in one
>   When they combine and mingle, bring

> A strong regard and aw: but speech alone
> Doth vanish like a flaring thing,
> And in the eare, not conscience ring.

The poem is concerned with the glittering power of rhetoric used to delight the ear but not to awaken the conscience; such sermons "ring" in the ear, but not in the heart. The temptation—familiar to one who had been Orator to Cambridge University—to use the "flowers of rhetoric" of known effect, those means of persuasion so artfully documented in manuals of oratory, would have been considerable, especially since the temptation would have presented itself as a means for serving God: why deny to his service those persuasive means that work so well to convince multitudes in secular life? But Herbert knew:

> The fineness which a hymne or psalme affords,
> Is, when the soul unto the lines accords.

What is true of a hymn or psalm is also true of a sermon.[11] Herbert begins *The Windows* in a tone of despondency at his own double unfitness to be a preacher: his temptation to use "speech alone" because of his gifts in that "ringing" speech, and his natural unsuitableness as a "brittle crazie" thing. The support for this conjecture about his state of mind comes chiefly from the "unhappy" ending of the poem but also from the decline into depression at the end of the second stanza. It is not clear in the poem what part in the redemption of the preacher can be played by the preacher himself, and what part must be played by God: from this confusion, the self-doubt and worry of the poem arise.

The first feeling of unworthiness, however, is briskly countered: though man, of himself, is no fit vessel for the Lord's "eternall word," still God, *through his grace,* has afforded man a place in the temple. This seems none of man's doing. Similarly, it is all God's doing when he chooses to "anneal in glasse" his "storie," "making [his] life to shine within/The holy Preachers." Holiness seems here a state caused by God, who makes his light/life shine in those preachers who move hearts and consciences. The third expression of the desirable state of the preacher, however, is not put as an act of intervention on God's part, as the previous two were; it is put impersonally:

Doctrine and life, colours and light, in one
When they combine and mingle, bring
A strong regard and aw.

What causes doctrine and life to combine and mingle? Herbert does not
say. In this formula, God would seem to contribute doctrine and light,
the preacher life and colors. But how is a preacher who feels, as Herbert
does when he writes this poem, "watrish, bleak, and thin" to bring his
necessary offering of life and colors? The whole ethos of the poem,
voiced in its consistent doublets, predicates a cooperative venture between God and man, or to put it in terms of selfhood, a better possibility than self-sufficient stoicism. Alone, man is brittle and formless
("crazie"), but God gives him a place both glorious and transcendent;
God's light and glory grows, through the holy preacher, more reverend
and winning. Doctrine joins with life, colors join with light, both
combine and mingle, the result in the congregation is regard and awe.
This parade of conjoined things going hand in hand to heaven is
broken only by the sullen triad "watrish, bleak, & thin," the first intimation of what may happen if God does not anneal his story. In the
second such intimation, all the conjunctions are disbanded into one
feared disjunction, that speech should ring in the ear but not in the
soul. The "alone" defining fraudulent speech intensifies its separation
from the desirable combinings throughout the poem, and is set off by
a contrastive rhyme with the mingled unity of "one." The poem, like
so many of Herbert's best, is a photographic double-exposure, where
we see the brittle, crazy, waterish, bleak, thin, flashy self of the un-
aided soul on one plane and superimposed on it the glorious, transcendent, holy, reverend, winning, awe-inspiring self of the shining
soul. Herbert's soul "knows not what it is," and his qualms of conscience over preaching religion without exemplifying it, and over
the question of his responsibility in the matter, cause the oscillations
in the poem between glory and ignominy.

Herbert's care for his emblems causes the final, and at first unsettling,
abandonment of the imagery of light and windows. The best life has the
colored glow of stained glass; less good is the pale and waterish light
from uncolored glass; even less good is the brittle crazed glass of natu-

ral man; but least good, and most hellish, is the false flare of hypocrisy, which flashes up in rhetoric, then "vanishes" like some spectacular firework, leaving the temple in total darkness. The implied image of the darkened temple is the final argument against trusting to rhetoric alone, and the terrible power of the unholy preacher—that he becomes opaque to God's light and therefore deprives his congregation in the temple of any light but his own *ignis fatuus*—haunts the poem. The sense of the poet's own unworthiness is matched by a yearning apprehension of the beauty and consistency in the life of preachers (and by extension poets) who have become transparent vehicles of God's light and selves colored with "his storie." In that sense, the poet is "wishing [himself] like to one more rich in hope/Featured like him . . ./Desiring this man's art and that man's scope." Like so many of Herbert's poems, this one hides its personal origin in generalized language, speaking of "man" and "holy Preachers," but as Herbert said in another poem about "man," "My God, I mean myself." The use of emblems to show contrary states of the soul is not new, but Herbert's use of these emblems to show two possibilities (or, counting the flare in the darkness, three) in his own evolution contributes that internalization of traditional materials which we have come to expect in *The Temple,* and adds another comment on his own poetics of sincerity.

In the most sophisticated of all his emblem poems, *The Rose,* Herbert triumphantly but silently make claims for language over seeing, for sustained experience over fleeting initial response. The quintessential emblem of the world's sweetness is a rose, but the rose has also been used emblematically to show the world's deceptiveness.[12] As an emblem, it first appears innocently, and we need the entire poem to tell us what it is to mean, how we are to "read" it:[13]

> Presse me not to take more pleasure
>   In this world of sugred lies,
> And to use a larger measure
>   Then my strict, yet welcome size.
>
> First, there is no pleasure here:
>   Colour'd griefs indeed there are,

Blushing woes, that look as cleare
  As if they could beautie spare.

Or if such deceits there be,
  Such delights I meant to say;
There are no such things to me,
  Who have pass'd my right away.

But I will not much oppose
  Unto what you now advise:
Onely take this gentle rose,
  And therein my answer lies.

What is fairer then a rose?
  What is sweeter? yet it purgeth,
Purgings enmitie disclose,
  Enmitie forbearance urgeth.

If then all that worldlings prize
  Be contracted to a rose;
Sweetly there indeed it lies,
  But it biteth in the close.

So this flower doth judge and sentence
  Worldly joyes to be a scourge:
For they all produce repentance,
  And repentance is a purge.

But I health, not physick choose:
  Onely though I you oppose,
Say that fairly I refuse,
  For my answer is a rose.

Although this is one of those poems in which Herbert set a stanzaic task for himself that not even he could fulfill (since he no doubt intended every stanza following the appearance of the rose to have a rhyme in *-ose*), the effect of the poem lies less in its softly insistent rhyme scheme (which includes, besides the rhymes in *-ose,* four stanzas with rhymes in *-ze,* as in "lies," "prize," "choose") than in its wordless gesture, to which the whole poem is accompaniment. The person to whom the poem is addressed (who could be any worldly tempter) has proffered, as a symbol of worldly joy, a rose, and the poem accompanies Herbert's gift back of the same rose. Herbert's first descriptions of the world represented by the rose are intensely severe. In each of them the reality (given by the noun) is wholly undesirable, and only the appearance (given by the deceiving adjective) is enticing: we have in the world, he says, sugared *lies,* colored *griefs,* and blushing *woes.* These may "look as cleare/As if they could beautie spare," but in reality there is no pleasure in them. The harshness of Herbert's initial perception of the world is betrayed in his "Freudian slip": intending courtesy and meaning to say, "If such delights there be," he lets fall the mask of politeness and instead says, "If such deceits there be." Though he corrects himself instantly, his *contemptus mundi* is evident. It is not clear, however, why he refuses to embrace worldly delights. First he says that he does take some pleasure in the world, but wishes it kept to his "strict, yet welcome size." Later he says that he does not take advantage of the deceits/delights because he has "pass'd [his] right away." Is he, then, a natural ascetic, or has he taken vows of asceticism? And do such tendencies, whether natural or religious, forbid *all* pleasure in the world or only an inordinate amount of pleasure?

The poem takes a new direction with the presentation of the rose. Though the rose had presumably supplied the imagery of colored griefs and blushing woes, it makes its first actual appearance in Herbert's ostensible refraining from argument. He will, he says, not "much" oppose to his seducer, only a "gentle rose." For the first time in the poem, something worldly has been given both an attractive noun and an attractive adjective: can the world, then, be good after all? Was Herbert's first vehemence, expressing itself in the rhetoric about sugared lies, only a response to his tempter's "pressing," a natural pressure of irritation in return? It seems so, because Herbert gives full appreciation to the beauty and sweetness of the gentle rose:

> What is fairer than a rose?
> What is sweeter?

For this and the next two stanzas, he counters the indisputable gentleness, fairness, and sweetness of the rose with its inevitable result when used as a purgative. The archaic notion that anything which acts as a purge does so out of natural "enmitie" to its host is essential to the poem, but there is also a suggestion, when Herbert says that the rose "biteth in the close," of the thorns which may prick the unwary grasper. Looked at, the rose is gentle, fair, and sweet; grasped and consumed, it bites and purges.

A new description of the world now surfaces in the poem; Herbert concedes that there are such things as "worldly *joyes*" (where "joy" is the noun-reality, "worldly" the accidental modifier)—an outright reversal of his original argument that any appearance of attractiveness in the world was a deceitful adjectival overlay upon a disappointing reality. There are, then, worldly joys, and they are real joys, and we joy in having them; but the aftermath makes us think twice. These joys contain their own medicine, as a surfeit of eating does, but still Herbert prefers to forego both the joy and the result, choosing health, not indulgence-plus-medicine. It is a reasonable argument, even if we choose to disagree with it, and Herbert cannot be accused of denying the appeal of the world, since he gives his mild answer in full view of the rose than which nothing is fairer or sweeter. His accents in praise of the rose show conviction. But with his more-than-delicate conscience, he perhaps knew what pangs of remorse indulgence would bring him. Even to a sturdier soul, the aftermath of joy can be daunting (Shakespeare's Sonnet CXXIX is a case in point), but the tempter here pretends that there is nothing to be had from roses except pure pleasure. He, of all people, should know better. Herbert nevertheless found it easier to reject the rose than would a poet more visual and more dependent on a daily submersion in natural beauty. *The Rose* deserves comparison with Hopkins' more anguished response to the vexed question of "mortal beauty":

To what serves mortal beauty/—dangerous, does set dancing blood—the O-seal-that-so/ feature, flung prouder form
Than Purcell tune lets tread to?/ See: it does this: keeps warm
Men's wits to the things that are,/ what good means—where a glance
Master more may than gaze,/ gaze out of countenance.

Hopkins is genuinely tempted by the mortal beauty of everything from stallions to ploughmen; Herbert's mind, we sense, is not under any such immediate assault. Emblems, in any case, do not arise under pressure; Herbert has reflected on the rose, its beauty and its properties, and has chosen it as the emblem fitting his notion of worldly delights. He has it to hand when the tempter appears, and the appeal of the poem lies not in any masterful effort to say "Retro me, Satanas," but rather in the imposition of elegance (there is no more elegant poem in *The Temple* than *The Rose*) on a situation more likely to provoke defensive expostulation. Not for Herbert the wrestling with the devil of the more primitive saints; a courtly bow and a rose is what the advocate of worldliness receives when he comes to call. The recovery of self-possession (after the initial quick temper) and the giving of the world its due (after the initial denial of its attractions) make the poem a small effort in the equilibrium of virtue; providing a stance is steadfastly held, there is no need to be violent in proclaiming it. Opposition and refusal can be as graceful as accommodation, given the right emblem and its right title; Satan is silenced by the presented rose.

Some of Herbert's allegorical narratives (*Humilitie* and *The World* among them) seem composed by formula, allegorically predictable and therefore uninteresting (though with incidental charm); but other comparable poems are undeniably successful. We have Coleridge's word for the appeal of *Love unknown;* and *The Pilgrimage,* like *Love unknown* not in the Williams manuscript and therefore among the later poems, is one of Herbert's most mysteriously powerful lyrics. It is impossible to paraphrase in full the unflagging particularity of *Love unknown,* but it is certain that the intense interest generated in the incidents and outcome of this "tale long and sad" springs from that particularity. "I well remember all," says the speaker, and indeed he does. One of his most endearing characteristics is the assumption that his listener is as eager to hear as he is to tell: "But you shall heare," "do you understand?" The assumption is natural, since his friend knows him, he says, as well as he knows himself. The passion for accuracy that informs the storyteller's language can be seen in the opening of his tale, full of qualifications and specifications (italics mine):

A Lord I had,
And have, of whom some grounds, *which may improve,*
I hold for two lives, *and both lives in me.*
To him I brought a dish *of fruit* one day,
And *in the middle* plac'd my heart.

The lord casts a glance at his servant, who seizes the heart and throws it "in a font, wherein did fall/A stream of bloud, which issu'd from the side/Of a great rock." The poor heart was there "dipt and dy'd,/And washt, and wrung"; later, as a result of that treatment, the heart characteristically became "well,/And clean and fair." For this narrator, one word will never do where three or four can serve. When he finds his heart callous, he describes the remedy at length and with zest:

But with a richer drug than scalding water
I bath'd it often, ev'n with holy bloud,
Which at a board, while many drunk bare wine,
A friend did steal into my cup for good,
Ev'n taken inwardly, and most divine
To supple hardnesses.

Such a passage is the equivalent of a recipe. In it, as in *Redemption* and *Love* (III), Herbert shows his willingness to let text and gloss intermingle. "A richer drug" is interpreted at once as "holy bloud," and later in the poem the speaker is allowed a *lapsus linguae* that betrays his full knowledge of allegorical equivalency:

I found that some had stuff'd the bed with thoughts,
I would say *thorns*.

Besides the speaker's loquaciousness (though his tale is said to be sad, there is an exuberance in the narration that belies the adjective) and his perfect acquaintance with both "levels" of his allegorical narrative, we also notice his undaunted purpose. He always has an end in view; and the frustration of each of his ends provides the lurking comedy of the poem, and its perpetual irony. He has in mind to bring, in placation, some fruit to his Lord—and what happens? His poor heart, in the middle of the fruit, gets thrown into a bloody font and washed and wrung. He wishes to present a sheep from his fold, "Thinking with that, which I did thus present,/To warm his love, which I did fear grew cold." Outraged, he narrates the sequel, with a pun on "tender" that also displays some outrageousness:

> But as my heart did tender it, the man,
> Who was to take it from me, slipt his hand,
> And threw my heart into the scalding pan;
> My heart, that brought it (do you understand?)
> The offerers heart.

That purpose frustrated, he goes home with another purpose in mind:

> Where to repair the strength
> Which I had lost, I hasted to my bed.
> But when I thought to sleep out all these faults
> (I sigh to speak)
> I found that some had stuff'd the bed with thoughts,
> I would say thorns.

He cannot even go to bed without a purpose—to repair lost strength, to sleep out faults. The poem exists to show that man proposes, but God disposes, and the narrator's little plans—involving a dish of fruit here, a sheep there, a good night's sleep elsewhere—are bound to fail. The equableness of the narration, in spite of the putatively horrible experiences it retells (being wrung and scalded and pricked with thorns), gives a melodiousness to the poem that belies its claims of suffering. This might seem to be a fault, and in fact did seem so to Coleridge, who said that the poem illustrated "the characteristic fault of our elder poets," namely, "conveying the most fantastic thoughts in the most correct and natural language."[14] Judged by Romantic expressive criteria, the poem entirely lacks fright and terror, imitative dislocation of speech, and evocative language. But the very notion of allegory is that what is being told *did not happen*. Nobody's heart was actually thrown into scalding water or washed in blood. A physical reaction to the physical events would be indecorous.

Again, it is characteristic of Herbert to recount his spiritual struggles in the past tense; they almost always are represented as having happened yesterday, so that the poem is giving today's view, a view tempered by knowledge of the purpose and result of each affliction. In this poem, the superior knowledge is not directly attributed in the first instance to the indignant speaker. Rather, his "friend" gently draws the moral: "Your heart was foul, I fear . . . Your heart was hard, I fear . . . Your heart was dull, I fear." To each suggestion, the poor speaker replies with willing admission: "Indeed it's true . . . Indeed it's true . . . Indeed a slack and sleepie state of minde/Did oft possess me." It is as though the speaker already knows the truth and only needs the friend's reminder to voice it. This degree of self-knowledge explains the quasi-apologetic tone that mingles with the indignation of the narrative, and it prevents the speaker from adopting a tone of active suffering. In point of fact, the narrator has been healed, as the conclusion points out:

> *Truly, Friend,*
> *For ought I heare, your Master shows to you*
> *More favour then you wot of. Mark the end.*
> *The Font did onely, what was old, renew:*
> *The Caldron suppled, what was grown too hard:*
> *The Thorns did quicken, what was grown too dull:*
> *All did but strive to mend, what you had marr'd.*
> *Wherefore be cheer'd, and praise him to the full*
> *Each day, each houre, each moment of the week,*
> *Who fain would have you be new, tender, quick.*

The poem may be seen as an internal colloquy, or dialogue of the mind with itself. In that colloquy, the reader is led to ratify the voice of the kind explanatory friend over the garrulous self-important voice of the narrator, at least when the speaker is at his most circumstantial and easily impressed:

> As I one even-tide
> (I sigh to tell)
> Walkt by my self abroad, I saw a large
> And spacious fornace flaming, and thereon

> A boyling caldron, round about whose verge
> Was in great letters set AFFLICTION.
> The greatness shew'd the owner.

The friend's voice is the voice of reflection, the speaker's the voice of immersion, and they must of necessity differ. Yet without the shamed admissions of the speaker, reflection could not arise. In spite of his disclaimer at the beginning ("In my faintings I presume your love/Will more complie then help"), the speaker needs the help of his "deare friend," nowhere more than at the end of his troubles, when his cry is heartfelt:

> Deare, could my heart not break,
> When with my pleasures ev'n my rest was gone?

The "compliance" he expects at the beginning from his "deare friend" is sympathy for his troubles: some remark affirming the worth of his own self-consciously worthy nature (all those dishes of fruit and sheep), and rebuking the impolite responses of his Lord (who ignored those gifts and practiced violence on his tenant). Instead, the friend courteously, but steadily, takes the Lord's part. The tentative ("I fear") and brief interpolations of the friend resemble nothing so much as the tentative interpretations proffered by an analyst: the sufferer is free to reject the interpretations, but is more likely to accept them, if only because he is struck by their hidden truth. We may, in the interests of historical accuracy, substitute "spiritual director" or "confessor" for analyst, but the result is much the same. And the wished-for end is also much the same—that one should be "new, tender, quick," responding not with clichés and old patterns of resentment, but with a fresher, quickened self.

In spite of the appealing realism of the narrator's voice and the healing gravity of the "friend's" replies, we must ask why, so late in his career, Herbert found this way of expressing affliction and redemption an attractive one, what it offered him that other modes (such as the ones found in the several *Affliction* poems) could not. I think that for Herbert the appeal of this kind of poem lay in distancing himself from himself. In effect, in poems like *Love unknown* Herbert is allegorizing not only his experiences but also himself. To allegorize oneself is different from writing about Everyman: it means to take one's own personality, exaggerate it, broaden it, delete its more eccentric specificities while retaining its individual character. In the latter aspect it differs from caricature, which is at pains to emphasize particular eccentricities. A self-allegory is recognizable as an individual person, yet not as wholly identical with the author. Many characteristics of the narrator in *Love unknown* remind us of Herbert: the liking for colloquy, the tendency to complain, the naïveté, the childlike speech, the forthrightness, the attacks of misery. All of these are represented in various Herbert lyrics by a genuine authorial "I." But in the first-person poems, Herbert is at the center of the stage; even in the impersonally phrased poems like *Prayer* (I) he often clearly "means himself." By inventing a genuine persona in *Love unknown* (as he also does, but less sustainedly, in *Redemption*), he achieves a detachment from self that we admire because it avoids a miserable concentration on the trivial events in one small life. We may regret the almost inevitable comic perspective that the entrance of a dramatized persona brings with it, and we may criticize a form which allows mildness of apprehension to coexist with images of boiling caldrons. But the allegorical narrative of *Love unknown* is an attempt and an approach which remains strangely winning and memorable, if not so immediately moving as the nonallegorical first-person lyrics. The greatest poem in *The Temple,* after all, depends on just such a dramatized persona, the self-conscious guest in *Love* (III). Even in that delicate poem there is a comic perspective. Herbert was never above humor at his own expense, and it is deeply characteristic of his self-irony that he, a person who so loved neatness and order, should invent a final banquet in which the guests must sit down just as they are, dusty and in travel garments. "I did expect a ring," says the narrator in *Hope;* the pilgrim in *Love* (III) "did expect" a final banquet where everyone would have a new white wedding garment; the speaker in *Love unknown* "did expect" that God would be pleased with his fruits and his sheep. These comic personae carry the burden of Herbert's ironies. We may prefer his miseries, or his joys, to his humor, but in his best poetry, as in *Love* (III), all three are found combined.

A sadder self-allegory appears in *The Pilgrimage:*[15]

I travell'd on, seeing the hill, where lay
      My expectation.
   A long it was and weary way.
   The gloomy cave of Desperation
I left on th' one, and on the other side
      The rock of Pride.

And so I came to Fancies medow strow'd
      With many a flower:
   Fain would I here have made abode,
   But I was quicken'd by my houre.
So to Cares cops I came, and there got through
      With much ado.

That led me to the wilde of Passion, which
      Some call the wold;
   A wasted place, but sometimes rich.
   Here I was robb'd of all my gold,
Save one good Angell, which a friend had ti'd
      Close to my side.

At length I got unto the gladsome hill,
      Where lay my hope,
   Where lay my heart; and climbing still,
   When I had gain'd the brow and top,
A lake of brackish waters on the ground
      Was all I found.

With that abash'd and struck with many a sting
      Of swarming fears,
   I fell, and cry'd, Alas my King!
   Can both the way and end be tears?
Yet taking heart I rose, and then perceiv'd
      I was deceiv'd:

My hill was further: so I flung away,
      Yet heard a crie
   Just as I went, *None goes that way*
   And lives: If that be all, said I,
After so foul a journey death is fair,
      And but a chair.

Joseph Summers described the presence in this poem of both the conventional (the pilgrimage) and the unconventional (the avoiding of the envisaged happy end);[16] Ryley pointed out its unusual beginning *in medias res*.[17] Beyond these larger observations, some inquiry is necessary concerning the success of the poem, achieved in unusual and unexpected ways. There are many things apparently "wrong" from an allegorical point of view about the way the poem is written. The first "wrongness" is the flouting of allegorical expectation described, but not explained, by Summers. "Is this the promised end?" we ask when we find first the brackish waters, next the inaccessible "further" hill, and finally the taunt of death. This is a grisly set of "dissolves," made more so by the perspective thus cast on the whole preceding "plot." This sequence of experiences has been, says Herbert, "so foul a journey." Such revulsion at the total Christian pilgrimage is, so far as I know, unheard-of outside this poem. The true wayfaring Christian may have his trials and his sloughs of despond, but it is unthinkable that Piers Plowman or Christian should fling out in anger, "After so foul a journey, death is fair." There is some global indictment of life here that a stricter "allegory" would forbid, because the trials of the pilgrim would, in a more traditional poem, fall under the generally approved rubric of Christian purification by suffering. But no good end is unambiguously attached to the afflictions in this poem; the journey is simply foul, in itself and in its result. It neither strengthens resolve, braces the soul, cleanses the heart, nor has any other moral effect. It only causes nausea, a revulsion which makes even that "uncouth hideous thing," death, seem fair: how much more hideous, then, is the life described as this "foul journey." In this access of felt truth, lyric response subdues allegorical expectation; what began as a pilgrimage (a noun that can scarcely take "foul" as a modifying adjective) ends as a journey, and a foul one at that. Whether the two perspectives—"the Christian pilgrimage" and "this foul journey"—can be reconciled, I am not sure. The poem attempts the rhetoric of pilgrimage, but abandons entirely the ascending tone of increasing faith which normally makes allegory close with Piers becoming Christ or trumpets sounding on the other side.

It is scarcely possible to read this poem and not think of Vaughan's

Regeneration, a poem following Herbert in the extreme simplicity of pilgrim narrative ("I came, I perceived, I entered, I said," and so forth) but which, in its descriptive fullness, causes Herbert's poem to seem a skeleton. The initial gestures toward description in Herbert (a gloomy cave, a meadow with "many a flower") are fatigued; the phases of the journey are labeled before we even have a chance to experience them. "The gloomy cave of Desperation," "the rock of Pride," "Fancies meadow," "Cares cops," "the wilde of Passion"—Herbert cannot wait to gloss his allegory, which he does more baldly and retrospectively here than anywhere else in *The Temple.* We can hardly imagine an allegory more perfunctory. The poem is like a game board, with areas staked out and labeled "Cares cops," "the rock of Pride," and so on. Flatlanders live here. Why, if he wanted to use it so blankly, did Herbert choose an emblematic landscape?

The answer must be sought, paradoxically, in Herbert's subsequent forsaking of labels in the second half of the poem. The gladsome hill, the lake of brackish waters, and the swarming fears remain allegorically unidentified, and by that very fact rebuke the earlier categories. The early stages are mapped out for the pilgrim, Herbert implies, by others. Any Christian knows that the straight and narrow path lies between presumption (or Pride) on the one hand and despair (or Desperation) on the other. The early "milk and sweetnesses" of "Fancie" are classically followed by periods of "Care." The fulcrum of the change from the general to the personal is the stanza on Passion, with its first clouding of the schema through the riddling paradox, "A wasted place, but sometimes rich." Nothing comparably mysterious inhered in the former cave, rock, meadow, or copse. The second mystery allowed into the poem is the mystery of deception. "At length *I got* unto the gladsome hill," says Herbert, and in a poem such as this, told in the past tense, we must take such a statement as true (otherwise it would read, "At length I got unto what I thought was the gladsome hill"). The simple form Herbert uses permits us, along with him, to be deceived, but it raises the query of the validity of this presumed "past" tense. All of Herbert's recapitulatory poems (of which *The Collar* is the most famous) purport to retell yesterday's events, but in fact seem rather to transport us back into yesterday as a present experience, tenses notwith-

95

standing. The formulation of experience into lyric is always at war with the lyric recreation of the experience. The surest way to "break" a past tense and transform it into the present is to insert direct discourse, which by its nature is forever "present." In *The Pilgrimage,* the immediacy of the poem is at its highest in the last three stanzas, which begin with an echo of the opening line of the poem (italics mine):

> I travell'd on, *seeing* the *hill, where lay*
> *My expectation* . . .

> At length I got unto the gladsome *hill,*
> *Where lay my hope,*
> *Where lay my heart;* and *climbing* still . . .
> A lake of brackish waters on the ground
> Was all I found.

The unexpected entrance of the present participle, absent from the poem since the first line, draws us into the action as we were not drawn in during the passage of the named stations. At the same time, the poignant displacement of the echo one metrical foot back in the line (an effect Herbert would have intended) exerts its own disappointment:

$$
\begin{array}{cc}
4 & 5 \\
\text{. . . the hill, where lay} \\
1 \qquad 2
\end{array}
$$

My expectation.

$$
\begin{array}{c}
5 \\
\text{. . . the hill} \\
1 \qquad 2
\end{array}
$$

Where lay my hope.

The other variations—the note of achieved joy in the adjective "gladsome" added to "hill"; the admission of emotion in the increasingly more passionate series "my expectation," "my hope," "my heart"— quicken the previous schematic weariness of the poem into feeling. Again, lyric impulse takes precedence over allegory, and bursts wholly out in the central line of the poem, a line entirely "present" and not at all "remembered":

Can both the way and end be tears?

Unanswered, Herbert rises bravely and then perceives he was deceived; but at the very moment of deception he makes his strongest claim— "the hill where" becomes "my hill." His hill it is, and he will have it yet. But the contest is a draw. The anonymous cry, "None goes that way and lives" (which may be taken either as taunt or warning), provokes Herbert into a piece of notable, if desperate bravado: "I cannot be worse treated than I have been; if that be your only threat, it is an empty one; after such a foul journey death seems fair." The horror of death is put aside here with quick *sprezzatura,* chiefly because death is not the real subject of this poem, whose theme is rather the foul journey, whose insight is the despairing one that both the way and end are tears.

The conquering of allegorical narrative by lyric dialogue, the transformation of past-tense recapitulation into present speech, the abandonment of manned stations in favor of anonymous encounter, all make this poem a very peculiar example of "allegory." In *Peace,* however, to cite a comparable poem, Herbert's allegory is tranquil. He seeks Peace in solitude, in the cosmos, and in nature, only to find, through the discourse of "a rev'rend good old man," that peace is to be found in the bread made of Christ's body. The didactic intent cohabits peacefully with the allegorical quest, and Herbert's first role as naïf seeker yields easily to his second, and silent, role as docile audience. *Peace* does not, in short, dispute its form in the way that *The Pilgrimage* does. If *The Pilgrimage* had continued as it began through its first half (excepting the paradoxical line about Passion), it would have been a wholly unremarkable poem. Vaughan learned from its mid-way change of styles to adopt its second form of unnamed experiences for the second half of his *Regeneration,* giving us by an unexpected restitutive kindness of literary history, the "successful" pilgrimage poem that the more saddened Herbert could not write. Without Herbert's example we could not have had Vaughan's heavenly grove and second spring:

> The unthrift Sunne shot vitall gold
> A thousand peeces,
> And heaven its azure did unfold
> Checqur'd with snowie fleeces,

The aire was all in spice
And every bush
A garland wore; Thus fed my Eyes
But all the Eare lay hush.

Vaughan's fountain, cistern, stones, and wind descend from Herbert's hill and lake and angel; if we prefer in some moments Vaughan's bank of flowers to Herbert's lake of brackish waters, we must at least acknowledge its lineage.

Herbert's exhausted language as the poem begins, his tired sense of the twice-told tale, his scrupulous but dry concessives ("but sometimes rich"), are phrased in an eternity of endurance. "I travell'd on . . . and so I came . . . so I came and there got through . . . that led me to . . . at length I got . . . when I had gain'd . . . I fell . . . yet taking heart I rose . . . and then perceived . . . so I flung away . . . yet heard a cry"—such a narrative form is unstoppable except by a declaration or a defiance, differing in that aspect from its vaguely felt model, the Passion of Christ, which also contained a fall at the top of a hill and a cry of abandonment. In this poem, Herbert re-examines the *Imitatio Christi:* the crucifixion is less painful finally, says Herbert, than the *via dolorosa.* Hopkins, perhaps learning from Herbert, said in *The Wreck of the Deutschland* that it is not the single extremity that prompts the heart to ask for ease; rather, it is "the jading and jar of the cart, time's tasking."

In *The Pilgrimage,* then, Herbert passes beyond his original allegorical schema (which may in itself have been initially a way to contain intractable emotion) and allows his emotion finally to overflow its vessels. A poem like *The Pilgrimage* constrains us to acknowledge the perseverance of Herbert's mind. Suspecting that both the way and end are tears, he not only does not bury and deny his intuition, but rather invents a table to embody it, and draws the tale out to its intolerable conclusion. As Stevens would say, he brings the storm to bear.

There are two conclusions to be drawn from Herbert's habitual resorting to allegorical and emblematic forms. The first affirms how much such forms pleased Herbert: he is perfectly at home in them, beginning, "I travell'd on" or "Having been tenant long," offering "this gentle rose," or musing, "As on a window late I cast mine eye." He launches with extreme ease and habituation into the genre, relishing the figurative possibility of emblematic description or allegorical narrative. But—and this must be the second conclusion—in almost every case he causes something odd to happen in the poem, bringing the form into question. In *The Windows,* a simple emblem (preachers are like stained glass) is bifurcated, trifurcated, and quadrifurcated, so to speak, into crazed glass, wat'rish glass, annealed glass, and no glass; in *Love-joy,* "misinterpretation" and "true interpretation" of a single emblem vie and are reconciled; in *Jesu,* emblems are rearrangeable in whole or broken forms; in *Humilitie* and *The Pilgrimage,* an "unhappy ending" is affixed to an allegorical form which normally would presuppose a cheerful resolution; in *Justice* (II), emblems are shown to be created according to one's angle of vision; in *The Agonie,* one emblem is shown to yield two "true" readings; in *Love* (III), text and gloss are strangely intermingled both with each other and with added elements; *Hope,* while maintaining the allegorical fiction of an exchange of gifts, takes no care that those gifts should be literally plausible; *The Rose* contains two entirely opposed emblematic truths in the same object; and *Love unknown* uses the mildest of tones to recount what, fictively speaking, are horrific sufferings. In short, any allegorical or emblematic form, in Herbert's hands, is undergoing a constant critique of its own possibilities comparable with, but not identical to, the continuing critique of his own feelings so pervasively conducted in the lyrics. The possible stodginess and complacency of these figurative forms, once they have been shorn of their narrative fullness, on the one hand, or their visual accompaniment, on the other, are skirted by Herbert with his customary penetration and grace. For him, figures and schemes are not the fixed result of inquiry, but rather the fluid means to discovery.

4

Imitators and Adapters

He that doth imitate must comprehend
Verse, matter, order, spirit, title, wit.[1]

Herbert's poetry has no clear immediate poetic antecedents. There
is no earlier religious poet in English whose work closely resembles
Herbert's, and the frequently drawn parallels between Donne and Herbert have to do more with large thematic resemblances common to
numberless religious poets in many languages than with any comparable
poetic or temperamental qualities. Donne's theatricality and morbidity,
in his best religious verse, are especially far from Herbert's inclinations.
In Harold Bloom's vocabulary of "poetic influence,"[2] the "covering
cherub" presiding over Herbert's verse, the force he must both incarnate
and resist, is received religious dogma, religious literature, tradition,
practice, ritual, and language. The Bible (notably the Psalms), the
Book of Common Prayer, homiletic practice, liturgical rites, religious
iconography, hymns, prayers, and meditations are Herbert's thematic
antecedents, as Rosemond Tuve has so definitively shown. That Herbert
learned from Sidney and Shakespeare, especially from their sonnets, from
Donne's secular lyrics (perhaps more than from his religious ones), and
from the various metrical translations of the Psalms cannot be doubted,
but the harmonious Mozartian inventiveness of his verse has more affini-
ties with musical rhythms and tempi than with any influence from a predecessor, with the possible exception of Sidney's songs in *Astrophel and
Stella*. Herbert's rhythms, insofar as they resemble Donne's or Sidney's,
probably owe that resemblance to a common source in song forms. The

result of drawing comparisons between Herbert and his poetic predecessors is the rather helpless admission of how little any of them truly resembles him in voice, nuance, structure, or effect. To define Herbert's special characteristics, it is more useful to turn to those poets, from Christopher Harvey on, who believed that they were writing poems *like* Herbert's. In one sense, they were: their poems share Herbert's themes and often look like Herbert's on the page. In more important ways, however, their poems are wholly unlike those written by their model. The difference resides in the area of poetic practice most difficult to identify: the specificity of genius in depth of feeling, originality of invention, and structural power. Herbert's early imitators, adapters, and revisers had not our disadvantages in distance of time and difference of culture. Their responses to *The Temple* can, by inference, tell us a good deal about what they saw, both good and bad, in Herbert and can reveal to us what qualities in Herbert they were unable to attain.

In 1640 Christopher Harvey published *The Synagogue,* a book of poems imitating Herbert, his "shadow of *The Temple.*" It was systematically enlarged in subsequent editions, and a comparison of the tables of contents of the 1640 and 1679 editions shows the sort of mechanical additions Harvey favored: by 1679 the list of ecclesiastical objects ensconced in the book has grown to include church-utensils, the font, the pulpit, the reading-pew, the communion-plate, the Book of Common Prayer, and the communion table; and ecclesiastical officers (sexton, clerk, overseer, warden, deacon, priest, and bishop) have been added wholesale. There is an implied reproach to Herbert, in both cases, for omitting from his temple so many sacred vessels, objects, places, and above all, ecclesiastical personnel. The festivals of the Church in Harvey's edition of 1679 have been expanded from two to nine, and even in the 1640 edition, Harvey has added to Herbert's modest threshold and Church-porch a Church-gate, wall, and stile. Our sense of Harvey's solemn tastelessness is borne out in the poems themselves, from which Herbert's inwardness is entirely absent. It is easy to mock Harvey's bizarre inventions:

> The Deacon! That's the Minister.
> True, taken generally;

And without any sinister
   Intent, used specially,
He's purposely ordain'd to minister,
In sacred things, to another officer.

At such moments, in ecclesiastical subject and didactic tone, Harvey is farthest from Herbert. He bravely attempts a poem on the Sabbath with an emblematic stanza of seven lines and an emblematic length of seven stanzas, but the final emblematic wish—that line 1 should have one syllable, line 2 two, and so on—combines metrical unhappiness with Harvey's foolishness of diction to make a lamentable poem:

Hail
Holy
King of days,
The Emperor,
Or Universal
Monarch of time, the week's
Perpetual Dictator.

It is impossible to write a poem so bad as this except through the desire to imitate. Harvey perceived, as such verses show, the external "constraints" that Herbert delighted to impose on himself, and knew them to be constitutive to Herbert's practice. These constraints did not disturb Harvey but on the contrary roused him to pleased emulation. He attempted a catena, for example, called *Church Festivals,* in imitation of Herbert's *Prayer* (I):

Marrow of time, Eternity in brief,
Compendiums Epitomized, the chief
Contents, the Indices, the Title-pages
Of all past, present, and succeeding ages,
Sublimate graces, antedated glories,
   The cream of holiness
     The inventories
   Of future blessedness,
The Florilegia of celestial stories,
Spirits of joys, the relishes and closes
Of Angels' music, pearls dissolvèd, roses

Perfumèd, sugar'd honey-combs, delights
　　Never too highly prized,
　　　The marriage rites,
　　Which duly solemnized
Usher espousèd souls to bridal nights,
Gilded sunbeams, refined Elixirs,
And quintessential extracts of stars:
Who loves not you, doth but in vain profess
That he loves God, or heaven, or happiness.

This perfectly external poem shows how little Harvey comprehended the passional components of Herbert's verse. The metaphors are dictated, in the first instance, by arid searches for figures applicable to liturgical feasts—Compendiums, Indices, Inventories, and Florilegia— but then Harvey's dim sense that his poem is not approaching Herbert's "softnesse, and peace, and joy, and love, and blisse" prompts him to a spate of images at first Herbertian ("the relishes and closes/Of Angels' music") but later tautologically saccharine ("roses/Perfumèd," "sugar'd honey-combs," "Gilded sunbeams," "refined Elixirs")— images that indeed gild the lily. The lack of spiritual elevation (though the state is mimicked in these phrases) is evident in the instructional complacency of the conclusion. *Church Festivals* is what *Prayer* (I) *seems* to be, an impersonal poem. Yet anyone examining the differences in the two poems is immediately struck by Herbert's organization of his figures around feeling, a structure to which, in this case, Harvey does not even pretend to aspire.

　　But there are instances where Harvey is attempting a genuine imitation of Herbert, feelings and all. The poems most like Herbert's appear in the 1640 *Synagogue,* before the spate of liturgical and ecclesiastical additions. One of the poems of 1640, *The Return,* is evidently inspired by *The Flower* and contains two stanzas (the first and third) of Herbertian "experience":

　　　Lo, now my Love appears;
　　　　My tears
　　　Have clear'd mine eyes: I see
　　　　'Tis he.

Thanks, blessed Lord, thine absence was my hell;
And now thou art returnèd, I am well . . .

> Who would have thought a joy
> So coy
> To be offended so
> And go
> So suddenly away? As if enjoying
> Full pleasure and contentment, were annoying.

The meditative stance here imitated from Herbert ("Who would have thought my shrivel'd heart/Could have recover'd greennesse?") is unhappily vitiated by the jog trot of the meter, which reads, to the ear:

> Lo, now my Love appears, my tears
> Have clear'd mine eyes: I see 'tis he.

It is characteristic of Harvey to "see" Herbert's disproportion in lines and to imitate their appearance (a "long" line followed by a "short" one), without noticing that Herbert, for instance, nowhere uses this particular rhythmic combination (trimeter followed by monometer). In the one poem, *Longing,* where Herbert uses a monometer refrain, he has the sense to perface it with a pentameter or tetrameter, thus "forbidding" the easy assimilation of two lines into one tetrameter, which happens in Harvey's verses. Normally, Herbert's "short" lines are dimeter or trimeter, and are prevented from coalescing with the lines preceding them because those lines themselves vary in length, a variation producing those effects of unpremeditated art we so prize in *The Temple.* However, even precluding from the metrical absurdity of *The Return,* we can perceive the gulf between Harvey and Herbert in Harvey's eagerness to leave behind the experiential origin of the poem and hasten to the didactic "lesson" (which in his hurry he even interpolates between the two experiential stanzas):

> By this I see I must
> Not trust
> My joys unto myself:
> This shelf,

Of too secure, and too presumptuous pleasure,
Had almost sunk my ship, and drown'd my treasure.

Harvey's irrepressible pulpit manner urges him beyond self-instruction into "a lecture," as he calls it, which still echoes Herbert in its attempts at metaphor:

> He that his joys would keep
>   Must weep;
> And in the brine of tears
>   And fears
> Must pickle them . . .
>
>   Learn to make much of care:
>   A rare
>   And precious balsam 'tis.

In making "care" at once a pickling brine and a precious balsam, Harvey stretches latitude in metaphor to the breaking point. He has understood Herbert's freedom in passing from metaphor to metaphor without caring for a consistent thread of imagery, so long as each metaphor illustrates a facet of the subject, but he has not comprehended the taste necessary to keep the varied metaphors from positive clashes with each other.

In *Comfort in Extremity*, Harvey attempts a version of *Dialogue*, which at least catches the naïve tone of Herbert's pleas. However, its halting alternation of trimeter and dimeter coalesce to form a "false" pentameter:

> Alas! my Lord is going,
>   Oh my woe!
> It will be mine undoing;
>   If he go
> I'll run and overtake him:
>   If he stay,
> I'll cry aloud, and make him
>   Look this way.

> O stay, my Lord, my Love, 'tis I;
> Comfort me quickly, or I die.

The undistinguished diction and lack of any real inner tension drop this stanza below the rank of its fine model, the deceptively self-exonerating first stanza of Herbert's *Dialogue:*

> Sweetest Saviour, if my soul
>   Were but worth the having,
> Quickly should I then controll
>   Any thought of waving.
> But when all my care and pains
> Cannot give the name of gains
> To thy wretch so full of stains,
>   What delight or hope remains?

The chief difference between these two poems appears in the dialogue attributed to Jesus. Harvey's Christ speaks in theological clichés about "mine all-sufficient merits" and "the throne of glory":

> *Cheer up thy drooping spirits,*
>   *I am here.*
> *Mine all-sufficient merits*
>   *Shall appear*
> *Before the throne of glory*
>   *In thy stead:*
> *I'll put into thy story*
>   *What I did.*

Herbert's Jesus, though he too refers to his redemptive act, does so in plain language:

> *What the gains in having thee*
> *Do amount to, only he,*
> *Who for man was sold, can see;*
> *That transferr'd th'accounts to me.*

Herbert's Jesus always carries on a true conversation, whether his intent is comfort, as in *The Collar,* or reproach, as in this poem:

What, Child, is the ballance thine,
Thine the poise and measure?
If I say, Thou shalt be mine;
Finger not my treasure.

Harvey's Christ speaks like a collect, Herbert's like a person. A *Poem to the Author* by one "R. Langford of Grayes-Inn, Counsellour-of-law," in the 1679 edition of *The Synagogue* rightly says:

He that doth imitate must comprehend
Verse, matter, order, spirit, title, wit.

Harvey understood Herbert's verse in part (its difficult metrical and stanzaic conditions) but did not see the harmonics that dictate which lines of differing lengths make acceptable sequences. As for the matter, he perceived Herbert's emblematic interest in poems like *The Church-floore,* and his liturgical inspiration in *Whitsunday, Trinitie Sunday,* and *Sunday,* but he was at a loss to understand Herbert's taste for prolonged introspection and revisionary interpretation of sacred things. Herbert's "order"—a convincing sequence of feelings—escaped Harvey entirely, and Herbert's "spirit" (whether his plain-speaking energy when addressing God, or his guilt and sorrow when addressing himself) is incomprehensible to Harvey's complacent, external, and officious mind. Herbert's wit, both in its power of invention as he "rewrites" religious clichés and in its local verbal playfulness, lies perhaps farthest of all from Harvey's timid reach. Harvey was no poet (unlike certain subsequent imitators of Herbert from Wesley through Taylor, Christina Rossetti, and Hopkins), and his resolute rewriting of Herbert into ecclesiastical propriety indicates how wholly, perhaps unconsciously, he rejected the Herbert of troubled meditation, the poet whose thoughts were all a case of knives, who called himself a wonder tortured. There are no wonders and no tortures in Harvey, and his lines imitating the true voice of feeling expose him in their hollowness.

The Samuel Speed who, in 1677, published many imitations of Herbert in *Prison-Pietie: or, Meditations Divine and Moral. Digested into Poetical Heads, On Mixt and Various Subjects* was a better versemaker

107

than Harvey. But what Speed understood of Herbert was also a matter of external characteristics, especially emblematic ones. Though it preserves the external form of Herbert's *Paradise,* Speed's *Petition* is incapable of thematic coherence:

> Stand by me, Lord, when dangers STARE;
> Keep from my Fruit such choaking TARE,
> That on Confusion grounded ——— ARE.
>
> Thou that from Bondage hast me BROUGHT,
> And my deliverance hast ——— ROUGHT,
> 'Tis thee that I will praise for OUGHT.
>
> O lord, to evil make me CHILL,
> Be thou my Rock and holy HILL,
> So shall I need to fear no ILL.

Speed is first a garden with Fruits and Tares, next a slave bought from Bondage, and finally a climber on God's holy Hill. The lines describing dangers that "stare" and the wish to become "chill" to evil are prompted solely by the needs of rhyme, and the poem, devoid of feeling, becomes merely an exercise in orthographical ingenuity.

In his *Antiphon,* imitating Herbert's, Speed does not even perceive Herbert's *terza rima.* He uses a less demanding rhyme scheme and yet cannot succeed in giving his lines any intellectual coherence:

> *Chor.* He that was bound to *Herod* sent,
>   *Men.* And spit upon,
>   *Ang.* He is our Tent . . .
> *Chor.* He that pardon can our sin
>   *Ang.* Hath broke our snare,
>   *Men.* But we fall in.
> *Chor.* He with whom none can compare,
>   *Men.* He gave us eyes,
>   *Ang.* He made us rise.
> *Chor.* He was scourg'd with heavy lash,
>   *Men.* For us lost blood,
>   *Ang.* And us did wash . . .

> *Chor.* He that wore a Crown of Thorns
> *Men.* That doth us keep,
> *Ang.* And us adorns.

It is difficult to see how Christ can be said to have broken the angels' snare, made them rise, washed them, or adorned them with a crown of thorns—except by a strained interpretation of these lines. Speed's sense of the Christian economy is vague by comparison with Herbert's strict intellectual precision, and reading Speed's feeble verse makes us prize the firm substructure of intelligence and the fineness of descriptive theology that underlie even Herbert's simplest poems. A clear idea of the relations obtaining between different orders of being is always present in Herbert, and he never sacrifices conceptual order and clarity to "poetic" needs of rhyme or metrics. The most rigorous, though unstated, condition preceding all composition for Herbert is the condition of intellectual and moral truth in its most discriminating apprehension. Nothing in the apprehension may be sacrificed, whether to "beauty" or to "ease." The expression is always adapted to the inspiration, rather than the reverse; such integrity prevails only in the most self-demanding of poets. Awkwardness, when it occurs in Herbert, is commonly in the direction of prosiness and disciplined thought, never in the direction of euphony or sentiment. For a poet so full of "passion and choler" (his brother's analysis), Herbert had established in himself, by the time he composed most of the poems in *The Temple,* a remarkable ascendancy of intellectual responsibility over momentary impulse.

Among Speed's more outright imitations of Herbert are pattern-poems in the form of a cross, an altar, or the Bible (in poems so called), poems with double-ended lines like Herbert's *The Water-course* (*Of God; Of Christ*), and a proverbial poem (*Knots,* imitating Herbert's *Charms and Knots*). These poems are sometimes so close to Herbert's practice that they might better be called plagiarisms than imitations. *The Altar,* for example, remains painfully close to the original:

> A broken ALTAR, Lord, to thee I raise,
> Made of a Heart, to celebrate thy praise:
>   Thou that the onely Workman art,
>   That canst cement a broken heart.

For such is mine,
O make it thine:
Take out the Sin
That's hid therein.
Though it be Stone,
Make it to groan;
That so the same
May praise thy Name.
Melt it, O Lord, I thee desire,
With Flames from thy Coelestial fire;
That it may ever speak thy Praise alone,
Since thou hast changed into Flesh a Stone.

At first sight, this poem seems almost indistinguishable, thematically, from Herbert's. But Speed's rationalizations of Herbert's oddities demand notice. If the altar is broken (as the heart is), it must be mended; and since it is irrational to say (as Herbert implicitly does) that man can mend his own broken heart, it must be God the workman who cements it (in lieu of Herbert's cementing it himself with tears). The forcible operations to be performed by God on Speed's heart take no notice of the autonomy of the human creature; God is to "take out" Speed's sin, "make" his heart groan, and in final incoherence, "melt" this strong heart back into flesh. Such a conception dismisses man's own cooperation and in fact rids the poem of any notion of sacrifice. The illogicality of the whole, coupled with Speed's emotionless lines, confuses the central metaphor of the altar, since it has no justification in either thought or sentiment. In Herbert's *Altar* we are puzzled; here we are simply unsatisfied.

Speed, like so many imitators, has no idea when to stop. "If an effect is good," his reasoning seems to go, "repeated five times it is better." Herbert's spare *The Call* is imitated *ad nauseam* in Speed's poem of the same name. The first stanza is typical:

Come away, my Lord, my Life,
Thy presence doth preserve from strife.
Come away, My Lord, my Way,
. . . my Truth,

> . . . my Light,
> . . . my Feast
> . . . my Strength,
> . . . my holy Joy,
> . . . my dearest Love,
> . . . Divinest Lamb,
> . . . my Shepherd
> . . . my Safeguard and my Shield.

Each epithet is then illustrated by a couplet, and in this abandon of Herbert's increasingly compact references, Speed eliminates forever the possibility of an intertwined synthesis like Herbert's "Such a Heart, as joyes in love." Herbert's economical principle of construction in *The Call* has been wholly misunderstood by his imitator, and an endless "invention" substituted for concern with substance, structure, sequence, and feeling. There is no reason for poems like Speed's ever to stop; epithets can go on forever, and so can explanatory couplets.

To pass from imitators to adapters of Herbert's verse is to encounter an equally curious set of poems and problems. The imitators were chiefly taken by Herbert's "eccentricities"—his pattern poems, emblematic stanzas, ingenious rhymes, parallelisms, and allegories. The adapters, however, were attracted by Herbert's Christian sentiments, and his ingenuities were to them rather blemishes than virtues.

The Dissenter who adapted for congregational singing thirty-two poems (in *Select Hymns Taken out of Mr. Herbert's Temple,* printed in London in 1697) chose his poems thematically, as his commentator William Stephenson suggests,[3] avoiding "oddities" like *The Quip,* which, although it uses psalm meter, creates an allegory too *outré* for inclusion in a hymn. After choosing his poems, the anonymous adapter regularized Herbert's meters.[4] In this collection, then, we have a relatively "pure" case by which to assess both metrical effects in Herbert and the effects on the poems of structural transposition. If anyone should doubt that Herbert's chain of metaphors in *Prayer* (I) represents a coherent spiritual evolution from dry recitation, through resentment, to spiritual refreshment, he has only to read the version of the poem adapted for hymn singing (the couplets are numbered to correspond with the line of the sonnet from which they are adapted):

Prayer the Churches Banquet is,
   Prayer the Angels Age   1
Prayer the Soul in Paraphrase,
   The Heart in Pilgrimage.   3

God's breath in Man returning thither   2
   From whence it had its Birth;
Prayer the Christian Plummet is   4
   That soundeth Heav'n and Earth.

Prayer reversed Thunder is,   6
   And Christ's side-peircing Spear,
Prayer's a kind of heav'nly Tune   8
   Which all things hear and fear.

Engine against the Almighty One,   5
   It is the Sinners Tower,
The World that was a Six-days Work   7
   Transposing in an Hour.

Softness and Peace, and Spiritual Joy,   9
   Prayer is Love and Bliss,
It is as 'twere the Milky-way,   12
   The Bird of Paradice.

Prayer exalted Manna is,   10
   And gladness of the best,
Heaven in Ordinary 'tis,   11
   Prayer is Man well drest.

The Church-Bell's heard beyond the Stars,   13
   It is the Souls Heart-blood,
A kind of Land of Spices 'tis,   14
   And something understood.

We may sigh at the repeated insertions of "Prayer is," while recognizing the need for some such expansion of the catena for hymnal intelligibility. Far more serious is the rearrangement of the components of the poem. The displacement of line 8 is awkward in the extreme: instead of serving, by its "heav'nly Tune," as a bridge to "Softness and Peace," it is misplaced between two images of aggression, the "reversed Thunder" and the "Engine." The similar displacement of line 12, which by its imagery of the Milky Way and the Bird of Paradise belongs to the Land of Spices and the realm "beyond the stars," shows this adapter's ignorance of Herbert's structural intent. A chain of metaphors, it seemed to this hymn writer, could be rearranged at will. We can conclude that he missed entirely the emotional coherence of Herbert's poem.

In *Home,* the adapter omitted Herbert's most individual and bitter lines:

> What is this weary world; this meat and drink,
>   That chains us by the teeth so fast?
> What is this woman-kinde, which I can wink
>   Into a blacknesse and distaste?

Though the "I" of the rest of *Home* speaks words generically suitable to fallen man, these lines startle by their personal distaste for "woman-kinde," a sentiment unpromising for a married congregation and therefore dropped. The last stanza of the poem, with its personal reference to "my verse," was also silently omitted, and a wholly innocuous invention added:

> O shew me, in thy Temple here
>   Thy wondrous Grace, thy special Love,
> Or take me up to dwell with Thee
>   Within thy glorious House above.

The adapter cannot rise above his feeble adjectival "special," and "wondrous," and "glorious," but seems unembarrassed to conjoin his tedious lines with Herbert's struggling ones.

When this adapter is confronted with a poem as complicated as *Longing,* he is daunted by the poem's eccentric range of metaphor. In reducing fourteen stanzas to a nine-stanza hymn, he was willing to include such pained words as "sick," "famished," "hoarse," "withered," "giddy," "bitter," and "troubled," not normally part of the vocabulary of hymns, so it was probably not Herbert's vehement diction but rather Herbert's conceits which made him drop some stanzas. In the deleted stanzas Herbert entwined sucklings, mothers, and Christ; the reined horse unable to run; the universe as an interlined book; guests nesting at God's table; a hard Savior; headless sin; a tear-filled bosom and tearful promises. This turbulent series of metaphors repels the neoclassical taste of the adapter; beside them, even the furnace and flames of Herbert's fourth stanza are liturgically acceptable, although for the sake of decorum Herbert's exclamatory sufferings are decently toned down. "What heat doth in my Heart abide," says the adapter, while Herbert says, both more fully and more enigmatically, "Mark well my furnace! O what flames,/What heats abound!"

The conceits omitted from *The Search,* reduced in *Select Hymns* to twelve stanzas, dwell speculatively on God's actions and his will. They seem to offend the adapter, not by their outlandishness of reference, like the far-flung net of metaphors in *Longing,* but by their metaphysical daring. In the seventh stanza of *The Search,* Herbert speculates, almost in anticipation of Hardy, whether God has gone off to create some new species,[5] and has consequently dropped man, his old "fabrick," from his regard and favor:

> Lord, dost thou some new fabrick mould,
>   Which favour winnes,
> And keeps thee present, leaving th'old
>   Unto their sinnes?

When Herbert suspects that it is God's will which has eclipsed God's face, he cries out that he could pass any other obstruction—brass or steel or mountains—but not the one unbridgeable abyss of God's will. So far the adapter follows him and allows Herbert his first metaphor, God's will as an "intrenching":

> The will such an intrenching is,
>   As passeth thought:
> To it all strength, all subtilties
>   Are things of nought.

However, Herbert's next two stanzas reach a level of abstraction and difficulty intolerable to his reviser, who silently drops them, perhaps afraid of their venture into the unverifiable:

> Thy will such a strange distance is,
>   As that to it
> East and West touch, the poles do kisse,
>   And parallels meet.
>
> Since then my grief must be as large,
>   As is thy space,
> Thy distance from me; see my charge,
>   Lord, see my case.

To conceptualize God's *will* as a *distance* is itself distinctly odd, and in a development odder even than Marvell's paradox of the planisphere, Herbert composes a planisphere flattened along both axes, and adds, for good measure, the meeting parallels. In the following stanza, Herbert dares to affirm that his feeling of grief is also a dimensional thing, as *large* (a word of area) as God's space or distance of will from him ("space" ambiguously implying either area or length, while "distance" measures the latter alone). Herbert compounds his metaphor in the next stanza by praying that God will remove "these barres, these lengths," and here God's will, which was previously distance and space, becomes as well a set of physical objects. Finally, God's "absence" is said to "excell/All distance known," so that absence itself becomes, by the comparison, geographical. These spatial fancies arise from Herbert's original constitutive metaphor, his unsuccessful search for God in all regions of the earth and sky. The paradoxes rise from Herbert's notion of an ever-present God, who, if he cannot be found, is nevertheless at hand, but veiling himself. Distance and absence cease to be functions of geographical placement, as they are with human beings, and become instead pure functions of will. God's (wrathful) will is the only distance between himself and Herbert.

I doubt whether to a modern reader the speculative freedom Herbert here assumes takes on so disconcerting an aspect as it did to his adapter. In retrospect, we can recognize the difference between Herbert's bolder lines, omitted in *Select Hymns,* and the more conventional supplications that surround them. Without this comparison, I think we would notice fewer of the internal "discrepancies" in the poem. Herbert's metaphorical speculativeness, when it passes beyond convention, was too much for a late seventeenth-century reader who wanted decorum in his divinity; but we, with a less-educated sense of that decorum, can pass, unseeing, lines that were intended to startle. The recovery of Herbert's "originality" is possible only if our sense of the decorous is recalibrated to seventeenth century standards.

It is astonishing how eager some readers have been to denature Herbert, to tone him down to their level of acceptability, to render him, in a way he never intended, "harmonious." A comparison of the two *Aaron*'s, Herbert's and the adapter's, clearly shows this denaturing:

Aaron, from *The Temple*

Holiness on the head,
Light and perfections on the breast,
Harmonious bells below, raising the dead
To leade them unto life and rest:
Thus are true Aarons drest.

Profaneness in my head,
Defects and darknesse in my breast,
A noise of passions ringing me for dead
Unto a place where is no rest:
Poore priest thus am I drest.

Onely another head
I have, another heart and breast,
Another musick, making live not dead,
Without whom I could have no rest:
In him I am well drest.

Christ is my onely head,
My alone onely heart and breast,
My onely musick, striking me ev'n dead,
That to the old man I may rest,
And be in him new drest.

So holy in my head,
Perfect and light in my deare breast,
My doctrine tun'd by Christ, (who is not dead,
But lives in me while I do rest)
Come people; Aaron's drest.

Aaron, from *Select Hymns*

Holiness written on the Head,
    Light and Perfections on the Breast,
Harmonious Bells raising the Dead
    To Life: Thus are true *Aarons* drest.

But, oh, prophaneness in my Head,
    Defects and darkness in my Breast,
A noise of Passions like a Knell;
    Ala[s], poor Priest, thus am I drest.

And yet I have another Head,
    Christ is my only Heart and Breast:
He is my Musick causing Life;
    In him alone I am well drest.

Now again, Holy in my Head,
    Perfect and Light in Heart and Breast,
My doctrine tun'd by Christ, who lives
    In me; Come People, *Aaron's* drest.

If the harmonious pole of Herbert's poem consists of the light and perfections, the opposite pole originates from words like "dead" and "no
rest." The poem depends, for its tension, on the fear of spiritual and
physical death, and on the horror of a place where there is "no rest."
The blandness of the adaptation for choral singing is perhaps understandable (though any congregation who could sing *Self-condemnation* should
be able to cope with all of *Aaron*), but it is less clear why Palmer should
have entirely deleted the rhyme-word "dead" in his description of
Herbert's five end-words, referring in his paraphrase only to "head,"
"breast," "rest," and "drest": "The standard of the priesthood being
one, is fixed in five rhyming words: in his own *head* and *heart* the priest
must be sound; from him music must go forth; it is his work to find *rest*
for the sinful; his *dress* or exterior must express an inner purity" (italics
mine).[6] There is something very Arnoldian about this comment. It is certainly not like Herbert, who is far more primitive, saying that there *is* a
hell, there are the dead, sins threaten an eternity of no rest, the priest
has the *super*natural power to raise the dead, and the priest should take
care not to be himself one of the dead. These thoughts, rather too

archaic for the nineteenth-century "enlightened" mind, are silently passed over in Palmer's note, where the priest emerges not as a sacred intermediary possessing supernatural power, but rather as a helpful minister—sound, harmonious, pure, engaged in finding rest for the sinful. Mary Ellen Rickey's summary of the rhyme lines is equally discreet: "The first ones [treat] the symbolism of the priest's *head,* the second ones, that of the *breast,* the third ones, that of the bells, the fourth ones, that of the *rest* afforded by the bells, and the last ones, the total *dress*ing of the servant of God" (italics mine).[7]

"Head," "breast," "rest," and "drest" (in its variant "dressing") are all explicitly repeated in this summary; "dead" alone, among the five rhyme words, is totally suppressed, and one would not guess, from this summary, the dark side of the poem. Summers, too, skips from the "cacophonous passions" in man's heart to the "hell of 'repining restlessnesse' " whither the passions lead man, omitting the various meanings of the word "dead" in the poem.[8] Ryley alluded to the Pauline "body of this death" (Rom. 7:24) to explain the use of "dead" in stanza two, but had no real interest in the perpetual stanzaic presence of "deadness."[9] The commentaries, by avoiding "deadness," avoid seeing the poem as a spiritual experience and treat it instead as a prescriptive description: "The profaneness in man's head, the defects and darkness in his heart, the cacophonous passions which destroy him and lead him to a hell of 'repining restlessnesse' *can* be transformed through the imputed righteousness of Christ into the ideal symbolized by Aaron's ceremonial garments."[10]

This is all very well as theology, but insufficient as a remark about poetry. Summers adds two literary comments: that the priest looks the same at the end as at the beginning (like the stanzas) and that the coincidence, at the end of the poem, of external dress and internal disposition makes the poem end in a "climactic synthesis."[11] Though these observations are true, it is never clear here or in other commentaries what motivates the changes from a poor priest to a true priest. Since poems are movements of heart, as well as constructions of a pattern, one cannot simply assert that the wicked *can* be changed into the just, since no one has ever doubted that as a proposition in theology. But why, *at this juncture,* do the wicked in fact change into the just?

The poem is a conversion poem: Herbert begins with holiness *on* the head and perfections *on* the breast, but he ends holy *in* his head, perfect and light *in* his *deare* breast. The adjective is as significant as the new preposition. Self-hatred has turned to self-tenderness, and the "body of this death" has become a breast Herbert can love. The Pauline complex of metaphor underlying the poem, but not generally perceived, is an elaborate interweaving of conversion, baptism, and resurrection (cf. Rom. 6:4–11). The poem also uses the Pauline formula of putting off the old man and putting on Christ, but that internal transformation (which may be called conversion) is metaphorically crossed in this poem with the resurrection of the natural body, as it is in St. Paul (1 Cor. 15:42–44):

> So also is the resurrection of the dead.
> It is sown in corruption; it is raised in incorruption:
> It is sown in dishonour; it is raised in glory:
> It is sown in weakness; it is raised in power:
> It is sown a natural body; it is raised a spiritual body.

The characteristics of the "spiritual body" are the holiness, light, perfection, and harmony possessed by the true priest. With these virtues, he can raise the "dead" to life; that is, sinners will be brought to spirituality by the priest, who, in raising these "dead," imitates and figures Christ. Christ, the priest, and the raised dead share in the perfect community of the saved.

But in the second stanza, the priest himself joins the unconverted "dead," and the community becomes disharmonious. If the salt lose its savor, wherewith shall it be salted? The subsequent interior process of conversion, in which the true moral and emotional interest of the poem resides, has three stages, each occupying a stanza. These stanzas may be thought of as variants of the same stanza: 3a, 3b, and 3c. If stanza one is perfection in the abstract ("Thus are true Aarons drest") and stanza two is imperfection in the personal instance ("Poore priest thus I am drest"), the three stanzas that follow are attempts to arrive at the single Pauline paradox: "I live, yet not I, but Christ liveth in me" (Gal. 2:20). Paul's gnomic expression is brief; Herbert needs three stanzas to approach and accommodate it. His first step, self-reproach following upon the harsh self-judgment in the second stanza, denies himself any part in the redemptive scheme. Justification comes by Christ, not by oneself, and Herbert claims to have *another* head, *another* heart and breast, *another* music. With the arrival of the mysterious Pauline phrase "in him," the poet is allowed a closer relation to Christ. The formulation, a revision of the previous stanza, nevertheless still excludes the natural. Herbert is no longer two-headed ("my" head and "another" head), but is now exclusively Christ-headed: "Christ is my *onely* head,/ My *alone onely* heart and breast,/My *onely* musick." The protestation is strained, and though the phrase "my ——— head" is more credible than "another head/I have," the convert has now entered into a fever of self-obliteration. After seeing, in stanza three, Christ as an *alternative* to the natural, he sees him in stanza four as a *substitute* for the natural. His relief at the discovery of the alternative to the defective self is succeeded by an immoderate enthusiasm which rejects the self, not now from the motives of self-reproach that prompted stanza three, but rather from an excess of humility vis-à-vis the glories of Christ. Herbert himself is "struck dead" (an uneasy, if Pauline, formulation) in this stanza, since being dead is associated with sin and mortality.

Once Herbert is "new drest" in Christ, however, he can with assurance allow a resurgence of the natural. Once again he can say simply, as in stanza two, "My head," and can add "my deare breast." Christ is no longer "another musick," nor Herbert's "onely musick, striking [him] dead." Rather, Herbert's own doctrine is now "tun'd" by Christ, who becomes a normative principle to the human rather than an alternative or subsitutive one. There may be a faint echo of the angel's words to the Marys at the tomb in Herbert's parenthesis about "Christ, (who is not dead/But lives . . .)", or Herbert may be remembering the Psalmist's "I shall not die, but live, and declare the works of the Lord" (Ps. 118:17), but in any case those words boldly announce the Resurrection of Christ within Herbert (the same Psalm, with its verse, "This is the day which the Lord hath made," is associated with the Easter liturgy). "Christ," says Herbert, "lives in me while I" ——— while I what? While I am dead, as Paul would have it? Not in Herbert's final formulation. "Oh rest in the Lord," "I will give you rest"—these and other texts supervene over the harsher Pauline metaphor of being struck dead; and freed from his excesses of self-reproach, self-obliteration, and self-abnegation, Herbert can at last re-enter his body and his poem, saying, "I rest."

The final stanza of the poem at first seems to be adopting a variant of the appositive-descriptive form in the first two stanzas: "*X, Y, Z*, thus are true/poor priests drest." However, the expected summary phrase does not follow the last series of parallel phrases ("holy," "perfect," "my doctrine tun'd"). Normally, such adjectives would be followed by "I" plus a verb: "So, holy, perfect, and light, I begin my ministry." But the very act of ministry itself precludes the singular pronoun. Herbert is now both himself and Christ, and he is also Aaron, the type of the true priest. His first word will be not "I" but rather the word of Christ, "Come." "Let the little children come," "Come unto me, all ye who labor"—"Come people; Aaron's drest."

Herbert's three formulations of his relation to Christ suggest both the influence of Paul and a resistance to Paul. The last stanza of the three is clearly the least Pauline, its musicality and lightness of diction distinguishing it from Paul's harsher mode. In Herbert's use and revision of Paul, he first of all adopts the most complex source of the theology of conversion, and then allows his own feelings to dictate a psychologically believable approach to and divergence from the Pauline position. Without knowing Paul (and the changes that Herbert rings on him) and without an appreciation of the stages of conversion conceived and represented by Herbert, we are in no position to perceive Herbert's art, which consists precisely in both the wit of his intellectual reformulation and revision of Paul, and in the accuracy of his psychological insight into the excesses of self-reproach and enthusiasm that beset the experience of conversion. Herbert's adapter probably saw neither his accuracy nor his wit. He conflated "another" and "onely," transmitted the self-reproach but not the self-forgiveness, shrank from the stern climax in which Herbert is "struck dead," and missed the resurrection of Christ in Herbert; in short, he omitted almost every item that makes this poem a movement of the heart rather than a proposition in theology.

John Wesley's rewritings of Herbert, such as his adaptations of *The Rose, Vertue,* and *The Invitation*,[12] have received less attention than the thematic reasons for his selection of certain poems from *The Temple*.

Elsie Leach mentions Wesley's "neo-classical distaste for the homely and particular" and his "cautious approach to the metaphysical conceit," citing certain of Wesley's omissions from Herbert, particularly from *Grieve Not the Holy Spirit* and *The Search*. She also singles out reversals of stanza order in the former poem, as well as instances in which a generalized eighteenth-century diction is substituted for Herbert's more concrete figurative language.[13] But my own main interest lies not in Wesley's choices from *The Temple* nor in his reasons for rewriting Herbert, but rather in those passages in the poetry that offended Wesley's religious or aesthetic sensibilities. What passes muster with Wesley, a devoted and sympathetic life-long reader of Herbert, is unfortunately that portion of Herbert's thought which is unexceptionable or at least acceptable from a conventionally religious point of view. Wesley is disturbed by Herbert's conceptual audacity in respect to religious matters, not simply by his seventeenth-century language and imagery. It is not enough to say that Wesley's neoclassical taste dislikes conceits, since innumerable conceits are permitted to survive his scrutiny.

Although Wesley's more elevated diction often works to destroy Herbert's colloquial effect, and is consequently the change first remarked, the wish for a more formal diction does not by itself explain all of Wesley's deletions, nor does his diction, taken alone, account for the generally insipid air of his hymns. I believe that Wesley was often taken aback by Herbert's plain speaking, his frankness about his own feelings, his outright complaints, and his unconventional attitudes toward God. Wesley could recognize an inadmissible tone or metaphor in a prayer, while we, unaccustomed to limits of decorum in colloquies with God, tend to assume piety in any example of the genre. The limits of Wesley's tolerance may be seen in his revision of Herbert's *Dialogue*.

Dialogue, by George Herbert

Sweetest Saviour, if my soul
    Were but worth the having,
Quickly should I then controll
    Any thought of waving.
But when all my care and pains

Cannot give the name of gains
To thy wretch so full of stains,
What delight or hope remains?

What, Child, is the ballance thine,
  Thine the poise and measure?
If I say, Thou shalt be mine;
  Finger not my treasure.
What the gains in having thee
Do amount to, onely he,
Who for man was sold, can see;
That transferr'd th'accounts to me.

But as I can see no merit,
  Leading to this favour:
So the way to fit me for it
  Is beyond my savour.
As the reason then is thine;
So the way is none of mine:
I disclaim the whole designe:
Sinne disclaims and I resigne.

That is all, if that I could
  Get without repining;
And my clay, my creature, would
  Follow my resigning:
That as I did freely part
With my glorie and desert
Left all joyes to feel all smart—
  Ah! no more: thou break'st my heart.

The Dialogue, by John Wesley

S.   Saviour, if Thy precious love
  Could be merited by mine,
Faith these mountains would remove;
  Faith would make me ever Thine:
But when all my care and pains
  Worth can ne'er create in me,

Nought by me Thy fulness gains;
  Vain the hope to purchase thee.

C. Cease, my child, thy worth to weigh,
      Give the needless contest o'er:
    Mine thou art! while thus I say,
        Yield thee up, and ask no more.
    What thy estimate may be,
        Only can by Him be told,
    Who to ransom wretched thee,
        Thee to gain, Himself was sold.

S. But when all in me is sin,
      How can I Thy grace obtain?
    How presume Thyself to win?
      God of Love, the doubt explain:
    Or, if Thou the means supply,
      Lo! to Thee I all resign!
    Make me, Lord, (I ask not why,
      How, I ask not,) ever Thine!

C. This I would—that humbly still
      Thou submit to My decree,
    Blindly subjecting thy will,
      Meekly copying after Me:
    That, as I did leave My throne;
      Freely from My glory part;
    Die to make thy heart My own—
S.   Ah! no more: Thou break'st my heart!

Stein and others have seen the disingenuousness of Herbert's sinner, whose "latent rebelliousness of the first speech," as Stein puts it, becomes in the second speech "active and open," while preserving "a certain cloak of appearances."[14] The most noticeable revision, in Wesley's version, is that the sinner is no longer the ingenious dialectician: he has become a humble soul, wishing to "win" Jesus, to "merit" his "precious love," to "purchase" him. Instead of disclaiming the whole design and "resigning" from it, like Herbert's petulant speaker, he "resigns" all to Jesus, a wholly different use of the word. Wesley's care is neither for diction nor for conceits; he cares rather for moral seemliness in an address to God. The only possible conclusion is that he found Herbert's rebellion too disturbing to include in a book of hymns.

But Wesley not only changes Herbert's sinner; he also changes his Savior. Herbert's Jesus is both ironic—"What, Child, is the ballance thine?"—and capable of the pun on "resign," while Wesley's Lord is far too solemn for either. More seriously, Wesley's Jesus asks what Herbert's would not: a blind subjection. The Jesus of Herbert's *Dialogue* asks that his clay, his creature, should follow *Jesus'* resigning, in *freely* parting with his glory, his desert, and his joys. Just as Jesus did nothing in blind subjection, neither should the sinner. Herbert's way is to persuade his sinner by Jesus' example, not to urge him to "submit" to "a decree," as Wesley would have it.

It follows that Wesley was not only taken aback by Herbert's argumentative sinner, but was also put out of countenance by Herbert's parleying Chirst, who uses all the most human of means—irony, pun, comparison with himself—to win the sinner. Herbert's Jesus is akin to the Jesus of the parables and to the Jesus who makes ironic rejoinders to those who seek to trap him with tribute money or reminders of the Sabbath. Wesley's Jesus, who addresses the sinner as "wretched thee," is altogether more removed from dialogue and from human interplay: a pedestal has been imported into the poem. Herbert's Jesus is credible as a projection of the self because he speaks the same language as the self, and the air of true conversation is maintained, even though two widely divergent attitudes are exemplified in this "dialogue of the mind with itself." The divine response, in words like "gains" and "resign," originates from the vocabulary of the sinner's complaint, consolidating the impression of an inner debate. Wesley, though he imitates the device in the first instance (but not in the second), destroys the effect of a single divided mind by his disparate levels of diction (cringing in the sinner, lofty in Jesus). The pleasure of the poem comes from seeing sophistry rebuked; poetry and sophistry are deadly enemies, and Herbert must have been able to recognize, sooner than most people on the defensive, the hollowness of his own self-justifications with their air of specious dialectic and special pleading. To undo his own false speech by countering it with an imagined speech above all self-interest meant to cancel a bad poem, so to speak, by a good one. No such poetic interest resides in Wesley's version, where the speech of the "sinner" is wholly "sincere" and humble, without any suggestion of sophistry. Therefore, in this version adapted for hymn singing, the worn convention of the supplicating sinner and the decree-pronouncing Savior replaces all human and poetic force and feeling, and one could read the hymn without feeling a flicker of poetic attention, derived though it is from a poem full of emotional and intellectual power.

Wesley's wish to revise Herbert did not spring only from his care for congregational singing. He also published two poems adapted from Herbert in *A Collection of Moral and Sacred Poems* (1744), retitling each *Anacreontick* and intending, as the title shows, to lighten Herbert's effect.[15] He is least successful in the second *Anacreontick,* his revision of *The Rose,* which strips Herbert of his playfulness and decoration, making him simply moral. Wesley assumed that if a poem has a moral aim, it needs nothing in itself beyond what is necessary to point the moral; and awkwardly enough, this aesthetic responds to certain of Herbert's own inclinations toward a minimal art, so that we can scarcely condemn it out of hand. Wesley's revision of *The Rose,* however, is so reductive of its original that even the moral is damaged:

> Never tempt me to caress
> Grief, disguised like Happiness:
> Earth to bless me wants the Pow'r,
> Take my Reasons in a Flow'r:
> Let the Rose its Beauty show,
> Emblem of the Bliss below;
> Fair and sweet, it yields Delight,
> To the Smell, and to the Sight;
> Yet the Bloom is quickly past,
> Yet 'tis bitter to the Taste.
> If then all that Wordlings prize,
> Biting ends, and sudden flies,
> Bear me, Friend, if I pursue
> Pleasure otherwise than you;
> Say, that fairly I oppose,
> Say, my Answer is—a ROSE.

The tempter is here addressed as "Friend," and the whole poem made more social; yet not these changes, but the skeletal nature of the whole, vitiates the poem. Herbert's original puritanism toward worldly pleasures, expressed in his condemnatory "sugred lies," "colour'd griefs," and "blushing woes," is here abstractly represented by "Grief, disguised like Happiness"; but his admission that the rose is *in itself* gentle, fair, and sweet (though acting *on man* as a purgative) distinguishes between the thing in itself and a natural enmity between it and man. Wesley muddles the issue by adding two *intrinsic* deficiencies to the rose—its transiency and its bitterness (Wesley's poem also implies that is is common for people to taste roses, surely an odd assumption, whereas Herbert's poem uses a flat medicinal fact, which implies no bizarre behavior). By the end of the poem Herbert has admitted that worldly joys are indeed joys, but that the rhythm of surfeit and purgative is not to be his, that he will keep to his "strict, yet welcome size." Nothing in this offends a reader's sense of truth or probability or aesthetics. Wesley's more crabbed version denies worldly pleasure altogether ("Earth to bless me wants the Pow'r," "I pursue/Pleasure otherwise than you"), offering a total asceticism based on an intrinsic repellency (transiency and bitterness) in the world's components. Such plainly false representations cannot receive any poetic assent from a reader, while even Herbert's unbelieving readers can find his representation of life true to fact, and his aesthetic asceticism plausible. Herbert's own understanding of the nature of the rose is conveyed by the exquisite grace and cadence of his verse, a fit enshrinement for the emblem of all beauty; Wesley's harsh tetrameter and closed couplets, by abandoning Herbert's recurrent phonetic charm (in quatrains and feminine rhymes), become pedestrian. What appeal there is in Wesley's poem, both in gesture and in rhythm, comes from echoes of Herbert still gracing the lines.

It is Wesley's early finality, his closing-off of the issues of a poem, which robs his versions of the continuing evolution that is one of the characteristic strengths of Herbert's poetry. A poem by Herbert is not finished, spiritually, until it ends; any new line may bring a sudden lithe twist of the whole. Wesley's impulse is always to close off the experiential and bring on the sententious. His first *Anacreontick,* adapted from Herbert's *Life*, is a sad example of the cruelty of the moral to the aesthetic. Herbert's poem is simple enough in its expression to be read by anyone, including the presumed readers of Wesley's *Moral and Sacred Poems*, so Wesley's motives in rewriting it can scarcely be attributed to care for its moral message. Neither does *Life* contain any "coarse" references to purges that must be obliterated, as does *The Rose*. In fact, it is hard to find anything to object to in Herbert's simple, transparent, and delicate poem:

> I made a posie, while the day ran by:
> Here will I smell my remnant out, and tie
> My life within this band.
> But Time did becken to the flowers, and they
> By noon most cunningly did steal away,
> And wither'd in my hand.
>
> My hand was next to them, and then my heart:
> I took, without more thinking, in good part
> Times gentle admonition:
> Who did so sweetly deaths sad taste convey,
> Making my minde to smell my fatall day;
> Yet sugring the suspicion.
>
> Farewell deare flowers, sweetly your time ye spent,
> Fit, while ye liv'd, for smell or ornament,
> And after death for cures.
> I follow straight without complaints or grief,
> Since if my sent be good, I care not if
> It be as short as yours.

It is true, as Stein remarked of this little allegorical poem, that the "main plot is crystal clear, while the actions that compose it are both genuinely and deceptively simple."[16] The first two stanzas seem to present a contrast between Herbert and Time: he plucks the posies; Time takes them away; and he is left, symbolically at least, empty-handed. The dazzling invention of the poem arises in the third stanza, where the flowers are *addressed*. There is always a formally invigorating effect when a poem turns from referring to a subject in the third person ("the flowers") to addressing the subject directly ("deare flowers"), but in this case the effect is both more surprising (since the flowers have been presented, then annihilated) and more touching (since though dead, they are imaginatively resurrected by being addressed and hailed for their virtue). By this address, the sense of immediacy, first evoked in the poem by the direct quotation in lines 2–3, is renewed, and the "pastness" of the inception of the poem ("I made a posie") and of its continuation ("I took . . . Times gentle admonition") is made to flow into a perception contemporary with the writing of the poem. The "pastness" of the poem consists of watching one's own death. The "present" of the poem consists, first, in valuing one's own life while alive (a value imparted in the quotation allying oneself to the posie) and, second, in valuing one's own life when dead (a retrospective judgment imparted by the quotation addressed to the flowers). The religious poet is more likely to value the obituary notice over the present alliance, and Herbert's appeal here arises from his perfect willingness to call his life on earth a gathered posy. Not a pilgrimage, not a sojourn in this vale of tears, not an ascetic *imitatio Christi,* not the good fight, not the race, not a purgation—but a gathered flowering. If life is a fragrant posy, then death can be a potpourri or a restorative; there is a proportion among these things. A fragrant life is continuous with a fragrant death, and as the flowers achieve the virtue of "physick" after death, though they had only scent and ornament while alive, Herbert may legitimately hope for a similar enhancement of function. The sense of things going beyond the function assigned to them in life, justifying the after-death "survival" of the flowers, arises from Herbert's initial emblem's having taken on a significance beyond that which he first attributed to it. The posy was meant to stand only for the form he would have his life take; but as it changes in his very hand, a new emblematic significance steals into his soul, through a conduit from hand to heart to head—that conduit kept open by Herbert's conscious wish to deepen his perception of significances. Herbert's characteristic conjunction of the aesthetic (smell or ornament) and the moral (cures) attributes a moral will to the flowers in praising them for having spent their time sweetly, for being fit for good in both life and death. This is like the charity that Smart attributes to his late-blooming Guernsey lilies, and is a fanciful attribution without Shakespeare's strict veracity in affirming that the summer's flower lives and dies only to itself. But the courtly "gentillesse" of the address to the flowers ensures that it is seen by indirection, as an imagined post-humous address of Herbert to his own soul; this is the obituary he would like to pronounce over himself.

Wesley's unfanciful mind finds the address to the flowers undignified; he thus allows only a brief "Adieu" to survive. The imaginative little playlet by which Time beckons to the flowers and then conveys a gentle admonition to Herbert, "sweetly" conveying death's sad taste and "sugring" the suspicion of decay, is also suppressed as unsuitably conjectural, playful, fanciful, or theatrical. In short, both drama and invention are deleted in Wesley's *Anacreontick* in favor of *sententiae*:

> I Pluck'd this Morn these beauteous Flow'rs,
>   Emblem of my fleeting Hours;
> 'Tis thus, said I, my Life-time flies,
>   So it blooms, and so it dies.
> And, Lo! how soon they steal away,
>   Wither'd e'er the Noon of Day.
> Adieu! well-pleas'd, my End I see,
>   Gently taught Philosophy:
> Fragrance and Ornament alive,
>   Physick after Death they give,
> Let me throughout my little Stay
>   Be as useful, and as gay:
> My Close as early let me meet,
>   So my Odour be as Sweet!

We can be certain that Wesley thought he was doing no violence to his admired George Herbert in altering this poem; what Wesley loved in the poem (and he knew much of Herbert by heart) he must have felt he had preserved. We can conjecture that the substance of Wesley's admiration went to the emblem of the posy itself, useful and gay, and to Herbert's almost light acquiescence in an early death. Both of these are preserved. What is not preserved is Herbert's sadness, that tone in the poem which made Palmer rightly call it a "lament."[17] The whole poem, in its original version, composes, for all its willing acceptance willingly expressed, a series of dying falls. The day runs by; the flowers steal away and wither; the poet takes an admonition; lines close with phrases like "deaths and taste," "my fatall day," "suspicion," "your time ye spent," "complaints or grief," and "as short as yours." Wesley's jaunty ending, in particular, with its line endings of "alive," "give," "Stay," "gay," "meet," and "Sweet," expresses what Wesley no doubt took to be proper Christian optimism in the face of death. Even Herbert's stanza itself is made up of two dying falls, reinforcing the many lamenting cadences found in the diction and syntax, while Wesley's daunting metrical regularity contradicts, rather than allows, Herbert's intent. Herbert is a master, as all his commentators have remarked, of metrical adequacy, and here the beautiful balance between aesthetic acquiescence and human regret needs the rhythmic, lexical, and prosodic lingering to validate the intellectual willingness to die. When the human is suppressed in favor of the intellectual, as it is by Wesley, we believe not at all in the sentiment voiced. By making Herbert "holier," Wesley destroyed credibility in his holiness, a paradox that we may be confident he did not himself recognize.

No poem by Herbert loses more by being fitted to the intolerant regularity of hymn meter than *The Collar*. Wesley's version, though unfaithful in some respects to Herbert's expression, was clearly meant to hew close to Herbert's thought; and we may conclude, from its banality, how much of Herbert's vehemence resides in his prosody. The restless metric of Herbert's poem, veering toward a norm but never, until the end, attaining it,[18] is matched by its erratic rhyming, which can delay for as many as ten lines (from "me" to "thee") to find surcease. Wesley tamed all this hectic speech, and his quatrains breathe an air of complacency even while theoretically expressing sinful rebellion:

> Conscience and Reason's power deride,
>   Let stronger Nature draw;
> Self be thy end, and Sense thy guide,
>   And Appetite thy law.

One who has made appetite his law is unlikely to talk in this stately language.

The Collar is in itself a paradox in that it recalls a past experience in language that is vividly present in the form of quotation. This retrospective immediacy, perfected by Herbert, partakes in one way of the convention of pure narrative: "I struck the board, and cry'd, No more." But by the time we reach the end of the poem, analysis has removed the narration from an unmediated form to a mediated form (italics mine):

> But as I *rav'd* and *grew more fierce* and *wilde* . . .
> Me thoughts I heard one calling.

These analytic phrases, which judge as well as narrate, impose a present judgment on a past experience. There are, then, three "times" in the poem. The most "present" in effect is the long self-quotation ("No more./I will abroad."); the next in remoteness is the pure narration ("I struck," "I heard," "I reply'd"); the most remote is the *post-hoc* analysis of action ("I rav'd," "I grew more fierce and wilde"). Intellectually speaking, however, the most *recent* "time" is the judgmental one, next the narrative one, and last the spoken one. Part of the equilibrium of Herbert's poetry comes, in general, from the judgmental frame accompanying it; yet the *post-hoc* judgment is not permitted to color in too evident a way the reproduction of the antecedent conflict. That it does color it cannot be doubted. We are never unsure whether Herbert will resolve his inner turmoil; he does not begin to compose the poem until he has resolved it. In resuscitating the conflict, however, he does not appear to recollect emotion from his present vantage point (as Wordsworth explicitly does in *Tintern Abbey*, for instance); instead, he gives emotion a fully resurrected image of its former self.

That this formulation is not quite exact can be seen in Wesley's attempt to come to terms with Herbert's rebelliousness. Wesley thinks that the savors of the world ought to be given a more vivid representation, if the poem is engaged in showing someone tempted by them. I emphasize by italics his attempts to give worldly pleasures voice:

> *Free* as the *Muse*, my *wishes move*,
> Through Nature's wilds they *roam:*
> *Loose as the wind*, ye *wanderers*, *rove*,
> And bring me *pleasure* home! . . .

Not so, my heart!—for fruit there is:
 Seize it with *eager* haste;
Riot in joys, dissolve in bliss,
 And *pamper every taste* . . .

And *give a loose to joy.*
Away, ye shades, while *light I rise,*
 I tread you all beneath!
Grasp the *dear hours* my youth supplies,
 Nor idly dream of death.

So much thought evidently went into this supplementing of Herbert's speech that Wesley must have believed Herbert's ascetic soul had no idea of riotings, dissolvings, roaming through wilds, roving for pleasure, pampering tastes, and lingering over youth's dear hours. Perhaps there is another reason for Herbert's reticence, however, since he could, after all, when he wished, summon up life's enticings better than Wesley:

I know the wayes of Pleasure, the sweet strains,
The lullings and the relishes of it . . .
My stuffe is flesh, not brasse; my senses live.

But before suggesting a reason for the absence in Herbert of enacted enticings, I must remark another "correction" of *The Collar:* Wesley's muting of Herbert's violent self-criticism. The passage in question reads, in Herbert's long excoriation:

Sure there was wine
Before my sighs did drie it: there was corn
 Before my tears did drown it . . .
Recover all thy sigh-blown age
On double pleasures: leave thy cold dispute
Of what is fit, and not. Forsake thy cage,
 Thy rope of sands,
Which pettie thoughts have made, and made to thee
Good cable, to enforce and draw,
 And be thy law,
While thou didst wink and wouldst not see . . .

> Call in thy deaths head there: tie up thy fears.
> He that forbears
> To suit and serve his need,
> Deserves his load.

Wesley's version omits the drying-up of wine and the drowning of corn, and as for the rest of the quotation, Wesley's version goes as follows:

> Riot in joys, dissolve in bliss,
> And pamper every taste.
>
> On right and wrong thy thoughts no more
> In cold dispute employ;
> Forsake thy cell, the bounds pass o'er,
> And give a loose to joy.
>
> Conscience and Reason's power deride,
> Let stronger Nature draw;
> Self be thy end, and Sense thy guide,
> And Appetite thy law.
>
> Away, ye shades, while light I rise,
> I tread you all beneath!
> Grasp the dear hours my youth supplies,
> Nor idly dream of death.
>
> Who'er enslaved to grief and pain,
> Yet starts from pleasure's road,
> Still let him weep, and still complain,
> And sink beneath his load.

While the "cold dispute" remains, the "cage," "rope of sands," "pettie thoughts," and "good cable" have vanished; Herbert's winking, refusal to see, contemplation of a death's head, and unloosed fears have likewise disappeared. The sarcasm of the self-address barely survives in phrases like "cold dispute" and "Still let him weep." Some of the omissions may be excused on the ground of Wesley's objecting to conceits (the cage, rope, cable, and death's head included), but the self-scorn that is the motive power of this passage is not in itself "conceited," and

Wesley is perfectly willing to keep the address to the self, without including the anger with which the "I" addresses its heart.

The original *Collar* expresses not attraction to the lullings and relishes of pleasure so much as impotent irritation at not being able to muster up enough response to them. "You are a poor thing," says Herbert to his heart, "preoccupied as you are with cages and cables and death's heads: why not resurrect some of that corn and wine that you drowned and dried up with tears and sighs? Why, O my temperament, are you not more cheerful, more sanguine, more energetic, more fearless, more *like other people? Is the year only lost to me?*" In this sort of useless railing against one's constitution and nature the circle of thought is self-closed and does not reach out to dream-visions of sensual satisfactions; Herbert has a negative motive here—self-hatred—not a positive one of yearning toward a definite something-else. If we did not sense that a futile self-destructiveness and an attempt to force a new untimely fruition on nature were at the root of the intemperate language, we would not be convinced by the famous two-word submission, "My Lord." We come to that submission with relief, because it means a return to Herbert's own nature, to which he has been so cruel in the course of the poem. We might almost see the poem as a war between the instinctual self and an "ideal" self, except that the second label is false in that the "ideal self" has, by this point in adult life, become more "natural," in its secondary autonomy, than the original primitive and instinctual self upon which it was grafted, and the ego cannot regress to its primitive state wtihout betraying its achieved adult integration. A charming recital of goods yearned for, after the Wesleyan model, would intimate a "schizophrenic" adult self, equally attracted to riotous pamperings and to dispute over right and wrong. For such a soul there would be no resolution possible, least of all a resolution effected by the one word "Child."[19]

These examples may suffice, though others could be advanced, to show Wesley's nervousness, even if dimly felt, in the face of Herbert's unconcealed humanity, and his wish to substitute for Herbert's unparalleled naturalness more acceptable sentiments of the unregenerate Christian sinner or the converted Christian soul. It is true that at first glance we are struck chiefly by Wesley's stilted, more abstract diction and his rejection of conceits, but those superficial qualities of style should not blind us to the more severe criticisms, not of Herbert's diction or imagery but of his inner self, that are evident in Wesley's revisions. Because he saw deepest into Herbert's intent, Wesley revised him most severely; from him we learn how open, true, human, natural, and explicit Herbert is. From his crampings of Herbert into orthodoxy, we learn that doctrine can, in Herbert's case, coexist with inner freedom and psychological accuracy. I have said earlier that in Herbert no intellectual truth is sacrificed for euphony, beauty of phrase, metrical or prosodic requirements, or ease of resolution; here I would add that in Herbert no human truth or truth of feeling is sacrificed for religious or doctrinal expression. To convince us that the intellectual and the beautiful, the natural and the doctrinal, can coexist, not only in mutual respect but in mutual buttressing, is the effect of Herbert's poetry at its best. Nothing need be sacrificed for anything else. If it appears that one of these values must "win" and the other must "lose," there is *a priori* something wrong with the way the problem is being seen or voiced. Herbert either works through his trouble until the resolution accommodates both values, or shows the falsity of the problem proposed. His imitators and adapters, having perhaps a less confident sense of Providence than he, more often opted for simpler solutions and simpler phrasings of problems. In so doing, they reduced Herbert to the capacities of their own minds, and scarcely realized how they were diminishing him.

5

"My God, I Mean Myself": Liturgical and Homiletic Poems

Herbert's poems on Church feasts or seasons, which form a distinct group in *The Temple,* are mostly to be found as well in the Williams manuscript (containing poems written before Herbert became a priest) and in them we can see his earliest known style of religious verse.[1] Though we might have thought to find more poems drawn from the Christian calendar among the lyrics written after Herbert's ordination, in fact the external stimulus of a given feast is generally replaced in the later poetry by internal promptings. The long dramatic effort of *The Sacrifice,* in a genre never again attempted by Herbert, is Herbert's most "external" early work, since even *The Church-porch* can be thought of, at least in part, as an ethical address to the self. Though no one can deny the finished elegance of *The Sacrifice,* it is not, in spite of its subject, one of Herbert's immediately moving poems. Its rather frigid ingenuity and stylization is at odds with the literary tradition of verbal simplicity in poetic treatments of Christ's Passion, a tradition respected by the *Improperia* or liturgical "Reproaches" from which the poem is drawn. Herbert's enjoyment of his own intellectuality reigns in *The Sacrifice* and shows one direction open to his talent—a talent schooled, after all, not only in divinity and patristic exegesis, but also in the periodic eloquence of Renaissance Latin prose and verse. Herbert's revulsion from the style in which he was bred is clear from his scorn (which inevitably in his poetry implies some measure of self-scorn) of the taste rebuked in

Divinitie: "With the edge of wit," he says, [men] cut and carve . . .
Divinities transcendent skie":

> Could not that Wisdome, which first broacht the wine,
>   Have thicken'd it with definitions?
> And jagg'd his seamlesse coat, had that been fine,
>   With curious questions and divisions?

By the time Herbert writes this poem (not in the Williams manuscript),
he has decided that it is not fine to invent "curious questions and divisions." But in fact, such curious invention was a constant temptation
to him, as we learn from *The Pearl, Jordan* (II), and other poems.
The extravagant thought and rhetoric of Herbert's Latin verse, orations,
and letters reveal his first literary mode, the bidding to which his mind
would naturally have been drawn by training and culture. To unlearn
a whole form of literary art and school himself in another, one that
would find its perfection in a poem like *Love* (III), was to be the task
of Herbert's literary life. He may have taken his conversational immediacy from Donne, but Donne's poems, on the whole, do not teach
transparency or self-effacement: these virtues Herbert taught himself.

To see Herbert's initial poetic difficulties with Church subjects and
his initial mistaken attraction to theological mysteries, we have only to
look at two liturgical poems in the Williams manuscript which Herbert
excluded, presumably as hopeless, from *The Temple.* In these poems
we discover that Christian topics could, before Herbert perfected his art,
prompt him to sterile versified theology. Nowhere in these pieces is there
the inner motivation of a private emotion, and doubtless for this reason
Herbert did not find it possible to revise them for *The Temple* as he
revised other early poems. Strictly speaking, in these two cases there is
no "poem" to revise, since feeling is absent. The first of these poems,
Trinity Sunday, draws attention by its intellectual sophistry and shows
how dangerous Herbert's relish for puzzles could be to his ultimate art.

> He that is one
>   Is none.
> Two reacheth thee
>   In some degree.
> Nature & Grace

With Glory may attaine thy Face.
　　Steel & a flint strike fire,
　　　Witt & desire
　　　Never to thee aspire,
　Except life catch & hold those fast.
　　　That which beleefe
　Did not confess in the first Theefe
　　　His fall can tell
　ffrom Heaven, through Earth, to Hell.
　　　Lett two of those alone
　　　To them that fall
Who God & Saints and Angels loose at last.
　　　Hee that has one,
　　　　Has all.

The external ingenuities here are evident. Metrical ones, twos, and threes make up all but four of the lines; couplets and a triad make up the rhymes, with one exception; the ending imitates the beginning; and three rhyme sounds interact in the last five lines to conclude the poem. These are the technicalities, engendered by the numerical compulsion of the Trinitarian subject. Within the poem intellectual invention searches, after the manner of Augustine, for natural analogies to the Trinity:

Nature plus Grace plus Glory
Steel plus Flint $=$ Fire
Wit plus Desire plus Life
Heaven plus Earth plus Hell
God plus Saints plus Angels.

Each of these *trouvailles* emphasizes a special aspect of Trinitarian doctrine. Nature, grace, and glory may be roughly seen as a paradigm of man's evolving perfectibility: in a parallel to the hypostatic union, man combines nature and grace; by the addition of glory he becomes immortal, the three principles uniting to form a saint. Fire is the "bridge," demonstrating the natural affinity of steel and flint, just as the Holy Spirit is the relation of love between Father and Son. Wit and desire (or in scholastic terminology, intellect and will) are two faculties that must inhere in a soul ("life") in order to exist, and life can only be manifest in its faculties, a relation of mutual inextricability comparable to the relations of the Trinity. All creatures must confess the Trinity, if not by profession, then by being used as emblematic examples: Satan's fall showed the three realms (Heaven, Earth, and Hell) which taken together comprise the universe; this relation may be compared to that of the three persons who comprise the Godhead. But here, in the lurking sense that Hell is becoming an analogy for one of the three persons, Herbert hastily abandons his threes. Presumably the inexorable God who decided that if Satan would not believe in the Trinity, he should at least demonstrate it by his fall, is not a *dramatis persona* to Herbert's taste, and certainly not consonant with a poem on the Trinity, a doctrine emphasizing the creativity and love present in the Godhead. Earth and Hell are rapidly banished from the poem, since the Trinity as a doctrine has to do only with the celestial aspects of the deity (the Incarnation—or God's other "cabinet full of treasure," as Herbert says in *Ungratefulnesse*—being the doctrine that deals with God's relations to men). At the close of the poem Heaven, the single remainder, is said to be all one needs. In its beginning and end the poem hints at the personal ("Hee that has one/Has all"), but the Trinitarian analogies that make up the body of the poem lose touch with their author's feelings.

The H. Communion, though it preserves an authorial "I," is another attempt to take a theological question as the subject of a poem—in this case the theories surrounding the manner of Christ's presence in the sacrament. Since Herbert begins with a disclaimer of the importance of the subject to true religion, we might ask his intent in writing the poem at all. The most Herbertian lines in the poem are the satiric rejections of theological debate:

> ffirst I am sure, whether bread stay
> Or whether Bread doe fly away
>   Concerneth bread, not mee . . .

> Then of this also I am sure
> That thou didst all those pains endure
>   To' abolish Sinn, not Wheat . . .

I could beleeue an Impanation
At the rate of an Incarnation,
   If thou hadst dyde for Bread.

Aside from these sallies, which make us wish we had more instances of Herbert's tart satire, the poem contains nothing of value. The logic by which Herbert decides that what is present in the Communion is neither flesh nor a glorious body is sophistic, to say the least, and tastes of clever wit. Even Herbert's devoted editor Hutchinson does not attempt to gloss the last three stanzas, though he offers paraphrases elsewhere of passages far less complicated.

In a way, Herbert rewrote this poem when he added a poem by the same title to *The Temple*. The later poem asks how Christ's presence in the sacrament refreshes both body and soul, but it gently assumes the existence of both functions, and more especially, there is no air of acrimony about the description of means:

. . . By the way of nourishment and strength
   Thou creepst into my breast . . .

Yet can these [nourishment and strength] not get over to my soul,
   Leaping the wall that parts
   Our souls and fleshy hearts.

Only thy grace which with these elements comes . . .
   [Opens] the souls most subtile rooms:
While those [elements of bread and wine] to spirits refin'd at doore
     attend
   Dispatches from their friend [grace].

This is not one of the more touching later poems: though Herbertian in its calm, it remains too exclusively in the realm of logic. Yet it shows a marked advance over the first poem of this title, its quietness rebuking the attention-claiming disputatiousness of the earlier verses.

It is odd to reflect how unsuited Herbert was to debate and dialectic of an intellectual sort, trained in it though he had been. Social exchange, however, is as congenial to him as life itself, and the tactical advances and retreats of poems like *Heaven, Love unknown, Dialogue, Conscience,*

Assurance, Hope, Love (III), and so many others are based on the infinite variety that social dialectic and response can take. Like Austen, Herbert has a genius for social inflection (without her genius for social types). Herbert's dialogues with himself and with God run such a gamut of moods as almost to exhaust one form of social life. The problem for Herbert as a religious poet was to find the mode that would allow him social discourse in religious forms. Theology, with its polemic, its self-involved definitions and divisions, allowed for no social element whatever. Herbert turned then to Church festivals, hoping by association in communal liturgical ritual and Christian narrative to find a social dimension for his verse.

One group of these liturgical poems, celebrating Easter, offer various solutions to a single problem: how to interiorize the meaning of a Church feast. In these poems, the feast is that of the Resurrection; the injunction, let us rejoice; the stumbling block, human misery. This stumbling block is nonexistent in the earliest Easter poem, the one in the Williams manuscript, where the only tension is that between the soul's self and its external offerings to Christ. Offerings, no matter how majestic, are negligible, but God will not despise a humble heart:

> I had preparèd many a flowre
> To strow thy way and Victorie,
> But thou wa'st vp before myne houre
> Bringinge thy sweets along wth thee.
>
> The Sunn arising in the East
> Though hee bring light & th'other sents:
> Can not make vp so braue a feast
> As thy discouerie presents.
>
> Yet though my flours be lost, they say
> A hart can never come too late.
> Teach it to sing thy praise, this day,
> And then this day, my life shall date.

Later, Herbert rewrote the poem as it now appears in *The Temple*:

> I got me flowers to straw thy way;
> I got me boughs off many a tree:

But thou wast up by break of day,
And brought'st thy sweets along with thee.

The Sunne arising in the East,
Though he give light, & th' East perfume;
If they should offer to contest
With thy arising, they presume.

Can there be any day but this,
Though many sunnes to shine endeavour?
We count three hundred, but we misse:
There is but one, and that one ever.

By the time Herbert revised the poem, it had, in its transformation from the weaker version in the Williams manuscript, engaged him in that self-criticism which always produced his best poetry. The self-regard of the earlier version, centering on his own heart, is purged, and the focus of the poem changed to the Resurrection proper. In the earlier second stanza, the sun is simply compared to its disadvantage with Jesus, but in the final version, the sun, and by implication Herbert himself, is *rebuked* for offering to contest with the rising of Jesus. *"I got me flowers,"* an innocent-seeming action, yields, with some thought, the conscious *"they* presume." A proper hierarchy has therefore been established in the poem: Christ's rising is better than other risings, cosmic or human—it "bears the bell," as Herbert says elsewhere, over them. But even such a hierarchy presumes a difference in degree only; seeing his presumption, Herbert proceeds to another self-rebuke. Many suns (including himself) endeavor to shine, but in counting three hundred in the year, we miss; there is but one. "Can there be any day but this?" Herbert asks, and we hear the echo, *"Haec* dies quod fecit Dominus," *"This* is the day." The pun on "Son" justifies the final claim of this sun to eternity—"There is but one, and that one ever." The delicate differentiation of *that* sun from *these* that we count points, too, to a difference in kind rather than in degree.

The grace of the revised *Easter* resides in its discretion. The aggrieved resentment at having been outpaced by the risen Jesus is barely suggested but not openly voiced, while the first version was more explicit both in its pluperfect first line ("I had prepared many a flowre") and in the statement, "But *thou* wa'st vp before *myne* houre." Also in the later version, the self-rebuke following on the resentment is only indirectly expressed, in terms of the presumption of the sun in contesting Christ's rising and of the fallibility of man's arithmetic, while in the first version the grievance holds, first in asserting, in a rather disgruntled way, that since even the sun's offerings are negligble, human flower-strewing is of little use, and second in emphasizing Herbert's "lost flowers. Perhaps the earlier and more discontented poem is closer to Herbert's original feelings, but there is a troubling inconsistency between the lilt of the meter and the baffled frustration of the speaker. In letting the lilt dominate, the artist in Herbert conquered the plaintive suitor, and the exquisite first stanza was made possible. The complaint hovers in the background of the second version in the words "contest," "presume," and "misse," but these hints of dissatisfaction only put into relief the initial graceful homage of "I got me flowers to straw thy way," and the final clear-sighted profession of faith, "There is but one and that one ever."

The poem paired in *The Temple* under the title *Easter* with "I got me flowers," like the earlier version of its companion, scants the problem of the human state. "Rise heart; thy Lord is risen . . . Awake my lute, and struggle for thy part . . . Consort both heart and lute, and twist a song." These comfortable adjurations presume no resistance in their addressees. God is enjoined in the same unquestioning way: "O let thy blessed Spirit bear a part." It is not clear what "our defects" are that the Spirit is to supplement with "his sweet art." Although the poem mentions suffering, it does so in a rather remote way: Christ's death is said to have "calcined" Herbert's heart to dust, and Christ's "stretched sinews taught all strings, what key/Is best." These are both highly intellectualized parallels, the first made so by its symmetrical placement:

> That, as his death calcined thee to dust,
> His life may make thee gold, and much more, just.

The second reference to Christ's death is intellectualized by the lack of any real comparison between his suffering body and the wood and strings of Herbert's lute.

Herbert, in effect, "rewrote" the first part of *Easter* when he later composed *The Dawning,* a far more emotionally truthful poem, which in spite of its beauty has received attention chiefly because of its notorious last two lines:

> Christ left his grave-clothes, that we might, when grief
> Draws tears, or bloud, not want a handkerchief.

In this poem the problem of misery is finally treated in full, but before approaching it, we must glance at the first genuine appearance of the problem of human suffering in the poem *Easter-wings,* where after an extremely conventional first stanza, Herbert bethinks himself seriously of the truths he has been rather emptily repeating:

> Lord, who createdst man in wealth and store,
>   Though foolishly he lost the same,
>   Decaying more and more
>   Till he became
>   Most poore:
>   With thee
>   O let me rise
>   As larks, harmoniously,
>   And sing this day thy victories:
> Then shall the fall further the flight in me.
>
> My tender age in sorrow did beginne:
>   And still with sicknesse and shame
>   Thou didst so punish sinne,
>   That I became
>   Most thinne.
>   With thee
>   Let me combine
>   And feel this day thy victorie:
>   For, if I imp my wing on thine,
> Affliction shall advance the flight in me.

The first stanza tells the Biblical story of man's creation in plenty, his fall from grace, and the possibility, through Jesus' atonement, that the fall can further Herbert's eventual flight to heaven, the redeemed soul being in the end more glorious than Adam in Eden. In this first stanza the fall is Adam's alone, without any complementary admission that in Adam's fall we sinned all, or any admission of personal suffering. The second stanza recapitulates the first, but this time, as though Herbert had glanced inward, he speaks in personal terms: *"My* tender age in sorrow did beginne." From sorrow to sin to sickness to shame—so Herbert sums up his life, till he became "most thinne." Though he had asked in the first stanza to "sing" Christ's victories, he now asks to "feel" them. Affliction had, till now, impeded his flight, since he was in opposition to God through sin; he senses that in "combining" with Jesus, who had to suffer before he could rise, he can turn even an affliction into an advance. It is his own affliction that prompts him to combine with the affliction of Christ, and we may assume, in the Christian economy, that there will be a resurrection after a passion. The poem, then, admits personal suffering and grief as apparent impediments to personal resurrection, but then explains them therapeutically as an imposition by God in just punishment for sin and as an imitation of Christ as well.

The explanation for suffering that views it merely as just punishment, present also in *The Flower,* is nevertheless insufficient: the causeless suffering of the good man, of which Job's trials are the type, must be dealt with. Herbert approaches this painful question in *The Dawning,* a poem which contains no mention of personal sin or divine punishment, but which rather places personal grief and the most powerful doctrinal injunction to joy, the Resurrection, in plain conflict. Using the same two commands, "awake" and "arise," as he had in *Easter,* Herbert begins an *aubade* entirely counter to his own present feelings: "Awake sad heart, whom sorrow ever drowns." The commands to the heart to feel mirth, though they are here outwardly sanctioned by religion, have a hectoring roughness about them that recalls *The Collar.* With impatience, the speaker passes from commanding to chastising his heart:

> Awake sad heart, whom sorrow ever drowns;
>   Take up thine eyes, which feed on earth;
> Unfold thy forehead gather'd into frowns:
>   Thy Saviour comes, and with him mirth:
>   Awake, awake;

And with a thankfull heart his comforts take.
But thou dost still lament, and pine, and crie;
And feel his death, but not his victorie.

The irritated scorn in "lament, and pine, and crie" gives us all the information we need about the "Christian" sentiments of the speaker. No sorrowful heart can be expected to break into instant mirth, Resurrection or not. The second stanza of the poem takes another tone altogether, abandoning the vision of the risen Savior as one attended by mirth and comforts. Herbert remembers instead Jesus' kindness to his sad followers —to Mary Magdalene, to the disciples at Emmaus—and shows us a Christ not absorbed in the joy of his own Resurrection, but one full of solicitude for others, "raising" them as he himself "rises." With this new sympathetic sense of the risen Christ, Herbert can cease to order his heart to be mirthful and can begin instead to entreat, to use the more gentle means of hypothesis and consolation rather than commands and scorn:

Arise sad heart; if thou doe not withstand,
    Christs resurrection thine may be:
Do not by hanging down break from the hand,
    Which as it riseth, raiseth thee:
        Arise, arise;
And with his buriall-linen drie thine eyes:
    Christ left his grave-clothes, that we might, when grief
        Draws tears, or bloud, not want a handkerchief.

To coax a sad heart to dry its eyes is very different from badgering it to take on mirth.

There is, Herbert recalls, one element in the story of Easter compatible with grief—the burial-linen of Jesus, which did not vanish but remained behind. By the Resurrection, then, Jesus did not intend to obliterate all recollection of his Passion: recollection and resurrection can coexist as well, then, in the heart. Grief, the last line reminds us, drew blood from Jesus in the garden of Gethsemane, and such griefs as we suffer are understood by him. He does not bid us repress them; he leaves us a sign, in his bloody shroud, of his own participation in them as a help to us in sorrow. Christ's "death" and "victory" are not so separate as the disjunction at the end of the impatient first stanza would suggest. Grief and sorrow are neither to be endured as punishment for sin, nor to be repressed as unworthy of a believing Christian, but rather to be incorporated into the Christian ethos, as they persist in the mind. At the same time, the second stanza, though subsiding in grief, burial-linen, tears, graveclothes, and blood, cannot be said to lack hope. The central image of the hand which, as it rises, raises, and the striking bracketing of the word "resurrection" with "Christs," on the one side, and "thine," on the other, initiate a lift toward consolation proper to the power of the feast. Despising neither the feast nor the grief, Herbert can celebrate Easter in good conscience.

The problem of proper interior celebration is also raised in the first part of *Good Friday*, where we see Herbert's mind occupied with seeking out a fitting meditation for the day, trying to "feel" the death of Christ, as later in *Easter* he will try to "feel" Christ's victory. Presumably this was Herbert's constant practice, not only on important feasts but also in morning and evening prayer, in reading the Scriptures, and in writing sermons. It is a crushing burden to put on oneself—to reinterpret in a personal, and personally acceptable, way every conventional liturgical and religious act: to make devotion always singular, never simply communal; to particularize, not to merge; to individuate, not to accede. Though religious life is no doubt more interesting and more valuable when lived in this way, it is also incomparably more taxing, and the instances of failure—when nothing in the feast, the season, the saint, the citation, or the concept strikes home—are inevitably more exhausting and fearful.

Good Friday begins as a search for "sparkling notions" and "lovely metaphors" by which to bring home in a personal way the sufferings of Jesus:

> O my chief good,
> How shall I measure out thy bloud?
> How shall I count what thee befell,
> And each grief tell?

Possibilities are enumerated: Christ's griefs may be aptly numbered by the number of his foes, the number of stars in the sky, the number of leaves in autumn, and the number of fruits on the vine. But these, Herbert grandly decides, are all too external to employ as figures: he would rather in his own person be the sole enumerator:

> Then let each houre
> Of my whole life one grief devoure.

An intimidating prospect, since given the statutory life of three-score and ten, Herbert could number some six hundred thousand griefs. Jesus' distress, he concludes expansively, will be his entire cosmos, the sun that numbers all his days. This grandeur of self-dedication is bound to go before a fall, and so it does. Between this third stanza and the last, Herbert realizes, with mortification, that this whole Good Friday meditation has been an exercise in narcissistic self-aggrandizement and has entirely departed from its original intent, to meditate on the sufferings of Christ. Any *real* attention paid to those sufferings would lead not to a sense of participatory glorification (as envisaged in the third stanza), but to a sense of remorse: Herbert, as a sinner, was the *cause* of those sufferings. In a sudden bitter "turn" (made possible, I suspect, by the echo from "sunne" to "sinne") Herbert places himself at last "correctly" vis-à-vis the Passion:

> Or rather let
> My severall sinnes their sorrows get;
> That as each beast his cure doth know,
> Each sinne may so.

Herbert's sins, finally, are the only adequate measure of Jesus' sufferings; for each sin, a scourge, since by his stripes we are healed. Demoting himself to a place among the beasts, Herbert finds his stall. By this time, in reaching the conclusion that his sins measure Christ's woes, being indeed their direct cause, Herbert has abandoned his fine conceits of foes, stars, leaves, and fruit in order to reside in simple fact. Though the ethical bent of the poem and its final total self-blame (in which Herbert's sins alone bear the burden of the Passion, and there is no hint at a shared collective responsibility with other "foes") are characteristic of Herbert's earlier self-abrasive style, the abandonment of conceits for a plainer truth represents that leaning toward sobriety which always seemed to him, in the end, finer and wittier than fine wit.

It is time to glance at some of Herbert's more unsuccessful attempts at individuating the liturgy of the Church. I hope I may be excused, in pursuing Herbert's failures for the sake of a complete picture of the poet, for quoting the worst of *Lent:*

> True Christians should be glad of an occasion
> To use their temperance, seeking no evasion,
>   When good is seasonable;
> Unless Authoritie, which should increase
> The obligation in us, make it lesse,
>   And Power it self disable.

The odd fact about these arid closing lines is that they describe Herbert's own case, since his agues and tuberculosis made fasting medically inadvisable.[2] Yet these lines are unconvincing, if only because Herbert would always rather exhort to good deeds than urge dispensations from them. Aside from a brief flare of wit on gluttony (whose "sluttish fumes" and "sowre exhalations" "revenge" the delight in eating), the poem fails to rise above the most unexceptionably dull homily until the last two stanzas. By then, although it is too late to save the dreary six stanzas preceding them, Herbert at last doggedly wins his way through to a glimpse of the rewards of self-denial, then to a mockingly satiric view of man's usual fasting and feasting. In the first of the closing stanzas, fasting is seen as an imitation of Christ, a going "in the way which Christ hath gone," and perhaps in his company:

> Perhaps my God, though he be farre before,
> May turn, and take me by the hand . . .

In the last stanza, the corporal fast is turned to a spiritual fast. Normally, Herbert suggests, we feed sin well; now let us "improve our fast/By starving sinne." Instead of feeding sin and starving the poor, let us reverse our acts, starving sin and feeding the poor:

> That ev'ry man may revell at his doore,
> Not in his parlour; banquetting the poore . . .

Herbert cannot resist the final irony; that among the needy poor, so long unfed, is of course the soul, neglected before:

> . . . banquetting the poore,
> And among those his soul.

The ending is so plain, dry, and fine that it deserves to belong to a better poem. As long as Herbert offers clichés about Christians and Lent, the poem falters; but as soon as he invents a personal relation to a wayfaring Christ and looks inward to the soul in its hunger, the poem becomes viable.[3] The peril of generalization for Herbert stands out clearly in this poem. A poem, for him, is only "helped to wings" when it is entirely personal (even if the personal is couched rhetorically in the abstract or the plural). In this sense, his mind is resolutely unphilosophic and wholly restricted to the private case, a turn of temper perplexing to a poet who wished to address himself to Christians in general.

A different problem of expression arises in *Trinitie Sunday,* where the difficulty is not with general reference to Christian practice, as in *Lent,* but with the impersonal surface presented by a peculiarly inapprehensible dogma. The poem offers one of the few instances in *The Temple* where Herbert's appetite for form—here, symbolic groups of three—hinders the poem. God formed, redeemed, and sanctified man; Herbert remembers, confesses, and promises to amend his sinful life:

> Lord, who hast form'd me out of mud,
>   And hast redeem'd me through thy bloud,
>   And sanctifi'd me to do good;
>
> Purge all my sinnes done heretofore:
>   For I confesse my heavie score,
>   And I will strive to sinne no more.

So far in the poem each line forms one element in a three-line stanza. But the last stanza compresses a triad into each *line:*

> Enrich my heart, mouth, hands in me,
>   With faith, with hope, with charitie;
>   That I may runne, rise, rest with thee.

The most awkward triad is that of heart, mouth, and hands; the most conventional is faith, hope, and charity; the most Herbertian is "runne, rise, rest," which recalls "glitter, and curle, and winde" in *The Starre* and other such Herbertian double or triple verbs. The problem with the poem is that it has little connection with the mystery of the Trinity, to which, as Herbert said in *Ungratefulnesse,* a "sparkling light accesse denies." There is in this poem no more personal recognition of the feast or the mystery than in the poem of the same name in the Williams manuscript. Perhaps one can scarcely think about or address oneself to three persons at once. In place of address or relation, Herbert seems to have resorted to the external homage of repeated threes, becoming himself, in the three triads of the last stanza, a verbal trinity-in-little.

The models for the first two stanzas are the uncomfortable ones of the Catechism ("Who made you?" "God made me." "Why did God make you?" "God made me to know him, to love him, to serve him," etc.) and the General Confession ("We acknowledge and bewail our manifold sins . . . We do earnestly repent, And are heartily sorry"). The weakness of Herbert's two poems on Trinity Sunday is the more surprising in view of the possibilities for poetry offered by the liturgy of that day, which uses the sight of the Heavenly Jerusalem in Revelations 4.1 for Epistle and the visit of Nicodemus for Gospel, passages put by other poets to dazzling use. But Herbert shuns both the apocalyptic and the mystical, nowhere more clearly than here. He is no visionary, and no ecstatic. Whole tracts of religious poetry are closed to him, but those of intimacy are his as if by eminant domain. His is the purest intimacy and vulnerability, not clothed in the powerful eroticism of St. John of the Cross and of Crashaw, but simply the bare and divested converse of the soul with itself. I say "itself" because for Herbert God does not seem a powerful other existing in a tension with the self comparable to the tension between lover and beloved; he is rather, potentially at least, Herbert himself. The ultimately desirable state of things for Herbert is one in which the self is indistinguishable from God, which is why, as Stanley Fish has pointed out, God can so often "collaborate" with Herbert in writing the poem or building the altar.[4] However, intimacy depends on a conversation between two people, and Herbert must have been at a loss when addressing three persons at once, even in singular form: the very notion abolishes that quality of privacy which is the deepest necessity for Herbert's best work, and prevents his making this feast an occasion for a true poem.

A happier liturgical occasion for Herbert than either Lent or Trinity Sunday was afforded by Christmas. The *events* of Christ's birth, like the events of his Passion, do not preoccupy Herbert, who exhibits, even in *The Sacrifice,* a feeble capacity for narrative. Result and meaning, not sequence, are his concern, and celebration—the mode of interior liturgy —always takes precedence over narration of the motive for liturgy. In *Christmas* there is a conventional sonnet-beginning, somewhat after the model of *Redemption,* but less animated in its narration and more thoughtless in its unoriginal reference to "my dark soul and brutish," for whatever qualities Herbert's soul might be thought to have, darkness and especially brutishness are not among them. But some time after composing the poems in the Williams manuscript, Herbert added to *Christmas* a far more idiosyncratic sequel, which conjures up a pastoral singing-contest—first between Herbert and the shepherds; then, surprisingly, between Herbert and the sun. This description of the poem is not really exact, however, both because concordance rather than competition seems at first to be Herbert's aim, and because the sun begins by shining, not by singing. Yet even this sentence fails of accuracy, since competition subtly underlies the concordance, and since the sun which finally is summoned into the poem is a miraculous stationary one, like Joshua's, rather than a natural sun. The poem, one of Herbert's lighter verses and yet undeniably characteristic of his feeling toward feasts, draws attention both by its gay reordering of the universe and by its increasing intricacy. It begins, oddly enough, with the singing not of the angels, as we might have expected, but of the shepherds, a pastoral importation into the Christmas story. Just as the songs of lovers prick Herbert's remorseful conscience in *Dulnesse,* so the imagined songs of the shepherds prompt him to a like response:

> My shepherds sing; and shall I silent be?
> My God, no hymn for thee?

The choice of shepherds is explained by the analogy, soon to be made explicit, of Herbert's soul to a shepherd. Too modest to compare himself to an angel (the true Christmas chorister), Herbert interpolates:

> My soul's a shepherd too; a flock it feeds
> Of thoughts, and words, and deeds.

Herbert had already read, and may have already written, Psalms in English verse paraphrase. The Twenty-Third Psalm comes naturally to mind in Herbert's pastoral analogy:

> The pasture is thy word: the streams, thy grace
> Enriching all the place.

The little allegory completed, a resolution follows:

> Shepherd and flock shall sing, and all my powers
> Out-sing the day-light houres.

So far, the poem is not memorable. The ingredients are familiar, the allegory not energetic, the conclusion predictable. The feast of Christmas has not, up to this point, produced anything more in Herbert than it could have evoked in any pious writer. Sensing this deficiency himself, Herbert advances one step further, prompted by his competitive verb, "out-sing." He wanted at the beginning to "out-sing" the shepherds (a legitimate impulse in a born poet), but now his ambition outraces the human: he wants to "out-sing" the day. What seemed at first modest humility—a declining to compare himself with the angels, and a simple grouping of himself with shepherds in a rustic human universe—has now become supreme self-vaunting: "Then we [his soul and his thoughts] will chide the sun." Herbert has leaped to a quasi-divine position, for who but God has the right to chide the sun? A spirited faith in his own poetic powers carries Herbert through the cheerful fantasy of the rest of the poem.

The chiding of the sun, which seems at first so lordly of Herbert, is really a self-chiding, since the visually "silent" sun may be said to represent Herbert's previous silence, while the shepherds alone kept up the angels' song. "We will chide the sun," says Herbert, "for letting night/ Take up his place and right"—just as Herbert had let the "night" of silence take up the place and right of human song, which should have joined the song of the shepherds. By now, Herbert has implicitly associated himself sufficiently with the sun so that his next "we" means not simply "my soul and my thoughts" but "my soul, my thoughts, and the sun":

> We sing one common Lord; wherefore he [the sun] should
> Himself the candle hold.

The universe is now harmonized: sun, shepherd, and flock are in accord. Though the poem has at this point stepped, in its bold familiarity with the sun, one degree beyond the conventional hymn, it is not yet beautiful. The "humble shepherd" is finally emboldened into a lighthearted ranger of the cosmos, a finder of suns, or rather an imaginative re-creator of them:

> I will go searching, till I finde a sunne
> Shall stay, till we have done;
> A willing shiner, that shall shine as gladly,
> As frost-nipt sunnes look sadly.

The unexpected negative comparison in the last line springs from Herberts' own previous "sad" and "frost-nipt" state, from which he has roused himself to sing. His new radiance must balance out his previous sluggishness; and having made the equation, he can enter into a happy twinship with the sun. At first, they could be considered merely "fraternal" twins:

> Then we will sing, and shine all our own day,
> And one another pay:
> His beams shall cheer my breast.

It is assumed that Herbert's notes will equally cheer the breast of the sun, and leaving this assumption for us to make, Herbert proceeds to the final harmonic synthesis in which he and his twin the sun become "identical" and indistinguishable:

> and both so twine,
> Till ev'n his beams sing, and my musick shine.

The poem has been so unremittingly literal in its vocabulary (as is the way of allegory) that what would be metaphor in another context (singing beams and shining music) comes close to surrealism here, the more so since the qualities are not subordinated as adjectives but are fully active as verbs: the beams *sing,* and the music *shines.* Herbert even forsakes his future auxiliary verbs, the governing form in the closing fantasy; by employing "till" with "sing" and "shine" alone, he gives a quasi-present tense to the final twinned-and-twined "identity."

To become indistinguishable from the sun, in a Christmas poem above all, is to become indistinguishable from the Son. There is no consistent correspondence of the sun to the Son in the poem, but the pun was surely the bridge by which Herbert crossed from the pedestrian pastoral beginning to a charming legend of cosmic rivalry. Since the meaning of Christmas is Christ's descent and assumption of human nature, only by the institution of the feast of Christmas does it become possible for Herbert in his own turn to scale the heavens and join forces with the sun. God's radiance at Christmas takes on a human voice, and human song shines with Christ's "glorious, yet contracted light." Herbert's last line—"Till ev'n his beams sing, and my musick shine"—is an incarnational metaphor infinitely more representative of the intent of the mystery than the dualistic incarnational formula in the earlier Christmas poem:

> Furnish & deck my soul, that thou mayst have
> A better lodging then a rack or grave.

In the later Christmas poem, Herbert has found his way to a meaning of the feast which, however fantastic in its twinship of the poet with the sun, is far closer to a personal truth. "I am all at once what Christ is, since he was what I am": Herbert's assumption of sunship reminds us of Hopkins' later claim to be "immortal diamond."

The difference between Herbert's lesser and greater penetration of the liturgy appears dramatically in the three poems *Mattens, Euen-song* in the Williams manuscript, and the later *Even-song* in *The Temple*. The first two, though by no means lifeless poems, are not particularly successful ones. Each has a rather simple intellectual premise. *Mattens* laments a human ingratitude: though God bends all his attention and art on man, man for his part studies the creation but not the creator. If man could learn God's love—God who sees and loves himself in his creation, man —man would in turn see God in the creation and aspire to him:

> Teach me thy love to know;
> That this new light, which now I see,
> May both the work and workman show:
> Then by a sunne-beam I will climbe to thee.

The pun on "sun" may again lie behind the conclusion.

In *Euen-song* the intellectual premise (one which led Vaughan to a greater poem) is that God is "Light & darkness both togeather":

> If that be dark we can not see,
> The sunn is darker then a Tree,
> And thou more dark than either.
>
> Yet Thou art not so dark, since I know this,
> But that my darkness may touch thine,
> And hope, that may teach it to shine,
> Since Light thy Darknes is.

Most of the rest of the poem is borrowed from the service for Evensong in the Book of Common Prayer, and the central Herbertian paradox of God's dazzling darkness is neither prepared for in the beginning nor used in the conclusion of the poem. Herbert's persistent wish to be a sun or a star appears again in his wish after death to "shine then more bright then he [the sun]," just as he wishes, in seeing the stars, to "glitter, and curle, and winde as they." But this habitual association of the self with "celestial quicknesse" is not sustained, and the poem ends with a conventional prayer against unholy dreams, as well as with the reassurance that though the "keyes" of the soul (presumably the faculties) are delivered over to dreams, the soul itself may "wake" (keep vigil) with God forever.

The case is different in the later *Even-song*. By Herbert's insertion of *Sinne* between *Mattens* and *Even-song*, we are surely meant to understand that man is unlikely to spend the time between dawn and dusk without some self-regarding acts. The problem in *Even-song*, then, is what to say to God at the close of day, when the brave resolves of the morning lie broken, and a sense of futility, shame, self-reproach, and fatigue overcomes the soul. We might expect words of self-blame and apology, but we receive instead, at first, nursery-prayer. Nowhere in Herbert, not even at the beginning of *Prayer* (I), is there a more toneless, unfelt, and unpromising beginning to a poem than in *Even-song:*

> Blest be the God of love,
> Who gave me eyes, and light, and power this day,
> Both to be busie, and to play.

But to be busy, to play—God's intent for man—has been vitiated by the sins committed this day. Herbert then decides, rather like an ostrich, that his sins can be seen only by himself:

> But much more blest be God above,
> Who gave me sight alone,
> Which to himself he did denie:
> For when he sees my waies, I dy:
> But I have got his sonne, and he hath none.

The palpable falsity of these lines—evident in their logical exclusiveness as well as in their apparent complacency—ensures their insufficiency as a solution to Herbert's own remorse. Herbert's self-reproach then surfaces: if God cannot see Herbert's faults, Herbert will tell him about them in full confession, ending with a passionate account of the true state of his mind—a state of anxiety and guilt, which would never have been deduced from the bland and ritualistic "Blest be the God of love" with which he began:

> What have I brought thee home
> For this thy love? have I discharg'd the debt,
>   Which this dayes favour did beget?
>   I ranne; but all I brought, was fome.
>   Thy diet, care, and cost
>   Do end in bubbles, balls of winde;
>   Of winde to thee whom I have crost,
> But balls of wilde-fire to my troubled minde.

These "great waves of trouble combating my breast," as Herbert described them in the Williams manuscript *Love,* preclude all thoughts of sleep, and we do not see how the poem can arrive at a peaceful close to its prayer.

"I have got his sonne, and he hath none," Herbert had boasted earlier. Herbert may *have* the sun, but God *is* the sun, and he *is* also the night, being the love that moves the sun and other stars. In the natural periodicity of the universe, God's gentle rhythms move on, taking no account of the fretful interpolations of his creatures. So Herbert's "balls of winde" receive no divine verbal reproach, and his "balls of wilde-fire" are soothed not by any self-exculpation but by the silent coming-on of night:

> Yet still thou goest on,
> And now with darknesse closest wearie eyes,
>   Saying to man, *It doth suffice:*
>   *Henceforth repose: your work is done.*

The undeserved tenderness of this response—that one's bubbles, "balls of winde," should be dignified with the name of "work" and found "sufficient"—comes as an "unmotivated" response on God's part. What guarantees for a reader the believability of God's words? After all, he has been "crost" (the pun is no doubt deliberate). Christ's words of forgiveness on the cross acknowledged, after all, the practical wickedness of men's acts, while excusing men on the basis of ignorance. Here, God's words are even more generous, relabeling foam as "work," and not forgiving indebtedness but rather acting as though it had been sufficiently repaid. We are meant to be struck, relieved, and yet mystified by God's attitude, not yet knowing exactly whence it proceeds. The commentary on God's words forming the latter half of the poem goes some way toward what is at least an analogical explanation of his motives:

> Thus in thy ebony box
> Thou dost inclose us, till the day
> Put our amendment in our way,
> And give new wheels to our disorder'd clocks.

God, in short, includes man in the universal heavenly and earthly law of things: the heavenly paradigm of sequence is Christ's own Resurrection after his death, while the earthly one is the constant setting and rising of the sun. Man, like the sun, dies and rises anew each day; coffined in sleep, he is resurrected repaired. The timely sun is a "new wheel" daily to the universe, and our soul, repaired by God's acceptance of our faulty days, is a new wheel or solar principle to our bodily mechanisms.

The "problem" of the poem has by now been "solved": worthlessness, by its inclusion in God's universal rhythms, has been restored to worth. Why, then, is there another stanza? Herbert writes it from a need to ratify in feeling what at the beginning of the poem was a mere form of words—"Blest be the God of love"—and to correct the false earlier presumption that there were parts of his life which escaped God's sight. The last stanza is cast in the form of a *débat:* which shows more love in God, his giving us the scope of day or the rest of night? At first, a remnant of the old self-reproach characterizes the day as a gale, but then, remembering those kind words "It doth suffice," Herbert subsides into kindness himself, toward the day as well as toward the night:[5]

> I muse, which shows more love,
> The day or night: that is the gale, this th'harbour;
> That is the walk, and this the arbour;
> Or that the garden, this the grove.
> My God, thou art all love.

Like all the greatest of Herbert's late poems, this is a poem of final self-acceptance. As he sits and eats, at last, in *Love* (III), so here he finally consents to cast off his trouble and rest:

> Not one poore minute scapes thy breast,
> But brings a favour from above;
> And in this love, more then in bed, I rest.

The "balls of wilde-fire" have been exorcised, and Herbert's "rest" is wholly credible. There is, in sober fact, three times as much "love" in the last stanza as in the first, and Herbert makes "love" a double rhyme sound in the last stanza as well, till the stanza too is "all love."

The poem *Marie Magdalene* is a curious case, because it is rare for poems written after the completion of the Williams manuscript to fail so signally. It is unique among Herbert's poems in addressing itself to a saint's legend, although saints' lives, like apocalyptic and mystical material, offered rich poetic possibilities (exploited by Crashaw and Hopkins, among others, after the Middle Ages). The reason for this unusual essay into hagiography was surely that Herbert's mother was named Magdalen. The subject of *Marie Magdalene* is social courtesy, so well suited to Herbert's mind and art. Yet something went desperately wrong with the poem, making it the nadir of Herbert's later period:

> When blessed Marie wip'd her Saviours feet,
> (Whose precepts she had trampled on before)
> And wore them for a jewell on her head,
> Shewing his steps should be the street,
> Wherein she thenceforth evermore
> With pensive humbleness would live and tread:
>
> She being stain'd her self, why did she strive
> To make him clean, who could not be defil'd?
> Why kept she not her tears for her own faults,
> And not his feet? Though we could dive
> In tears like seas, our sinnes are pil'd
> Deeper then they, in words, and works, and thoughts.
>
> Deare soul, she knew who did vouchsafe and deigne
> To bear her filth; and that her sinnes did dash

Ev'n God himself: wherefore she was not loth,
  As she had brought wherewith to stain,
  So to bring in wherewith to wash:
And yet in washing one, she washed both.

The problem Herbert encountered in writing this poem is put grossly
in the passage that says of Mary Magdalene, in shocking contradiction,
that she was a "Deare soul" full of "filth." This grotesque verbal colloca-
tion is the image that undoes the poem. "Womankind" that Herbert
"can wink/Into a blacknesse and distaste" (*Home*) is too oppressively
present in the equivocally sexual figure of the stained yet repentant Mary
Magdalene, and Herbert, so seldom graceless, becomes in this poem
positively incoherent. From the beginning, relations between the elements are confused: it sounds, at first, as if Jesus' feet had precepts, and
second as though Mary's feet could trample precepts, and third as
though someone's feet could be worn on one's head.[6] Uncharacteristic-
ally, Herbert continues the confusion, comparing tears to "seas," which
are then said to be "piled" less deep than our sins—a verb hardly con-
ceivable, even metaphorically, of seas. Although Herbert indeed tries to
relate the elements of Mary Magdalene's story to each other and to all
men's sins, and even to quarry a small paradox for his ending (that in
washing Jesus, Mary cleansed herself too), the poem nevertheless per-
ishes, not for want of pains but for want of empathy.[7] Herbert may say
in *The Forerunners* that his words, before his employ, knew only stews
and brothels, but it would seem that he knew just enough to have a
perfect horror of such places and of their inhabitants. The word "filth"
is significantly used in one of the early sonnets that Herbert sent to his
mother:

Why should I *Womens eyes* for Chrystal take? . . .
Open the bones, and you shall nothing find
  In the best face but *filth*.

Perhaps Herbert could never conceive a tarnished female sympathetically,
even one who was to become a saint. Writing the poem may have been

ambiguously inviting: unconsciously Herbert may have welcomed the chance to write about the subjugation of a "filthy" woman (with Christ's feet on her head), but consciously he denies his revulsion (in "Deare soul").[8] Herbert had no secure mastery over this particular corner of hagiography; yet caught between the wish to honor his mother and his own intractable response to sexual sin, he produced an uneasy poem.

It is not possible to distinguish in any certain way Herbert's homiletic poems from his liturgical ones. Though Herbert spoke of his poems on his deathbed as a picture of his own spiritual conflicts, many of the lyric verses in *The Temple,* especially the later ones, as Rickey notes, can be read as small sermons.[9] Herbert presumed as much in hoping as he died that his poems might be of use to some "dejected poor soul," and he thought it true that "a verse may catch him who a sermon flies." Though he abandoned, after *The Church-porch,* the long homily, he kept some homiletic impulse both in the form and in the content of a number of poems. Such poems assume a special audience and a particular relation to that audience, as well as a certain dignity and office in the speaker. The poet can, in specific cases, go so far as to assume (disastrously) the mentality and voice of the average parishioner, as in *Praise* (II), where Herbert successfully occludes all his own gifts by assuming a very limited voice.[10] A purely homiletic purpose by itself never engenders a successful poem, but the habit of preaching perhaps caused Herbert to write some of his verses addressing himself as he would address a congregation. It is one of the ironies of literary history that "dejected poor souls" have been helped more by Herbert's troubled accounts of his own pained struggles than by his more affirmative and public verse-homilies.

It is characteristic of Herbert's more public poems to be metaphorically explanatory, glosses on some occasion or some truth unfolded in all its implications to a simpler soul. These poems afford an occasion to enquire into Herbert's use of metaphor: his sources of comparison, the audiences implied by his figures, the extent of his daring, and the conviction attending the reaches of his imagination. *Sunday* and *Mortification* can serve as contrasting examples, if only because the second is so universally considered a symmetrical, grand, and mysterious set of metaphysical metaphors, and because the first is so confusing and heterogeneous in its use of figures.

All readers of Herbert know the childlike lilting end of *Sunday:*

> O let me take thee at the bound,
> Leaping with thee from sev'n to sev'n.
> Till that we both, being toss'd from earth,
> Flie hand in hand to heav'n!

Everyone knows as well that the poem is written in emblematic seven-line stanzas, though it is surprising to find nine rather than seven stanzas making up the whole, especially since the somewhat random organization of the poem could well spare two stanzas (stanzas two and five, perhaps). There seems in the poem a superfluity of metaphor, as though two poems were being written at once. The second, simpler, poem (stanzas six, seven, and eight) compares Sunday to Easter, and shows Christ taking the resting-day of our creation, which we had sullied by original sin, unhinging it from its position as the end-of-the-week Sabbath, and at the same time clothing us anew so that we can be "fit for Paradise." This compressed typological reprise, which by way of a bridge between Genesis and Easter invokes the Old Testament type of Samson, has a long iconographical history[11] and belongs to the expository tradition. It is the least original and most public part of Herbert's poem, and contains the least memorable lines. Such a passage, once undertaken, more or less writes itself, the ingredients being so familiar and, in this instance, being in no way "reinterpreted" or "reinvented" by Herbert.

But bracketing this Biblical and typological passage are stanzas more recognizably Herbertian, coexisting somewhat uneasily with the traditional meditation on redemption. Strangely enough, even Herbert's "own" stanzas do not live very happily with each other here. The poem begins in an almost ecstatic vein, reminiscent of the close of *Prayer* (I):

> O day most calm, most bright,
> The fruit of this, the next worlds bud,
> Th'indorsement of supreme delight.

It is hard to credit the fall in the poem from this language of Platonic perception to a narrative analogy in which the weekdays and Sunday "make up one man," whose face is Sunday and "the worky-daies are the back part."[12] It is as though Spenser inserted the House of Alma into one of the *Four Hymns*. This deviation into pictorial allegory renders Herbert almost speechless, and losing his original *élan,* he lapses into one of his most pedestrian stanzas:

> Man had straight forward gone
> To endlesse death: but thou dost pull
> And turn us round to look on one,
> Whom, if we were not very dull,
> We could not choose but look on still;
> Since there is no place so alone,
> The which he doth not fill.

In the face of such flagging language, Herbert seems to gird himself up to seek more metaphors, looking for a middle ground between the brief rapturous figures with which the poem began and the wooden extended allegorical figure on the man. The first metaphor he finds (perhaps an architectural echo from Bacon, as Hutchinson noted) is a particularly congenial one:

> Sundaies the pillars are,
> On which heav'ns palace arched lies . . .
> They are the frutifull beds and borders
> In Gods rich garden.

The second metaphor is as disastrous as the first was attractive:

> The Sundaies of mans life,
> Thredded together on times string,
> Make bracelets to adorn the wife
> Of the eternall glorious King.

Since we never think of God as enthroned in heaven with a wife, this domesticity, even when we recall the *Song of Songs* (explicitly invoked in the Williams manuscript version of line 31, "ye spouse & wife"), jars our sense of propriety. Leaving his metaphors, Herbert resumes his typology and three stanzas later closes the poem with one final burst of invention, sponsored, like so many of his other successes, by the notion of a celestial flight. The lilting end may have too whimsical a suggestion of the nursery, but at least it finds an achieved lightness and vivacity and eagerness.

What are we to deduce from the problems posed by so inchoate a poem? There is no reason to object to any single element (except perhaps the one dull stanza), but there is reason to object to their sequence and juxtaposition. In a writer usually so careful of structure, climax, and feeling, the plain incompetence of *Sunday* in these respects must claim attention. There seems to be no internal reason why the idea of a poem on Sunday should be repellent to Herbert, nor was he incapable, as the Easter poems show, of writing well on redemption and Resurrection. What, then, went wrong?

I suspect it was his public homiletic intention that defeated Herbert. The encapsulated narration of Genesis, the Fall, Samson, and the Redemption; the reminder of the Sabbath yielding to Sunday; the labored comparison of the week to a man—all these unhappily recall the Bible class. The illustrative metaphors, too, especially the bracelets, have an air of being invented as "concrete examples" for a dull-witted congregation. The gardens escape tediousness only because of Herbert's native delight in their neatness. In short, the only parts of the poem that do not betray a studied homiletic intent (or a false self-assimilation to the audience, as in "if *we* were not very dull") are the first rapid linked metaphors (rapid enough to be incomprehensible to an audience requiring the painful spelling-out of the other metaphors) and the final abandonment of the homiletic persona as Herbert, well out of the pulpit and no longer accompanied by a congregation, goes "leaping . . . from sev'n to sev'n." I am reminded of Hopkins' disastrous experiences with sermons, as when he compared the Church to a milch-cow with seven teats (the seven sacraments), which dispensed grace to all who would suck. A similar attempt to reach the imagined understandings of an uneducated audience results in the defects of *Sunday* as a lyric.

This is not the case with *Mortification*, which yet on the surface might seem to resemble *Sunday*. It too consists of a series of metaphors; it too is consistently homiletic in tone; and it too is found in the Williams manuscript and is therefore not a late poem:

> How soon doth man decay!
> When clothes are taken from a chest of sweets
>   To swaddle infants, whose young breath
>   Scarce knows the way;
>   Those clouts are little winding sheets,
> Which do consigne and send them unto death.
>
>   When boyes go first to bed,
> They step into their voluntarie graves,
>   Sleep bindes them fast; onely their breath
>   Makes them not dead:
>   Successive nights, like rolling waves,
> Convey them quickly, who are bound for death.
>
>   When youth is frank and free,
> And calls for musick, while his veins do swell,
>   All day exchanging mirth and breath
>   In companie;
>   That musick summons to the knell,
> Which shall befriend him at the houre of death.
>
>   When man grows staid and wise,
> Getting a house and home, where he may move
>   Within the circle of his breath,
>   Schooling his eyes;
>   That dumbe inclosure maketh love
> Unto the coffin, that attends his death.
>
>   When age grows low and weak,
> Marking his grave, and thawing ev'ry yeare,
>   Till all do melt, and drown his breath
>   When he would speak;
>   A chair or litter shows the biere,
> Which shall convey him to the house of death.

Man, ere he is aware,
Hath put together a solemnitie,
And drest his herse, while he has breath
As yet to spare:
Yet, Lord, instruct us so to die,
That all these dyings may be life in death.

It might be urged that, unlike *Sunday, Mortification* has an underlying pattern to follow (the ages of man) and that its stanzas, linked by repetitive rhymings of "breath" and "death," are more adroitly constructed than those of *Sunday*. While these remarks are true, it is also true that repeated rhymes and a progressive linear structure alone never made a good poem. What is important, in a comparison with *Sunday,* is that the origin of metaphor in *Mortification* is far deeper, and it is the path to that origin which we must discover.

Although as Arnold Stein says, *Mortification* is not "a poem of spiritual conflict," it must nevertheless, since it succeeds, be more than what Stein calls it, a rehearsal of "theme and plot . . . fixed by religious and rhetorical traditions."[13] A poem so "traditional" might be thought uninspired, but Stein solves this difficulty by asserting that "the argument, and its conduct, addresses itself to the inescapable human problem of how to live without being dominated by the fear of death." Herbert, says Stein, exposes "the secret forms of death, imagining them into familiarity, so that they can be recognized and mastered." Though *Mortification* does adopt a stance of detachment in presenting its typical instances, there is no such thing in Herbert (or perhaps in literature) as a successful "detached" poem. The "subject" of *Mortification,* in spite of its title, is neither death nor decay, but rather the burden of poetic significance borne in the mind of the poet.

When swaddling-clothes are taken from a "chest of sweets" to wrap a baby, for whom is it true that "those clouts are little winding sheets"? Certainly not for the baby; still less is this gruesome perception attributable to the baby's mother or nurse; I would hesitate even to attribute this conclusion to God, since Herbert's God does not elsewhere engage in morbid comparisons. No, this equivalence, asserted so unequivocally, is believed in—and first noted—only by the poet, who sees a correspondence unperceived by anyone else. The startling resemblance between swaddling-bands and a shroud is one that only a poet would be struck by, or capitalize on. The ironic imagination thinks back to its own origins and reflects sardonically: "I thought I was being warmed: I was really being embalmed." The literal translation tells us that each stage in living is a stage toward death, that metabolism is itself "mortification" or putrefaction. "No young man," says Hazlitt, "believes he will ever die," and this poem is written by someone once a young man, who now has passed the watershed, knows he will die, and wonders how he could not always have been aware of that truth, which is as true in infancy as it is in middle age. The poet takes a cruel self-lacerating pleasure in looking back over all the "innocent" phases of his life, seeing in each, hidden in some corner, a clue, cunningly planted there by the Master of Significances, which shows the destiny of the thoughtless soul.

Had the soul been a master of significance then as it is, being a poet, now, it would have remarked the clues which it now retrospectively uncovers and names. In this sense, the poem is a triumph of knowledgeable mental malice, since in the most trivial scenes—bedtime, parties, moving into a house—it finds a sinister significance. Do you lie down? You are stepping into a "voluntary" grave as later you will be cast into an involuntary one. Do you call for music? You are anticipating a music that will be tolled for you and for which you have not called. Do you build a house? Your last house will be your coffin. Do you order a litter to carry you? You will be carried on a bier to your grave-house. There is an implicit taunt in such a list; the poet coerces each man into a role in a willfully imagined *Totentanz*. No action, not even the most innocent, is left untainted by the odor of mortification. Most tainted of all, however, is the poetic mind, which cannot look anywhere without being haunted by correspondences. Once death is on the poet's mind, it clouds everything he sees.

The burden of this somber overlay is insisted on in the poem by the compulsive invariant rhyming of "breath" and "death," verbally representing metabolism as mortification. Such a mental burden cannot be exorcised, nor can it be denied. But, as perception merely, it is blighting and useless: "It forces us in summer skies to mourn,/It spoils the singing of the nightingale," as Keats said of a moment of similar perception, when he "saw too distinct into the core/Of an eternal fierce destruction." Herbert cannot dismiss his insight as a mood of his own mind, as Keats tried to do, since the insight connects with too many webs of religious meaning—thoughts of the corruptibility of the body, of the "blight man was born for" (to quote Hopkins), and of man's natural destiny (were it not for grace). In a conclusion which does not materially change the morbidity of the poem, Herbert asks that the burden of insight at least be amenable to a religious purpose: *"Memento mori"* says the poet's mind to him ceaselessly; perhaps this distressed consciousness can be a spur to an amended life. The collect-like clause of hortatory purpose ending the poem imitates a ritual form of collective prayer in keeping with the ostensibly impersonal vein of the poem, but it does not carry any freight of personal help for the personal morbidity of consciousness in the poem.

It may be urged that this Jacobean vision of omnipresent death is not personal at all to Herbert but rather typical of his predecessor Donne, among others, and derives from a general relish in the funereal. It is also true that this poem has a public "homiletic shape," both in its collection of typical instances and in its liturgical close. Nevertheless, something personal distinguishes *Mortification* as art from a homiletic poem like *Sunday,* and that something is a consistent individual vision, even if impersonally expressed. In *Sunday,* the metaphors are taken literally, and univocally predicated as true for everyone everywhere: everyone can see equally well that Sunday is care's balm and bay, or that heaven's palace is supported by Sundays as pillars, or that Sundays could be threaded together to make a bracelet. Though these metaphors are fantastic, it is assumed that to any worshipper they would be equally welcome as "poetic ways" of putting a universally shared belief. But the grim metaphors of *Mortification* are deliberately repugnant to common feeling: the preacher is imposing on his audience a blighted private vision, not elucidating for them their own received ideas. And the vehicles chosen in *Mortification* are not fanciful and unconnected variations, as in *Sunday,* but the insistently coherent facets of a single lens, more intense for being phrased in a relentlessly invariant structure, bereft, after the first line, of any rhetorical exclamations, rebuttals, or questions. There is only the inexorable declarative narration of a reality so all-embracing that it suppresses all protest and surprise. Needless to say, it is such "homilies," informed by a strong private feeling, that are the most searching and unforgettable.

At times, in the homiletic poems, Herbert's personal feeling supervenes over what we must imagine to have been the original theme of the sermon. The result is a distortion, more or less painful, of the expected discourse, "as if a greater eye looked through her eye," as Yeats said on another occasion. The ostensible intent of the poem called *Mans medley* is to show how man occupies a middle position in creation, between the beasts and the angels, and to say that though he may taste some earthly joys, his fuller joy will be hereafter. These sentiments seem to be expressed in the first two stanzas in an unremarkable way:

> Heark, how the birds do sing.
>   And woods do ring.
> All creatures have their joy: and man hath his.
>   Yet if we rightly measure,
>   Mans joy and pleasure
> Rather hereafter, then in present, is.
>
>   To this life things of sense
>   Make their pretence:
> In th'other Angels have a right by birth:
>   Man ties them both alone,
>   And makes them one,
> With th'one hand touching heav'n, with th'other earth.

The arrangement of this last line, we see by hindsight, is ominous. Had the stanza closed otherwise, we might have read:

> In th'other Angels have a birthright giv'n:
>   Man ties them both alone,
>   And makes them one,
> With th'one hand touching earth, with th'other heav'n.

But with the choice of "earth" over "heaven" to end the line, Herbert adopts the voice of compulsive anticlimax, repeating, in spite of his wish to demonstrate joys hereafter, the earthbound pattern he has established:

> In soul he mounts and flies,
>   In flesh he dies . . .
>   [He] should take place
> After the [heavenly] trimming [of his dress], not the [earthly] stuffe
>   and ground.

For the more cheerful notion of man's uniting earth and heaven, making them one, Herbert has substituted the figure of the flesh as the body of death, a coarse stuff. Frightened at his own denigration of the earthly, Herbert hastens to re-establish its worth:

> Not that [man] may not here
>   Taste of the cheer,
> But as birds drink, and straight lift up their head,
>   So he must sip and think
>   Of better drink
> He may attain to——

So far so good: but the line ends, "after he is dead." Not a reassuring thought. Let us once again imagine the stanza rewritten (with the usual apologies to Herbert):

> But as birds drink, then lift their head to see,
>   So he must sip and think
>   Of better drink
> He may attain to when his soul is free.

The poem, it is clear, keeps attempting a balanced description of a true medley, appropriate to the Spenserian "Heark, how the birds do sing/ And woods do ring." But as Frost would say, truth keeps breaking in. In the fifth stanza, the undertheme of death (already seen in "earth," "in flesh he dies," and "after he is dead") becomes at last dominant: the usual effort to insist on man's joy is followed by a slide into depression more precipitous than anything preceding it:

> But as his joyes are double;
>   So is his trouble.

Herbert explains grimly:

> He hath two winters, other things but one;
> Both frosts and thoughts do nip,
> And bite his lip;
> And he of all things fears two deaths alone.

Nothing in this stanza convinces us that man indeed has "double joys," but we are only too well assured of his double troubles,

It is not easy to know how much Herbert realized his own descent into gloom in this poem. He knew enough at this point, however, to stop insisting on unfelt double joys. The poem collapses into the optative:

> Yet ev'n the greatest griefs
> May be reliefs,
> Could he but take them right, and in their wayes.
> Happie is he, whose heart
> Hath found the art
> To turn his double pains to double praise.

As if in a weak effort to turn about-face, the poem rises from griefs to reliefs, from pains to praise, reversing its previous direction from joy to pain, but the deliberateness of the effort robs it of success, as Herbert's reach exceeds his grasp. The homiletic effort is subverted by the lyric truths that keep reshaping the sermon form (which, conventionally, is a balanced and even optimistically hortatory one) into a lopsided expression of grief. It is as though Herbert adopted the homiletic form here in order to talk himself into balance and apportionment, but even the strictest container cannot wholly distort its contents. The way in which the form of this poem works against its content, or vice versa, tells us something about how Herbert may have viewed the sermon: it was an occasion to step back from the personal, to adjust perspectives, to see if possible through God's eyes, and to take the lessons that sprang from such correction (the perfection of the form is reached in *Love unknown*). But the attempt to see through God's eyes, in *Mortification* as in *Mans medley*, reverts to a personal vision.

The unhappy results of too strenuously attempting the strained perspective of the homiletic stance can be seen in *The Bag*. Though Robert Graves' notorious commentary is full of special pleading, he is not wrong in remarking the peculiarity of this poem.[14] It is a sermon—"a strange storie"—preached to despair:

> Away despair! my gracious Lord doth heare.
>   Though windes and waves assault my keel,
>   He doth preserve it: he doth steer,
>   Ev'n when the boat seems most to reel.
>   Storms are the triumph of his art:
> Well may he close his eyes, but not his heart.
>
> Hast thou not heard, that my Lord JESUS di'd?
>   Then let me tell thee a strange storie.
>   The God of power, as he did ride
>   In his majestick robes of glorie,
>   Resolv'd to light; and so one day
> He did descend, undressing all the way.
>
> The starres his tire of light and rings obtain'd,
>   The cloud his bow, the fire his spear,
>   The sky his azure mantle gain'd.
>   And when they ask'd, what he would wear;
>   He smil'd and said as he did go,
> He had new clothes a making here below.
>
> When he was come, as travellers are wont,
>   He did repair unto an inne.
>   Both then, and after, many a brunt
>   He did endure to cancell sinne:
>   And having giv'n the rest before,
> Here he gave up his life to pay our score.
>
> But as he was returning, there came one
>   That ran upon him with a spear.
>   He, who came hither all alone,
>   Bringing nor man, nor arms, nor fear,
>   Receiv'd the blow upon his side,
> And straight he turn'd, and to his brethren cry'd,

If ye have any thing to send or write,
  I have no bag, but here is room:
Unto my Fathers hands and sight,
  Beleeve me, it shall safely come.
That I shall minde, what you impart,
Look, you may put it very neare my heart.

Or, if hereafter any of my friends
  Will use me in this kinde, the doore
Shall still be open; what he sends
  I will present, and somewhat more,
Not to his hurt. Sighs will convey
Any thing to me. Harke, Despair away.

The story told to despair is indeed strange, in several ways.[15] The
first part of the poem answers the question, "How did God divest himself of his Godhead and become simply man?" The answer is deliberately winsome: "He gave his rings and his glory to the stars, his bow to
the clouds, his spear to fire, and his blue cloak to the sky." The con-
naturality of these gifts is evident, and they provide the answers to
other questions: "Where did the rainbow come from?" "Why is the
sky blue?" Whether Herbert ever spoke so freely in the pulpit we may
doubt; but mythical explanations, as we can see from *The Pulley* and
Peace, are very congenial to him. The myth-making tone is preserved
in the second episode of the poem, the account of the Passion of Christ,
and the event is retold in a childlike tone, so reducing the trauma of the
Passion as to make it invisible. It is the Passion seen from a celestial
perspective, in which "God's death is but a play," to adapt Yeats's words.
Death is simply not permitted to happen: as soon as Jesus receives his
death-wound, he turns and cries, "Here is room." The naïf speaker here
may succeed in domesticating the events of Jesus' life, bringing them to
a rustic level of understanding, but he loses something by his assimilation of grand redemptive events to simple undressings, journeyings, and
the "receiving" of blows. Awe and majesty vanish: even pathos vanishes.
Neither Miltonic sublimity nor Franciscan empathy exists in the poem;
instead, there is a denatured, if appealing, fairy tale. It is hard to believe

that this miniaturizing of the Incarnation, Passion, and Death of Christ was Herbert's sole intent in the poem. There has to be a reason for his deliberately simplified homiletic posture. What does Herbert feel uttering these anecdotes? Certainly not personal guilt for the sufferings of Christ, since there is no evident suffering here. How can this tranquil narrative be reconciled with Herbert's expressed need for a medicine against despair? Where, for that matter, has his despair gone?

I am not sure that all these questions are answerable within the confines of this single poem. However, a few facts are clear. The uncanonical event introduced by Herbert into the poem is the transformation of Jesus' side-wound into a bag for the conveying of messages to heaven: this, if anything, represents "the triumph" of Jesus' "art" in dealing with "storms." "Do, deal, lord it with living and dead,/Let him ride . . . in his triumph," said Hopkins, asking Christ to preserve another keel through winds and waves; but Hopkins' energetic verbs stand in strong contrast to Herbert's more neutral "preserve" and "steer," verbs denoting a conservative rather than an active part. Hopkins was depending on the Gospel story in which Christ actively stilled the waves; Herbert shows the winds and waves unabated, but the craft nevertheless preserved. How, in the midst of the winds and waves, can despair then be banished? By what art will Jesus triumph in this storm?

The primal fact, one might think, is that the soul is assured of salvation by Christ's death, as in *Redemption:* "Thy suit is granted" is the word from the Cross. That contractual release is not, however, the subject of *The Bag.* The problem of the poem is not, "What is my ultimate destiny?" but, "How do I stay courageous through despairing times?" This explains the strange response to despair at the beginning of the sermon: not, "Hast thou not heard, that my Lord JESUS di'd for me?" nor, "Hast thou not heard, that my Lord JESUS redeemed me?" but simply, "Hast thou not heard, that my Lord JESUS di'd." It is the death of Jesus that matters, as the whole poem bears out. Nowhere do we see the resurrected Jesus, nor Jesus in heavenly triumph after his death and resurrection. Herbert's version of the Passion of Christ ends with a permanently stricken Jesus, one who will act, in his wounded self, as a permanent messenger to the Father, one whose "door" will "hereafter . . . still be open." This is to arrest the Gospel story halfway and, by minimizing the trauma of the events of the Passion itself, to set in relief the generous eternal passion, so to speak, of the eternally wounded Christ. No more than Herbert himself, perpetually assaulted by winds and waves, can Jesus, eternally wounded, change his state. Jesus' response to grief is to put it to use, not to wish it away, and Herbert's lesson is to do the same.

The difference in Jesus' two stanzas ending the poem is marked. The first offers the general principle of conveyance in solicitous but stately language, rationally ordered in end-stopped lines. The second of Jesus' stanzas applies more directly to Herbert's case, since Herbert is one of those later "friends" who "hereafter" may wish to use Jesus "in this kinde." Suddenly the verse, which till now has been predictable and measured, with generally end-stopped lines and a degree of self-containment in the opening quatrain and the closing couplet of each stanza, forsakes both terminal punctuation and the two-part division for a final stanza in which the spirit bloweth where he listeth.

The phrase-units strain, in fact, to obliterate the stanza form:

Or if hereafter any of my friends will use me in this kinde,
the doore shall still be open;
what he sends I will present,
and somewhat more,
not to his hurt.
Sighs will convey any thing to me.
Harke,
Despair away.

It is extremely rare that Herbert ever violates his stanza form in such fashion, and he would not do it unknowingly: a sense of spontaneity, of afterthought, of codicil, animates the passage. It is rather like Herbert bethinking himself on his deathbed of "any dejected poor soul" who might thereafter profit from *The Temple*. "What is man, that thou art mindful of him?" asked the Psalm, and the kindness of Jesus, in remembering that there will be needy souls like Herbert "hereafter," is what consoles Herbert now. For his sake, Christ is willing that the wound remain perpetually open, and demands no formal messages, but only the sighs of the heart assaulted by grief.[16]

In the imagining of a perpetually wounded Christ receiving the perpetual sighs of the troubled, Herbert finds a Christ congenial to his grieving state, as a handsomely resurrected Christ, installed at the right hand of the Father, would not be. There is, by the end, no real distinction between Christ's condition and Herbert's, except that Christ is free to move as messenger between heaven and earth. The earlier Christ, who in no way resembled Herbert while he was descending from heaven or traveling on earth (and was therefore presented in mythological terms), has been remolded to Herbert's suffering image, and in this coalescing of ego and divinity lies the resolution of the poem. It is not a "public" resolution, which assumes a neutral audience expecting to hear the familiar end to the redemptive act—a resurrection and a new covenant. Instead, the end is intimate and conversational, with Jesus, in his last words—"Harke, Despair away"—wholly identified, by his human conversation, with the poet, whose first words were "Away despair!" So homily becomes communion, and the frightening disjunction in the universe with which the poem began—a soul assaulted and an absent God—has been healed.

In each successful homiletic case, then, as in each successful liturgical case, Herbert has entered in a personal sense into the problem set by the poem. The honesty we prize in the incorporation of misery into Easter in *The Dawning* is the same as the honesty we praise in the intensity of *Mortification* or in the dejection of *Mans medley*. Herbert often resisted successfully the temptation to let the homiletic or liturgical form impose on him socially acceptable sentiments or religiously praiseworthy attitudes. He even allowed the grotesque, like the bag of Christ's wound or the handkerchief of Christ's grave-clothes, to appear in his homiletic or liturgical poems, no matter how unsuited it appeared to his public subject and stance, if it answered to the human needs voiced in the poem. The public occasions of these poems (whether a Church feast or a prospective sermon) were not hindrances to Herbert's genius: he needed the outline of received belief to provoke him into asking how much of that received belief he could make his own, or what additions, suppressions, corrections, or enhancings the doctrine or feast would need to become part of his own religious experience. These "conflicts" with received religious sentiments, celebrations, rituals, and exhortations are as much a source of the poems in *The Temple* as are the more famous "conflicts" between self-will and obedience, between ambition and humility.

6

Configurations and Constellations: Ethical, Discursive, and Speculative Lyrics

Although Herbert's ethical, discursive, or speculative lyrics are not easily separated from his more personal devotional verse, in certain poems we can see a concentration on intellectual enquiry or speculation take precedence over purely devotional expression.[1] The odd thing about these poems is that they are not, for all Herbert's intellectual brilliance, very successful. Readers with a philosophical bent, like Coleridge and Emerson, may be attracted to a poem like *Man,* and we may all be initially pleased by the tireless ingenuity of *Providence,* but these poems are not the first we would anthologize. And yet, most of these efforts are not early compositions; they were written, presumably, at the same period of life in which Herbert searched out his most expressive means for poems like *The Crosse, The Flower, Discipline,* and *The Collar.* The speculative poems are not, on the whole, good enough to solicit or reward sustained attention: they versify what they mean, sometimes unremarkably and sometimes well, but they rarely contain those crosscurrents of powerful feeling that vex and freshen Herbert's best poetry. Once we have read all the curious natural lore in *Man* or *Providence* and approved the compactness and symmetry of the presentation, there is nothing more, no echoing residue or precipitate of feeling. In worse cases, the motivation of the poem itself is entirely obscure. Why did Herbert feel moved to write *Avarice?* And in sonnet form?

> Money, thou bane of blisse, & source of wo,
>   Whence com'st thou, that thou art so fresh and fine?
> I know thy parentage is base and low:
>   Man found thee poore and dirtie in a mine.

The paradox of man's creating gold in his own image by stamping his face on coin makes up the body of the poem, which closes with man falling into the symbolic filth of the mine:

> Man calleth thee his wealth, who made thee rich;
> And while he digs out thee, falls in the ditch.

There is no breath of temptation in the poem, nothing to show that Herbert himself ever thought money powerful or attractive. Though Herbert, in short, seems to have had some inclination, judging by poems like *Avarice,* to write discursive or speculative poems, a degree of anxiety about the poetic legitimacy of pure speculation tended to tame his enquiries or to end them prematurely by imposing a rapid close to speculation in favor of moral approval or censure.

  Too many of the discursive poems fail to enter into their subject, as Herbert adopts a spectator's stance. Herbert's tone in *Vanitie* (I), for example, gives in general an appearance of moral neutrality amounting to pure discursiveness, but since the tone falters in the second of the three stanzas describing the Diver, we begin to suspect the putative neutrality of the opening and closing stanzas bracketing the middle one. The "fleet Astronomer" surveying the spheres and the "subtil Chymick" or chemist stripping creatures naked are both described attentively, if not enthusiastically, but the Diver, bound for a pearl, is harshly reproved, together with the lady who will wear the jewel:

> The nimble Diver with his side
> Cuts through the working waves, that he may fetch
> His dearely-earned pearl, which God did hide
>   On purpose from the ventrous wretch:
> That he might save his life, and also hers,
>   Who with excessive pride
> Her own destruction and his danger wears.

If God may be said to have hidden the pearl on purpose, has he not equally purposefully hidden the motions of the spheres and "the callow principles within their nest"? Does not pursuing that which God has hidden make the Astronomer and Chymick equally "ventrous" wretches? Though Herbert does not draw this conclusion explicitly, it seems the only explanation for the wicked Diver's presence in the poem, since a form of innocent undersea exploration could surely have been found to match the "innocent" exploration of sky and earth. At best, the intellectual Astronomer and Chymic are "poore men" who search round "to find out *death*" while missing *"life* at hand."

The fearful repudiation, however masked, of intellectual enquiry under these apparently detached criticisms is not restricted to *Vanitie* (I); it appears unmasked in *Divinitie,* with its outright scorn of theological speculation, and, metamorphosed into a critique of anxiety, in *The Discharge.* In each case, possibilities of thought are abruptly and peremptorily closed off, without being given a chance to express, let alone defend, themselves. The poem by which to try, and condemn, these others is Herbert's fine repudiatory poem, *The Pearl,* which casts off the world while yet recognizing its appeal to the full, using in that recognition an almost excessively synonymic spate of definition:

> I know the wayes of Pleasure, the sweet strains,
> The lullings and the relishes of it;
> The propositions of hot bloud and brains;
> What mirth and musick mean; what love and wit
> Have done these twentie hundred years, and more:
> I know the projects of unbridled store:
> My stuffe is flesh, not brasse; my senses live,
> And grumble oft that they have more in me
> Then he that curbs them, being but one to five:
>   Yet I love thee.

Yet even in *The Pearl,* at one juncture, Herbert is almost too quick to dismiss the pleasures he wishes to evoke, when he allows Honour to become morbidly suspect. "I know," he says,

> How many drammes of spirit there must be
> To sell my life unto my friends or foes.

But at least, during most of the poem, the world is given its due, as it is even more powerfully in two equally successful poems, *The Quidditie* and *The Quip,* which, like *Vertue,* reveal in all its attractiveness the world that must be either transcended or rebuked by the soul intent on independence. These poems show how Herbert's true "temptation poems" are wholly unlike the more impatient and detached self-condemnation in poems like *An Offering* and *Businesse.*

The Quidditie (called *Poetry* in the Williams manuscript), in a fling of grammatical wit, finally shows the world to be only a sequential procession of single nouns and verbs, whereas a poem, it tells us, contains all of those things and actions simultaneously:

> My God, a verse is not a crown;
> No point of honour, or gay suit,
> No hawk, or banquet, or renown,
> Nor a good sword, nor yet a lute:
>
> It cannot vault, or dance, or play;
> It never was in *France* or *Spain;*
> Nor can it entertain the day
> With my great stable or demain:
>
> It is no office, act, or news,
> Nor the Exchange, or busie Hall;
> But it is that which while I use
> I am with thee, and *most take all.*

The very indirectness and inarticulateness of the final definition, coupled with the large claim of the last three words, limits the secular world suddenly to its own now impoverished inventory, which until this moment had seemed the spirited sum of all things and all doings. The closing definition is careful not to make verse a means of passage to God. Not "By using verse, I can reach thee" but "While I use verse, I am with thee," says Herbert. The final revenge on all those nouns and verbs is fairly earned.

In *The Quip* revenge is envisaged, too, but never really taken, since this poem shows the final style of the "sweet and vertuous soul." Nevertheless, the brief processional masque of Wordly Delight is given insidious verbal and emotional power:

> The merrie world did on a day
> With his train-bands and mates agree
> To meet together, where I lay,
> And all in sport to geere at me.
>
> First, Beautie crept into a rose,
> Which, when I pluckt not, Sir, said she,
> Tell me, I pray, Whose hands are those?
> *But thou shalt answer, Lord, for me.*
>
> Then Money came, and chinking still,
> What tune is this, poore man? said he:
> I heard in Musick you had skill.
> *But thou shalt answer, Lord, for me.*
>
> Then came brave Glorie puffing by
> In silks that whistled, who but he?
> He scarce allow'd me half an eie.
> *But thou shalt answer, Lord, for me.*
>
> Then came quick Wit and Conversation,
> And he would needs a comfort be,
> And, to be short, make an Oration.
> *But thou shalt answer, Lord, for me.*
>
> Yet when the houre of thy designe
> To answer these fine things shall come;
> Speak not at large; say, I am thine:
> And then they have their answer home.

The taunts of the "merrie world . . . with his train-bands and mates" make up the small four-stanza drama, but we should not mistake the form for the content: the dramatis personae actually live within Herbert's own consciousness, and a good part of the tension of the poem comes from our sense that Herbert is here successively incarnating several of his possible selves. The first is the rash gazer before the rose, tempted to pluck it; the second, the young musician with the chink of money in his pockets providing his "closes"; the third, the brave courtier in silk, aspiring to glory; the fourth, the poet and university Orator. No wonder Herbert says that the tempters met together "where I lay": they met in his soul, body, and life-history. The intimacy of the taunts alone proves them to be self-lacerations, while the defensive posture of the victim, propitiating the bullies by pretending to believe that they are simply "merry" mates meeting "in sport," is adopted in part at least to enable Herbert to deny the undoubted interior power of the temptations. The tempters impugn, in turn, Herbert's aesthetic sense, his skill in music, his aristocratic birth, and his elegance in wit, all qualities so much inherent in him that insults given to them had to be taken as insults to the roots of his being. So much the more reason for a splendid justificatory Last Judgment, complete with "Come, ye blessed" and "Depart, ye accursed." In his last two lines, Herbert defeats that expectation by a counterclaim. The train-bands have claimed him as one of themselves and have jeered at him for refusing to belong to their group; God's counterclaim, "I am thine" (not "Thou art mine"), is so much a reversal of expectation that clearly the gift outweighs the attractions of the world, whose mocking presence has nonetheless so shaken the soul in uncomfortable and despondent moments that the soul has momentarily wished for some large public divine vindication. It is the wish for that vindication, along with the interior nature of the temptations, which validates the reality of the experience in the soul, so that we feel (as we never felt in *Avarice*) the chinking of money intimidating Herbert's music, and his spurt of self-defense in "But thou shalt answer."

Against such felt expansion and realization of temptation may be set Herbert's impatient trouncing of his "silly soul" (*Vanitie* [II]), whose delays and backslidings he treats with no sympathy at all. Such poems as *An Offering,* though they can be construed as self-criticism, are not really so directed, or if they are, the self has so split off from itself that it no longer knows the part it is criticizing. The poem shows an ill-tempered Herbert not often brought to view by critics:

Come, bring thy gift. If blessings were as slow
As mens returns, what would become of fools?
What hast thou there? a heart? but is it pure?
Search well and see; for hearts have many holes.

In a series of superficially-conceived stanzas, Herbert wishes that hearts
could propagate themselves and therefore their gifts, fears lest the heart
be divided into parcels of lust and passion, and recommends Jesus' blood
as a cleanser and closer of wounds. But the wounds are not described as
they would be by the wounded soul; all is surveyed from the outside:

But all I fear is lest thy heart displease,
As neither good, nor one: so oft divisions
Thy lusts have made, and not thy lusts alone;
Thy passions also have their set partitions.
These parcell out thy heart: recover these,
And thou mayst offer many gifts in one.

The cold detachment here is equally visible in *Businesse,* a poem
which, in its logical "plot" and hectoring tone, makes Herbert into an
unpleasant schoolmaster:

Canst be idle? canst thou play,
Foolish soul who sinn'd to day?

Rivers run, and springs each one
Know their home, and get them gone:
Hast thou tears, or hast thou none? . . .

Hast thou sighs, or hast thou not? . . .

But if yet thou idle be,   ·
Foolish soul, who di'd for thee?

Who did leave his Fathers throne,
To assume thy flesh and bone;
Had he life, or had he none? . . .

Did he die, or did he not? . . .

186

> He that sinnes, hath he no losse? . . .
> Brings thy Saviours death no grain?

These rapid and impatient questions, which do not stay for an answer while flogging the soul into shame, are embarrassing to read, and recall comparable injunctions to hapless souls in Herbert's lesser poems, as in *Vanitie* (II):

> O heare betimes, lest thy relenting
>   May come too late! . . .
> Then silly soul take heed; for earthly joy
> Is but a bubble, and makes thee a boy.

Herbert writes in these poems as though he and his soul had yet to make each other's acquaintance.

Still more grotesque in this respect is the poem *Self-condemnation,* which busily condemns the soul for preferring the world's delights and gold over Christian joy: the world, displayed in all its real luxuriance in *The Pearl,* is here reduced to a vulgar siren, an "ancient murderer" with an "enchanting voice," and her allies are simply the unregenerate, who make a "Jewish choice." Nowhere is Herbert more the Pharisee and less the Publican, nowhere does he seem to feel less guilty himself of the sins he condemns:

> He that doth love, and love amisse,
> This worlds delights before true Christian joy,
>   Hath made a Jewish choice . . .
>
> He that hath made a sorrie wedding
> Between his soul and gold, and hath preferr'd
>   False gain before the true,
> Hath done what he condemnes in reading:
> For he hath sold for money his deare Lord,
>   And is a Judas-Jew.

In this same harsh vein Herbert offers no comfort to the troubled soul that weeps. Rather than wail, he says coldly in *The Water-course:*

187

Turn the pipe and waters course
To serve thy sinnes, and furnish thee with store
Of sov'raigne tears, springing from true remorse:
That so in pureness thou mayst him adore,
Who gives to man, as he sees fit, $\left\{\begin{array}{l}\text{Salvation.}\\\text{Damnation.}\end{array}\right.$

These are hard sayings, and no gentle recourse is offered to the troubled soul in this rigid minatory criticism.

There exists a considerably more agreeable group of poems which, though remaining outside a center of feeling and tending to retain forms of investigation, query, or description, reveal a genuine aspect of Herbert, showing him in his less passionate moments, meditating rather than pleading or expostulating. Most of these poems are less compelling than the personal poems, and they range from known forms of exercise ("Who is the virtuous man?" answered in *Constancie* with a description of a stoic man such as the volatile Herbert no doubt sometimes wished to be) to reconstructions of typological parallels (*Decay, Sion, The Bunch of Grapes*) to rather stately examinations of standard religious topics—faith, sin, the Holy Scriptures, and prayer (in the poems by those names, including the second *Prayer*). No doubt some or all of Herbert's less-than-inspired poems, including the ill-tempered ones, were written in periods of tiredness or illness, as attempts to keep the poet's hand in when imagination or feeling flagged. Several have unhappy endings (*Self-condemnation, Avarice, Businesse, Decay,* and *Sinne* [I and II]), and these endings are generally a sign, in Herbert, of discouragement and discord within the self. *Ungratefulnesse,* for instance, after beginning in spontaneous gratitude ("Lord, with what bountie . . ./ Hast thou redeem'd us!") and offering a meditation on God's "two rare cabinets full of treasure,/The Trinitie, and Incarnation," ends on an oddly gloomy note:

But man is close, reserv'd, and dark to thee:
When thou demandest but a heart,
He cavils instantly.
In his poore cabinet of bone
Sinnes have their box apart,
Defrauding thee, who gavest two for one.

Nothing in the poem, except its title, prepares us for this closing condemnation of man, and no solution is proposed for this dark state of affairs. God is left defrauded; man unredeemed. A poem ending in personal despair is more bearable than a poem ending in speculative mistrust, since the emotion of despair authenticates itself in language, whereas if a poet assumes the question of ungratefulness as a speculative problem, the least we expect of him is a speculative solution (of the sort given in *Even-song,* for instance, when God kindly, in spite of our ingratitude, says "It doth suffice," and gives new wheels to our disordered clocks).

Similarly, the historical speculation in *Decay* closes with the whole world turned to coal and not even the virtuous soul left thriving:

> Sweet were the dayes, when thou didst lodge with Lot,
> Struggle with Jacob, sit with Gideon,
> Advise with Abraham, when thy power could not
> Encounter Moses strong complaints and mone:
>   Thy words were then, *Let me alone.*
>
> One might have sought and found thee presently
> At some fair oak, or bush, or cave, or well:
> Is my God this way? No, they would reply:
> He is to Sinai gone, as we heard tell:
>   List, ye may heare great Aarons bell.
>
> But now thou dost thy self immure and close
> In some one corner of a feeble heart:
> Where yet both Sinne and Satan, thy old foes,
> Do pinch and straiten thee, and use much art
>   To gain thy thirds and little part.
>
> I see the world grows old, when as the heat
> Of thy great love, once spread, as in an urn
> Doth closet up it self, and still retreat,
> Cold Sinne still forcing it, till it return,
>   And calling *Justice,* all things burn.

For Herbert, the attractive part of this speculative reconstruction of Old Testament days was clearly the representing of colloquial relations between God and his creatures. Moses complained and God said, "Let me alone"; God made frequent stops at bushes and wells; and one could casually ask his whereabouts, which gossip would provide. These childlike relations with God have disappeared as a real possibility, but Herbert delights in reasserting them by creating, over and over in his poems, occasions where God appears and speaks familiarly to the soul. He thus takes pleasure in reimagining the Mosaic intimacy with God; and since that intimacy was, for Herbert, a better state of affairs than now obtains, he has reason to call the poem *Decay*. But he omits, in this poem, all mention of the cheerful resolutions that exist for this misfortune. God has not abandoned his creatures permanently, and an intimacy has been promised in heaven which will replace that lost on earth.[2] These remedies, often invoked by Herbert himself in other contexts, here seem unavailable to him, for reasons (no doubt personal) which the poem itself does not provide. Granted, Sin and Satan are said to "straiten" God, but they both were equally present in Moses' day, and the real "straitening" appears, in this poem, to be effected at God's own pleasure. It is God who "immures" and "closes" himself up; his love "doth closet up it self, and still retreat"; and the remark about Sin's forcing it to do so, in the light of the active reflexive verbs attributed to God, is somewhat disingenuous, especially since God's "Love" seems to have the power, if it wishes, to return at any time. In the cruel ending of the poem, "Love" indeed returns, but only in vengeful guise, not as heat but as fire, consuming, with the aid of Justice, the whole world. This inflammatory return seems unmotivated in the poem, as though Herbert's speculations, free and pleasurable when ranging in the time of Moses, need to be strictly repressed when they touch the present. The anger of God seems explicable only as a projection of Herbert's own anger against God for the abandonment of his creatures; but Herbert's speculation here does not extend to his own motives. Herbert's avoidance of self-scrutiny prevents this poem, for all its initial charming reconstruction, from being ranked among the greater poems where Herbert is transparent to himself.

Decay belongs in a group of typological poems, perhaps conceived together, which hover around speculations concerning the Mosaic dispensation: *Sion, The Bunch of Grapes,* and *Josephs Coat* are the others.³ *Sion* shows the same pattern of nostalgia and mystification as *Decay,* but ends with an extended, curious, and unconvincing excursus on groans, a subject that preoccupied Herbert (*Sighs and Grones, The Cross, The Flower,* and *The Search*) rather more than he could easily absorb poetically. *The Bunch of Grapes,* unlike *Decay* or *Sion,* attempts a "happy" ending, but cannot make its resolution convincing. Herbert, having paralleled his sorrows with those of the Jews in the desert, then wants to complete the typology:

> But where's the cluster? where's the taste
> Of mine inheritance? Lord, if I must borrow,
> Let me as well take up their joy, as sorrow.

Herbert's answer to himself, "But can he want the grape, who hath the wine?/I have their fruit and more," stands simply as an assertion, not a feeling; his sad preceding lines do not read as the utterances of someone who "has" wine. Suspicion of this resolution is reinforced by the flatness of the lines following it and concluding the poem:

> Blessed be God, who prosper'd *Noahs* vine,
> And made it bring forth grapes good store.
> But much more him I must adore,
> Who of the Laws sowre juice sweet wine did make,
> Ev'n God himself being pressed for my sake.

Though the coherence of the imagery is irreproachable, and the illusion of a satisfying insight maintained in the substitution of the superior wine for the inferior grape, nevertheless the central assertion of would-be feeling expresses itself in utter clichés: "Blessed be God . . ./But much more him I must adore." There are depressing resemblances here to "We adore/And we do crouch." In short, the end, where we least expect clichés in Herbert, remains only an intellectual conclusion, following on the intellectual typological comparison with the Jews, and though feeling surfaces throughout the suffering body of the poem, it does not penetrate the would-be self-reassuring conclusion.

Of all these poems, only *Josephs Coat* refuses the speculative in favor of the direct expression of feeling. The typological relation is referred to only in the title, and no superstructure of narrative historical explanation is constructed, as it is in the other poems of the group. *Josephs Coat,* however, finally finds a resolution adequate to the terms of the central difficulty enunciated in all these poems: the estranged and deprived condition of the soul today. God used to be familiar to his subjects (*Decay*), he used to live in visible temples (*Sion*), and he used to reward his pilgrims with bunches of grapes. But now he has withdrawn his external presence and allowed Sin and Satan to torment the heart in which he lives (*Decay*); forsaking his external temples, he exacts a temple of sighs and groans (*Sion*); and he keeps his people in seeming deprivation (*The Bunch of Grapes*). The external resolutions so far offered (God will burn all evil things; God is pleased by the temple of sighs and the music of groans; God's sacramental presence in the Eucharistic wine ought to suffice for the absence of the bunch of grapes) are all far removed from the essential problem—the impoverished state of the poet's soul, when he finds his God invisible, inaccessible, and unrewarding. As Herbert writes poem after poem of complaint, the real insight of resolution finally strikes him, and he cries, "Wounded I sing, tormented I indite." Since no connective such as "though," "because," or "when," unites the adjective and verb, the relation of adjective and verb becomes a wholly cohesive and inseparable one, while the contrastive surprise (that anyone wounded should sing) reinforces the paradox—which would really be no paradox if one took the meaning to be, "Though wounded, I nevertheless sing." The rest of *Josephs Coat* explores this central insight: that Herbert is prompted to sing by suffering, that the relish of versing is his only by the anguish of torment, and that the repose of expression in available only after having been cast down:

> Wounded I sing, tormented I indite,
> Thrown down I fall into a bed, and rest:
> Sorrow hath chang'd its note: such is his will,
> Who changeth all things, as him pleaseth best.
>   For well he knows, if but one grief and smart
> Among my many had his full career,
> Sure it would carrie with it ev'n my heart,
> And both would runne untill they found a biere

> To fetch the bodie; both being due to grief.
> But he hath spoil'd the race; and giv'n to anguish
> One of Joyes coats, ticing it with relief
> To linger in me, and together languish.
> I live to shew his power, who once did bring
> My *joyes* to *weep,* and now my *griefs* to *sing.*

Verse is, in fact, as Herbert says, his life-principle: the poem hovers perilously near to death in its "full career" of grief in lines 5–9, saved only from expiring, heart and body, by the coat of Joy, which makes anguish linger by giving it sporadic relief. As long as Herbert thought of the outcome of his sufferings as sighs and groans alone, his resentment persisted, but once the groans become not only "musick for a King" but also music for Herbert himself, a component of joy is added, in spite of anguish, and resentment ebbs.[4]

The reason that Herbert could not resolve speculative poems with speculative resolutions, as Donne or Marvell could, is surely that the speculative problem did not possess for him enough reality, or did not engage him enough, to press him to an intellectual conclusion. The poems in which he sets forth a subject for intellectual perplexity pass hastily from enquiry to assertion, or embed enquiry in a matrix of inner complacency. So, in *To All Angels and Saints,* the glory of angels, saints, and the Virgin Mary is freely conceded and even expatiated on, but the problem —what sort of veneration is then due to these "glorious spirits"—is dismissed with a logic that could not bear serious examination for a moment, a trivial logic of which Donne or Marvell would have been ashamed. "Chiefly to thee," says Herbert to the Virgin Mary, "would I my soul unfold":

> But now, alas, I dare not; for our King,
> Whom we do all joyntly adore and praise,
>   Bids no such thing:
> And where his pleasure no injunction layes,
> ('Tis your own case) ye never move a wing.
>
> All worship is prerogative, and a flower
> Of his rich crown, from whom lyes no appeal
>   At the last houre:

Therefore we dare not from his garland steal,
To make a posie for inferiour power.

The position is not original with Herbert, but then many of his positions
are not; the trouble seems to be, in this early poem, that he has not subjected the question to any serious personal scrutiny.

In like manner, Herbert's poem *Faith* would rather rejoice in the possession of faith than enquire into its meaning. In fact, faith is rapidly
assimilated to something resembling the magic in fairy tales:

Hungrie I was, and had no meat:
I did conceit a most delicious feast;
I had it straight, and did as truly eat,
    As ever did a welcome guest.

There is a rare outlandish root,
Which when I could not get, I thought it here:
That apprehension cur'd so well my foot,
    That I can walk to heav'n well neare.

I owed thousands and much more:
I did beleeve that I did nothing owe,
And liv'd accordingly; my creditor
    Beleeves so too, and lets me go.

After these fanciful bits of sleight-of-hand, Herbert turns to a momentarily "metaphysical" comparison, after the manner of Donne:

When creatures had no reall light
Inherent in them, thou didst make the sunne
Impute a lustre, and allow them bright;
    And in this shew, what Christ hath done.

Unable to sustain this level of theological abstraction, and having for-
saken the level of fairy tale, the poem ends, not spiritually, but in a
more satisfying Herbertian materialist view of faith, closer to Herbert's
natural inclination than speculative talk of imputed luster:

> What though my bodie runne to dust?
> Faith cleaves unto it, counting ev'ry grain
> With an exact and most particular trust,
> Reserving all for flesh again.

The entire poem is uncertain in stance and cannot decide whether Faith is childlike (as in the fairy tale) or uneducated (making "proud knowledge bend & crouch" as Herbert unfeelingly puts it) or theological (needing a vocabulary like "imputed lustre" to express itself) or simply economical (counting out grains of dust to restore them again). No personal mystery or personal urgency motivates the poem, and as an enquiry it falters and stumbles.

But perhaps the strangest example of Herbert's constitutional inability to sustain speculation appears in *Praise* (III), a poem supposedly discussing God as the prime mover of the universe, caring for all things. The subject has a history in philosophical poetry, but Herbert's speculations remain almost grossly literal, and never did such an exalted subject receive more deliberately rustic treatment:

> When thou dost favour any action,
> It runnes, it flies:
> All things concurre to give it a perfection.
> That which had but two legs before,
> When thou dost blesse, hath twelve: one wheel doth rise
> To twentie then, or more.
>
> But when thou dost on businesse blow,
> It hangs, it clogs:
> Not all the teams of Albion in a row
> Can hale or draw it out of doore.
> Legs are but stumps, and Pharaohs wheels but logs,
> And struggling hinders more.

Not only are God's intentions toward men shown only by their speedy or lumbering earthly results, but even his actions in heaven are represented in strangely materialistic forms. He saves Herbert's tears in a heavenly bottle (like a poor-box, Herbert tells us), but the bottle is so large that Herbert's fears do not fill it:

But after thou hadst slipt a drop
From thy right eye,
(Which there did hang like streamers neare the top
Of some fair church, to show the sore
And bloudie battell which thou once didst trie)
The glasse was full and more.

All of these efforts toward literalness represent an effort toward the roughening of language. "I like our language," said Herbert in *The Sonne,* and he tries again and again to use more of that language than his speculative subject—the soul's relation to God—easily encompasses. Legs and clogs, teams of Albion, stumps, bottles, streamers and bloody battles—all of these terms reach out to vocabularies not ordinarily found in verse about divine things. These incursions into foreign territory surely gave Herbert satisfaction when they were successful—when he could put, for instance, "a ragged noise and mirth/Of theeves and murderers" into a poem concerned with redemption. Nonetheless, even this understandable wish to broaden the diction of devotional verse, so awkwardly overworked in *Praise* (III), is alien to speculative enquiry: Herbert here chooses elaboration of verbal range over refinement of mental distinctions. It is a viable choice, but it precludes a certain sort of poetry.

Herbert's "philosophical" poems (works as different as *Providence, Man,* and *Church-monuments*) tend to be elaborate multiplications of instances rather than constantly deepening meditations. Herbert was never at a loss for instances, as he himself recalls in *Jordan* (II):

I sought out quaint words, and trim invention;
My thoughts began to burnish, sprout, and swell,
Curling with metaphors a plain intention,
Decking the sense.

This is a perfectly accurate description of one sort of Herbertian poem: a plain intention decked and curled. What else, after all, is the famous *Church-monuments?* There is not a notion in it that is not a commonplace of the literature of *memento mori;* and nowhere in it is there any radical rethinking of a traditional view (as in *Dooms-day,* for instance, with its human pageant and human fears). But the commonplaces of decay are rehearsed in *Church-monuments* with elaborate attention to linked verbal details and mimetic syntax, all the burnishing and swelling remarked by Joseph Summers.[5] Herbert's own dissatisfaction with this sort of poem can be seen not only in his invention of a different kind of religious poetry—the kind in which he sets forth the received position and then, examining it, modifies it radically to suit his individual perception of the truth—but also in his expressed conclusion that the matter of poetry does not reside in the embellishments of rhetoric, but lies deeper. When he says, in *A true Hymne,* that "The finenesse which a hymne or psalme affords,/Is, when the soul unto the lines accords," the statement is a wholly serious one. Poetry is more than the exquisite statement in rhyme of what everyone knows, though Yvor Winters, in praising *Church-monuments* as Herbert's greatest poem, seems to have taken this as his definition of poetry.[6] If the words only rhyme, and individual engagement of mind and soul are missing, God "justly complains," and so do Herbert and his readers. The "sweetnesse readie penn'd" exists in the single soul to be copied, and a faithful tracing of the interior disposition of the unique individual soul, with nothing concealed of what it felt and thought, is the best and most original achievement of Herbert's poetry. It is understandable, given the sacredness of divine subjects, that Herbert might have initially considered his poetic vocation to consist only of decking the given, as he does in *Church-monuments,* but the relative shallowness of such verse, no matter how intricate and polished, made Herbert turn eventually to searching interior enquiry. The pull of the homiletic and the discursive in the other direction, away from personal questioning and toward received opinion, could not wholly be resisted, however, and came to the fore, naturally, in moments of less-than-adequate insight or inspiration.

Herbert's consciousness of the crucial boundary between ordinary meditation and original insight is expressed many times in the poetry as a change in visual perspective, most directly seen in *The Elixir:*

> A man that looks on glasse,
> On it may stay his eye;
> Or if he pleaseth, through it passe,
> And then the heav'n espie.

The same notion is suggested in *H. Baptisme* (I), where "He that sees a dark and shadie grove,/Stayes not, but looks beyond it on the skie," and it reappears in another form, in Herbert's praise of the Holy Scriptures as "the thankfull glasse,/That mends the lookers eyes." Though Herbert was glad to gain more than ordinary insight into a given text, feast, prayer, or mystery, he sensed that beyond the original separate insights there existed a system of interconnected relations, if only he could grasp it. If he could succeed in a personal interpretation of each point of sacred light, there remained still an interpretation to be made of the interconnections of these separate stars. *The H. Scriptures* (II) compares Biblical exegesis with self-examination:

> Oh that I knew how all thy lights combine,
>   And the configurations of their glorie!
>   Seeing not onely how each verse doth shine,
> But all the constellations of the storie.

In answer to the imagined charge that generalized exegetical systems of interconnection are only invented by the poet and are unverifiable, Herbert replies that his insights are "more than fancy" because they are vindicated by his lived experience:

> Such are thy secrets, which my life makes good,
>   And comments on thee: for in ev'ry thing
>   Thy words do find me out, & parallels bring,
> And in another make me understood.

Such searching out of parallels and confirmations can issue in fantastic and far-fetched "correspondences," but Herbert, though he usually does not go beyond the first step in this poetic method, seeing only "how each verse doth shine," in what we might call the personal reinterpretation of the sacred, does that so well that had he lived longer, we might have had configurations as well as single shining verses.

The early speculative poem that most clearly shows Herbert "passing through" a given phenomenon in order to "espie heaven" beyond it is *Death,* but in this poem Herbert distinguishes only the appalled natural perspective from a calm supernatural one, and lacks that individual penetration into new truth which he would later win:

> Death, thou wast once an uncouth hideous thing,
>   Nothing but bones,
>   The sad effect of sadder grones:
> Thy mouth was open, but thou couldst not sing.
>
> For we consider'd thee as at some six
>   Or ten yeares hence,
>   After the losse of life and sense,
> Flesh being turn'd to dust, and bones to sticks.
>
> We lookt on this side of thee, shooting short;
>   Where we did finde
>   The shells of fledge souls left behinde,
> Dry dust, which sheds no tears, but may extort.
>
> But since our Saviours death did put some bloud
>   Into thy face;
>   Thou art grown fair and full of grace,
> Much in request, much sought for as a good.
>
> For we do now behold thee gay and glad,
>   As at dooms-day;
>   When souls shall wear their new aray,
> And all thy bones with beautie shall be clad.
>
> Therefore we can go die as sleep, and trust
>   Half that we have
>   Unto an honest faithfull grave;
> Making our pillows either down, or dust.

Later in his career Herbert will tend to extend a received supernatural perception with a privately reinterpreted one, but even in *Death*, though the familiar contrast of earthly and heavenly perspectives gives the poem its basic structure of "once" versus "now," a closer look at Herbert's representation of the "supernatural" point of view shows his native originality at work. In seeing dust on the hither side of death, he is conventional; even in the formulation of "shells of fledge souls left behind" there is a natural extrapolation from the old image of the butterfly-soul escaped from its chrysalis. However, the next two stanzas aim not merely at the escape from death but at its transfiguration. Christ, by freely embracing Death, has changed our notion of it from something to be shunned to something to be welcomed, says Herbert, but this sentiment in itself is not particularly surprising: Herbert reserves his conviction for the following stanza, which follows the "fledge souls" into their new state of being. Three things come together in this beautiful stanza: those escaped fledge souls, whom we, in our ignorance, had thought already sufficiently clothed in their feathers, by analogy with the butterfly; the bones left behind, which we had earlier dismissed as "sticks"; and Death itself, an "uncouth hideous thing/Nothing but bones," the bones in this case being emblematic rather than real. Now both real and emblematic bones are re-clad, and the winged souls too have their further "new aray" of resurrected flesh. The spirited juxtapositions in "gay and glad,/As at dooms-day" and in "bones with beautie" permit the coexistence of the fact of death with the sight of resurrection. Herbert is influenced here by St. Paul, as his corruption puts on incorruption, but it is not quite incorruption or immortality that both Death and the soul put on; it is rather gaiety, gladness, beauty, and a new array—terms quite literally resurrective of the body, unlike the terms of perfection-by-negation ("in-" and "un-") preferred by St. Paul. The quiet trustful ending depends on that vivid conviction of the real bodily and substantial nature of the resurrection, affording its sufficiency to the imagination which, in Herbert, is unlikely to be satisfied by abstractions like incorruptibility and immortality, for all their rhetorical Pauline splendors. There is really no difference, by the end of this poem, between down and dust, dying or sleeping, since the dust of dying has been shown to be so wholly resurrectible into feathers, flesh, energy, and beauty.[7] As Herbert says, Jesus' death "did put some bloud" into the face of Death; so Herbert himself puts new blood into the notion of Dooms-day, changing it from the day of wrath in which the whole world turns to coal to a day populated by the "gay and glad."

Poems like *Death* are "speculative" in one sense, in expressing a meditation on a common topic, but Herbert's speculations, when they are most his own, do not need increasing degrees of abstraction, hermetic or learned diction, a reasoned weighing of debatable alternatives, or a survey of available positions. These discursive means, though they have served other poets well, and though they were plentifully available in Renaissance poetry and even occasionally attempted by Herbert, were finally not channels of immediate feeling for him, as were forms of colloquy or devotional address. The picturing of his own conflicts, as Herbert said (if we are to believe Walton), was his main poetic intent, and it is to the poems which record Herbert's varieties of personal religious experience that we must turn to find his chief mastery.

7

Fruit and Order: Formal Patterns

Each critic presents what he believes to be the centrality of his poet, the kernel or seed of that originality which makes the poet memorable. George Herbert's critics have in the past concentrated on the sweetness and discipline of his character, the traditional and yet personal quality of his piety, the exemplary qualities of his life and ministry, and the powerful influence for consolation and conversion found in his poetry. A strong private attachment to Herbert's personality (an attachment often stimulated by contrast, as in the cases of Cowper and Coleridge) appears throughout the writings of his best critics, and indeed, in the case of George Herbert Palmer, a name conferred at baptism ensured the critic's link to his poet. It is not because I do not share these feelings that I should like to present Herbert somewhat differently. When the man is the focus of attention, his forms seem merely inheritances from his age, the sometimes regrettable accidents of a rhetoric bewitched into eccentricities. The pattern poems appear therefore as charming vagaries, quaint examples of barbaric impedimenta, and the more striking examples of "closed form" are fastidiously relegated to a second rank. Arnold Stein comments, for instance on the "arbitrary choices that fix the internal order of a poem":

> In poems like "A Wreath," "Sinnes round," "The Call," and "Trinitie Sunday," the expressive elements are severely limited, as the obstacle created by strict form take over the oppositions normally furnished by individual thought and feeling. These poems deserve our interest, and admiration too; besides they make it plain

how much Herbert values the discipline of his craft and the necessity of obstacles and opposition in his art. But measured by the standard of his best poems the triumph over technical difficulties will seem relatively cold and thin.[1]

The theoretical confusion lying behind such a judgment is self-evident. To think of "strict form" as offering only "obstacles," to suggest that such "obstacles" preclude "individual thought and feeling," to conclude that such poems must seem "cold and thin"—this expressive theory can scarcely accommodate poets of Herbert's sort. Though it is true that some of Herbert's most highly wrought poems are not among his most successful, it is also true that some of his loosest poems are not successful. To attempt to find the formal cause of poetic failure in structural organization is to pursue a will-o'-the-wisp. Stein's admission that *Aaron* is one of Herbert's greater poems would in itself defeat his argument, but even there Stein's reluctance to like such poetry is felt: the repetitive form of *Aaron* astonishes, he says, "not for its virtuosity but for the latent power brought out of its deliberately limited materials."[2] Economy and spareness are once again seen as limitation rather than as virtue. Such principles are not stable ones for evaluation. Through a consideration of both happy and trivial examples of formal order in Herbert, I shall attempt a judgment of the practice of strict form so essential to his innermost sense of both himself and his poetry.[3]

It is tempting to begin with Herbert's greatest triumphs of order, but I would rather have "a feast as mends in length" and so will keep the best wine till the last. However, it would be unfair to Herbert to begin with his failures, which should take a modest inner place. Let me open, then, with a poem about which Stein tepidly remarks that the closed form "does less to confirm the development of the poem than to confirm the procedural method."[4] This poem, *The Call,* can serve as a touchstone for one's attachment to Herbert. If one likes it, one likes Herbert; if one does not like it, one simply likes a more complicated-seeming sort of poetry and rejects Herbert's wish for simplicity-in-complication:

> Come, my Way, my Truth, my Life:
> Such a Way, as gives us breath:

Such a Truth, as ends all strife:
Such a Life, as killeth death.

Come, my Light, my Feast, my Strength:
Such a Light, as shows a feast:
Such a Feast, as mends in length:
Such a Strength, as makes his guest.

Come, my Joy, my Love, my Heart:
Such a Joy, as none can move:
Such a Love, as none can part:
Such a Heart, as joyes in love.

The poem does not appear in the Williams manuscript, and so may be thought to be one of Herbert's later works. The initial scheme, marked by an initial restriction to monosyllables (with one exception), reads as follows, with X, Y, and Z standing for nouns, P for pronouns, V for verbs, O for objects of verbs, and subscripts for rhyme sounds:

Come, my X, my Y, my Z:
Such an X as $V-O$
Such a Y as $V-O_z$
Such a Z as $V-O$.

Stanza two introduces two refinements. Line 2 reads, "Such an X as V-Y" and line 3 reads, "Such a Y as V-in-O." In the third stanza, the variations go:

Come, my X, my Y, my Z:
Such an X as $P-V_y$
Such a Y as $P-V_z$
Such a Z as X's in Y.

The algebraic difficulty of writing such a stanza as the last, with its interlocking chimes, cannot be overestimated. However, since difficulty in itself never made a good poem, nor did musicality in itself (though that goes further than difficulty), the poem must be scanned at the expressive level as well. It begins, as do so many of Herbert's poems, with a Biblical reference, Jesus' saying, "I am the way, the truth, and the life" (John 14:6), which absolutely determines the basic stanzaic form and indeed the nouns themselves in the first stanza. So Herbert's problem was simply to fill out the scheme:

> Come, my Way, my Truth, my Life:
> Such a Way, ————
> Such a Truth, ———— -ife:
> Such a Life, ————.

We may believe that the word "Life," climactic in Jesus' description of himself, engendered the word "death" and caused the second schema:

> Come, my Way, my Truth, my Life:
> Such a Way as $V-O_{eath}$
> Such a Truth as $V-O_{ife}$
> Such a Life as killeth death.

The inner end-nouns are invented arbitrarily, since way and truth are not normally associated with breath and strife. Jesus' words are the unchangeable matrix here, and the rest of the stanza has to be tailored to fit them.

If the poem went no further than this, it would remain piety and no more, the sort of versification of the Gospels found often in hymns. The genuine oddness of the second stanza, and its tiny movement toward further interlacing, give us a glimpse of Herbert's tendency toward redefinition of Jesus and by extension a redefinition of himself. If Jesus is the Way, the Truth, and the Life, then the poet is the strayed sheep, the mind in darkness, and the soul imprisoned by the body of this death. The poet's state is a joyless one, unredeemed, and one conscious of a profound dualism between earth and heaven. He is without "breath" or "spiritus"; he is in a condition of strife; he is the captive of death. Jesus will give him breath, end strife, and kill death. Theologically this is all very well; temperamentally it is a vision of the religious life fundamentally alien to Herbert's nature, which more closely conjoined man and God. With his usual audacity, Herbert in the second stanza, writes new lines, so to speak, for Jesus to say.

The first two lines are quite close to things Jesus did in fact say—"I am the light of the world," and "I am the living bread"—but still there is a departure from scriptural authenticity. Jesus nowhere said, "I am the Light, the Feast, the Strength." Even to put the line in this way shows the skewing of origins taking place in the poem: the exclusiveness of the definite article in the formulation from John from which the poem derives is already being lost. "I am the light" still passes, and even perhaps "I am the Feast," though "I am *a* Feast" is more idiomatic. "I am the Strength" is of course ungrammatical, and the underlying sentence is becoming "I am *X*" rather than "I am the *X*." "I am Joy, I am Love" is almost Blakean and shows how far from Biblical probability Herbert is willing to stray (though not from Biblical authority, using as he does John's words "God is Love" and imaginatively reattributing them to Jesus after the manner of stanza one).

The putative imagined sentence of Jesus' from which "Come . . . my Heart" may be said to derive is more difficult to formulate. "I am Heart" and "I am the Heart" are both ungrammatical; "I am a Heart" is simply foolish; "I am your Heart" is the only logical possibility. For the first time, Jesus' description of himself, "I am your Heart," coincides with an attribute of Herbert's: "Come . . . my Heart." I do not think this accidental. From the beginning, Herbert's effort has been to make intimacy from dogma, and Jesus' stern implication in the original Gospel source that unbelievers will perish if they do not find the way, the truth, and the life has become impossible as a sequel to Jesus' self-definition as Herbert which we see in the end of the poem.

From the strictness of the first stanza, with its contests between truth and lies, life and death, journey and perdition, the poem passes to a "better world," the world of courtesy, in the second stanza. Man is invited to a feast; a light shows the way; the feast is one where the best wine is brought out at the end, and the nourishment not only mends but makes the guest: "A guest, I answer'd, worthy to be here./Love said, You shall be he." It might be thought, in view of Herbert's exquisite apprehension of the metaphor of courtesy, that intimacy with Jesus could go no further, or rather, to put it in terms of selfhood, that no better condition could be imagined than that of the guest, so welcomed and fed by the divine host. Here, in this stanza, there is no suspicion that man's estate is dark, strife-filled, uncertain, and death-like; the implications of Jesus' first utterance are erased by Herbert's substitution of the metaphor of the feast, where man is the honored guest.

But even this Biblically sponsored metaphor of man's condition does not satisfy Herbert. With an intimacy foreign to the original words of Jesus with which the poem began, Herbert creates a wholly human tenderness between Jesus and man, and claims for man the right to be the true love of his redeemer. There really is no inequality between the two partners in the last stanza of the poem, not even the social inequality of host to guest, to say nothing of the inequalities of stature between God and man implicit in the first stanza. For the first time, the titles by which Jesus is addressed come from the speaker himself rather than from his Scripture reading. "Come, my Joy, my Love, my Heart" comes close in feeling to "My true love hath my heart and I have his." Something strange has also happened to the personal pronoun in this final stanza. The "my" in the first two stanzas can be translated by various forms:

> my Way—the Way for me
> my Truth—what shows me truth
> my Life—what gives me life
> my Light—what gives me light
> my Feast—where I banquet ("Feast" refers to the event, not to
>   what is consumed, since it "mends in length")
> my Strength—what gives me strength

But in the last stanza, these translations do not work:

> my Joy—what I joy in
> my Love—what I love
> my Heart—me

The redundancy and tautology of these phrases show that the identity of self and Jesus has finally been achieved. Both "Joy" and "Love" are words that can be either nouns or verbs, and unlike the nouns used in the first two stanzas, they are susceptible to the fundamental change in status marked by a change in grammatical function. In the line, "Such a Heart, as joyes in love," even the final "love" is probably to be taken as a verbal, so that it would be translated, "Such a Heart, as joyes in loving." However, by the parallel construction with "in length" in the second stanza, "in love" keeps its nominal status as well. When nouns and verbs are indistinguishable, it means, metaphysically, that what I love is my love, what I enjoy is my joy, the heart loves joy, the heart joyes in love; "My Joy, my Love, my Heart" *is* "Such a Heart, as joyes in love."

This is a figure for total self-completion, when the subject and his actions are perfectly congruent, and when the actions and their object are also perfectly congruent. The confidence sponsored by this congruence enables the bold exclusive claims of the last stanza: Herbert knows that "none can move" this joy, "none can part" this love. I do not think it is too fanciful to see the last line, with its perfect employment of all three epithets in one assertion, as a figure for the Trinity, where the heart may resemble the Father, the love the Son, and the "joying" the Holy Ghost. Because the heart "joyes" in love, there is no reason for the love ever to cease, by moving or by parting: the activity is perfectly self-contained, self-enabled, and self-delighting. There are no more possibilities in the stanza for the heart; all its "words" have been literally used up; in this little cosmos there are no other choices open to it but to go on loving. The self-exhausting of the terms of the stanza in the last line precludes any exceptions to the rule that the line enunciates. Selfhood is defined, finally, as having a heart that joys in loving, and this selfhood is identical for Jesus and the poet. The poem enacts the Pauline claim, "I live, now not I, but Christ liveth in me." The identity of man and Christ is not at all evident in the first stanza, still unachieved in the second stanza (though at least a reciprocity of host and guest has been established), but is wholly present in the final stanza. It is good, the poem says, to be on the right way, perceiving truth and gaining life; it is better to be a guest at the wedding feast; but it is best of all to be indistinguishable from one's beloved. "No better serves me now, save best," says Hopkins, and this poem is an example of the same assertion. Why, in religion, should man be satisfied with any metaphor less than the humanly best he can imagine for himself? Pilgrimage and replenishment are all very well, but love-joy, to use Herbert's term, is better. This tiny, almost wholly monosyllabic poem, with its stunning economy of means, will serve as an example of Herbert's punctilious but weighted poetry. Lightly read, it seems a trivial hymn, but the enchantment of its last stanza, by its implicit rebuke to the stiffness of the preceding verses, tells us that Herbert never wrote lightly, and rarely wrote conventionally.

The alternatives the poem presents are not just alternatives. There is a sequence; one proposal is put aside and a next, new one, entertained; and the poem ends where it does because no more proposals are possible. The heavenly love-bond is the "music beyond which philosophy cannot go," and there we halt. Even the halt criticizes, by implication, the earlier formulas: "Jesus said thus and so," say stanzas one and two; "but I say something else, and something more," says stanza three: "*My* Jesus would say, 'I am your Joy, your Love, your Heart.' " Nothing here lacks Biblical authorization, exactly, but the ending is far less "Biblical" and far more "Herbertian" than the beginning.

The end of *The Call* comes as a pure satisfaction, but the satisfaction arises from more than the fulfillment of the exigencies of form. Something internal has to have happened in the poem as well; there has to have been a movement of the mind and feelings in harmony with the form. Sometimes Herbert tries to suit a form only to a construct in the mind, without including the indispensable element of personal feeling, and such "forms," no matter how ingeniously worked out, are empty disappointments. The strangest of these in *The Temple* is *Antiphon* (II). It is certainly the most peculiar example of terza rima in English, and is a poem needing music to flesh it out:

> *Chor.* Praised be the God of love,
>   *Men.*   Here below,
>   *Ang.*   And here above:
> *Cho.* Who hath dealt his mercies so,
>   *Ang.*   To his friend,
>   *Men.*   And to his foe;
>
> *Cho.* That both grace and glorie tend
>   *Ang.*   Us of old,
>   *Men.*   And us in th'end.

Cho.   The great shepherd of the fold
    Ang.   Us did make,
    Men.   For us was sold.

Cho.   He our foes in pieces brake;
    Ang.   Him we touch;
    Men.   And him we take.
Cho.   Wherefore since that he is such,
    Ang.   We adore,
    Men.   And we do crouch.

Cho.   Lord, thy praises should be more.
    Men.   We have none,
    Ang.   And we no store.
Cho.   Praised be the God alone,
    Who hath made of two folds one.

There is no point in scrutinizing such a poem for purely aesthetic reasons, but I think it has something to tell us about Herbert's mind. Oddly, Palmer does not seem to recognize Herbert's intent in using terza rima: he says tortuously that the poem is "an exquisite case of inwoven rhyme. The second, fourth, and sixth lines of each stanza rhyme together; but the fifth of each with the first and third of the following stanzas."[5] The reason the poem does not *sound* like one written in terza rima is that it is "really" written in tetrameter couplets:

Praised be the God of love,
Here below, and here above:
Who hath dealt his mercies so,
To his friend, and to his foe;

That both grace and glorie tend
Us of old, and us in th'end . . .

The eye and the ear are at war in the poem, so that the only adequate means of helping the ear to distinguish what the eye sees would be a musical setting, in which presumably the angels would sing up high, the men down low, and the chorus would blend the two. If, then, one were to list the conditions of composition that Herbert set himself for this apparently simple poem, the list would go something like this:

(1) Terza rima.

(2) Antiphonal chanting between the joint chorus of men and angels, on one hand, and men and angels, on the other.

(3) The length of line for the chorus to equal the combined lengths of the lines for men and angels.

(4) Antiphonal chanting—a sub-antiphony—between men and angels.

(5) The length of the men's lines to equal the length of the angels' lines.

(6) The men to speak first in the first and last stanzas; elsewhere the angels to speak first.

(7) The lines of the chorus to be equally applicable to men and angels.

(8) The lines of the men and the angels to show the differences in their separate states under the broader rubric of the identity among creatures asserted by the chorus.

(9) The poem to be concluded by the chorus, breaking the previous stanzaic pattern of closure by men, and thereby affirming unity above disparity.

This is a truly torturing set of conditions, as anyone can see by trying to write a poem on this pattern. There are metaphysical reasons for all the conditions. Herbert chooses terza rima because it represents the three components (men, angels, and their combined position as spiritual principles and creatures of God); he measures line length by quantity (men + angels = chorus); God's mercies are the same to all his creatures, hence the univocal predications of the chorus; God specifies particular mercies to particular needs, hence the separate statements of men and angels; God is the principle of unity in the universe, hence the unified conclusion; the special remarks begin and are concluded by men, since poems are human things; in the middle, the angels speak first, as having hierarchical preference. Some of these conjectured reasons are debatable, but I do not doubt that Herbert had firm reasons for each of his structural conditions. The only genuinely metaphysical insight the poem might be said to embody is the notion that things in heaven are in truth identical to things on earth. God is praised in both places, deals his mercies in both, gives grace and glory to both, shepherds both, defeats foes in both, and unites both. In short, there are many things that angels and men can say in chorus, for all the differences that separate them. "Insofar as I can say these things, I am like an angel; I live, in part, with the angels; God treats me as he treats the angels"—such would seem to be the human message of the poem. However, the peculiar tonelessness of the poem prevents that message from appearing really felt. A sense of brotherhood with angels ought to have more elation about it, if it were being experienced and not merely enunciated. "Whether I flie with angels," Herbert says elsewhere, and we believe him; but here there are no wings. The meter is peculiarly heavy-footed in its trochaic insistence, and for once Herbert's euphony and gracefulness have deserted him, especially in lines like "Wherefore since that he is such,/We adore,/And we do crouch."

For all its faults, the poem is wholly characteristic of Herbert's mentality in its fierce principles of construction. Its armature of historical dogma, however, is *not* characteristic of Herbert, and it is that unsympathetic center which prevents his entering more fully into the poem. "The relations between men and angels in respect to God's treatment of them" is scarcely a personal or poetic subject. It would do better as the subject of a theological essay. And Herbert did not have a particularly theological mind. Dogma interested him less than ethics, and ethics less than religious experience; he had none of Donne's intrepid fascination with fine points of theological speculation.

Nevertheless, it is not only dogma that can ruin a poem. *Praise* (II) suffers a different, if obscure, unsuccess. Its intent seems plausible: it is personal; it is a colloquy; it concerns that quintessentially Herbertian subject, the relief of the heart after being "heard" by Christ; and it formally enacts the transactions between Christ and the soul:

> King of Glorie, King of Peace,
>   I will love thee:
> And that love may never cease,
>   I will move thee.

> Thou hast granted my request,
> Thou hast heard me:
> Thou didst note my working breast,
> Thou hast spar'd me.

The poem continues in this vein, with alternate stanzas of "I" and "Thou," the "I" using the future tense of resolve, the "Thou" shown in a series of past-tense mercies, each stanza alternating masculine and feminine rhymes. Finally, after six "tensed" stanzas, comes the final "untensed" stanza, employing the "eternal" infinitive:

> Small it is, in this poore sort
> To enroll thee:
> Ev'n eternitie is too short
> To extoll thee.

It is hard to say what goes wrong, but one could venture some guesses. The relation between God and man is phrased in clichés about sin and mercy; the poem remains static and shows no change of heart or advance of mind; the same awkward trochees that marred *Antiphon* (II) exist here—but such guesses are never wholly satisfactory. The one thing that can be said with certainty is that the poem does not fail (given its stringent set of satisfied conditions) for lack of planning. Nor does it seem to have been considered a failure by at least one of Herbert's admirers, since Vaughan imitated it in his *Praise,* though without perceiving several of its structural principles and clearly caring more for its sentiments than for its art. Rickey refers to Herbert's structural conditions here as evidence of "the greatest ingenuity," in a paragraph of praise beginning, "He also learned to make the technical aspects of his verse count for more in conveying meaning."[6] This praise does not to me seem applicable to the poem, since no special meaning inheres in the structural elements themselves.

It is a relief to pass from *Antiphon* (II) and *Praise* (II) to happier examples of Herbert's serious games. In *Grace,* the self-imposed conditions are as usual multiple:

(1) The theme to be the need for grace.

213

(2) The stanzas to have an inflexible (but not self-sufficient) refrain, "Drop from above."

(3) The rhyme for "above" to be chosen from words ending in "-ove" but only from those in which "-ove" is pronounced "uv" or "oov," not those pronounced "ōv" (as "grove," "wove").

(4) The stanza to consist of four lines, including the refrain.

(5) The meter to be iambic tetrameter.

(6) The word "grace" (or a homonym) to be mentioned in the third line of each stanza, except for the last, where in heaven the need for grace vanishes.

(7) The first two lines of each stanza to be statement, the last two lines prayer (except in the last stanza, which is all prayer); the prayer form to use "let" if possible.

The marvel of the poem is that with all its iron conditions, *Grace* reads as pure colloquial spontaneity, unpremeditated meditation:

> My stock lies dead, and no increase
> Doth my dull husbandrie improve:
> O let thy graces without cease
>   Drop from above!
>
> If still the sunne should hide his face,
> Thy house would but a dungeon prove,
> Thy works nights captives: O let grace
>   Drop from above!
>
> The dew doth ev'ry morning fall;
> And shall the dew out-strip thy Dove?
> The dew, for which grasse cannot call,
>   Drop from above.
>
> Death is still working like a mole,
> And digs my grave at each remove:
> Let grace work too, and on my soul
>   Drop from above.
>
> Sinne is still hammering my heart
> Unto a hardnesse, void of love:
> Let suppling grace, to cross his art,
>   Drop from above.

O come! for thou dost know the way:
Or if to me thou wilt not move,
Remove me, where I need not say,
    Drop from above.

The problem for the poet in composing this poem is first to amass all possible rhyme-words (within the given conditions) for "above." Herbert would have made the following exhaustive list (there are really no other suitable common words), sufficient for seven stanzas:

improve
prove
dove
remove
love
reprove
move

He even wrote seven stanzas, as we learn from the Williams manuscript, then rejected the penultimate one (in spite of his wish to use up all his rhyme-words) because it accused God of "seeking" delays:

What if I say thou seek'st delayes:
Wilt thou not then my fault reproue?
Prevent my Sinn to thine owne praise,
    Drop from above.

Consistency in imagery is not so important to Herbert as is musicality.[7] We are variously given, in sequence, images of fruitfulness versus "dull husbandrie," sun versus night, freedom versus captivity, dew versus dryness, a mole underground versus a soul aimed toward heaven, hammering to hardness versus suppling to meekness, and coming to earth versus going to heaven. The allusions in these antitheses, easily grasped by the reader Herbert had in mind, are mostly Biblical (Job, the parable of the sower, man's flesh like grass, Jesus leading captivity captive, the heavens dropping down dew). The elements of structure added by Herbert, as works of supererogation, to his already elaborate scheme are not structures of imagery so much as structures of thought. The poem proceeds as an argument, with the first stanza presenting the whole in little: Herbert's sorrow, and the wish for its remedy, grace. Then the rest follows:

Stanzas 2-3: Other things than grace still come from heaven (sun and dew).

Stanzas 4-5: But enemies encompass me (death and sin).

Stanza 6: Move thyself to remove me.

It cannot be accidental that the small psychomachia in the poem between the forces for good and evil makes a little poem in itself—sun and dew versus sin and death—in which the alliterations and an assonance scarcely arrive by chance. These are natural, quasi-homonymous enemies. Herbert "thickens" the texture of his poem even further by having the rhyme-words of stanzas one and two resemble each other ("increase," "cease," "face," "grace"), as also do those of stanzas three and four ("fall," "call," "mole," "soul"). Finally, we can scarcely doubt that just as "grass" came into Herbert's mind in stanza three as a homonym for "grace," so "grease" (however absurd) was hovering somewhere in the penumbra of the poem and summoned up (however unconsciously) the notion of "suppling" the heart (as one might "supple" leather by oiling it). Christ's blood, as Herbert's speaker in *Love unknown* tells us, is "most divine/To supple hardnesses."

These may be called the "nonsense" elements of the poem: elements of game, of sound pattern, of hieroglyph, of puzzle. They in some sense preceded the composition of the poem proper. But they alone do not make the poem, and it is once again to those components of mind and feeling that we must look to vivify the arrangements, no matter how charming, in which they this time appear. Herbert wrote greater "dejection odes" than *Grace* (*Affliction* [I], *The Forerunners*), but the passage from ingenuousness to self-severity in this poem is a theme he never tires of. Here he begins with himself as a husbandman cultivating his garden. True, his husbandry is "dull," but his dead stock nevertheless seems scarcely his fault, as it would not be the fault of a real husbandman whose stock died, if the cause of that death were perpetual night and drought. If "still the sunne should hide his face," no stock could thrive; if the dew did not fall, the grass would die. There is probably a pun, as usual, on "sun," since without the sun, God's works are said, mysteriously, to remain the captives of night in a world that is but a dungeon. "He hath led captivity captive," and the harrowing of hell are not far from Herbert's mind.[8] The *Rorate coeli*, "Drop down, ye heavens, from above," of Isaiah (45:8) has also long been associated with the coming of the Son and may provide the link between the second and third stanzas, from the hidden "sun" to the falling of the dew. The third stanza, with its repeated invoking of "the dew," "the dew," "the dew," has the freshness of the reawakening in *The Flower:* "I once more smell the dew and rain,/And relish versing." There is scarcely anywhere in Herbert a better triple invocation of man's misery, God's mercy, and nature's emblematic power than in his gentle rivalry between the dew and the Dove. The artless observation gained from morning walks, the mild reproach, the parched muteness of the grass (more harshly sensed in *Longing* and *Deniall*), all follow each other in such musical euphony that we hardly notice the modulations.

Speculation on the cause of the dead stock has so far stayed aboveground: no dew, no sun, dull husbandry. But plants can as well be undermined from below, and Herbert's gaze, having descended with the dew to the level of the grass, now passes like an X-ray through the soil and sees the leveler beneath—Death, working "like a mole." It might seem that the real cause of the dead stock has been reached, Death being the natural enemy of life and the putative cause of anything's being dead. But Herbert's allegories often operate in both the literal and the figurative realm at once, so we need, besides a natural villain in the form of Death, a spiritual villain in the form of Sin. The allegory of the dead stock is abandoned, and we enter the realm of direct statement: Sin is hammering Herbert's heart unto hardness. The usual figure for a hard heart (a heart of stone) will not do here, since Herbert wants an active agent who can turn something soft into something hard, as a blacksmith turns something malleable into tempered metal. Though this imagery is not consistent with the subsequent "suppling," and we do not know exactly what metaphor may lie behind the use of "suppling," still there is a clear intent to show active forces, negative and positive, striving to induce changes in Herbert's heart. Grace, Herbert insists, works pointedly and not at random: "Let grace work *too*"; "Let suppling grace, *to crosse his art,*/Drop from above."

Sometimes Herbert concentrates almost too much on his own guilt, to the exclusion of circumstances and of the nature of human life. Here, with the introduction of Death and Sin, forces are suggested which modify the first view, that God's withholding of grace is responsible for Herbert's sterility. Nevertheless, the first view is not denied: the world *is* dark, the world *is* dry, and also the mole Death *is* digging, and Sin's hardness *is* being hammered in. Yet the very placement of the four causes implies a passage, characteristic of Herbert, from external causation to an internal one, as he attributes "spiritual dryness" in the end to human mortality and human sin. The helplessness of the human being reduced to this primal level of deprivation surfaces in the poverty of the repeated prayer. There is only one thing to say:

> O let thy graces without cease/Drop from above!
> O let grace/Drop from above!
> The dew . . ./Drop from above.
> Let grace work too, and . . ./Drop from above.
> Let suppling grace . . ./Drop from above.

It is no wonder that at the end, seeing that on this earth, given the reiterated persistence of Sin and the irremediable presence of Death, the only thing left to pray for is removal: "Remove me, where I need not say,/*Drop from above.*" This is poverty's definition of heaven—the place "where I need not say/*Drop from above.*" This parched negative description is a more haunting version of bliss than any positive claims, at this point, could be. Yet the confidence that such a state exists steadies the poem and validates its trust in external relief. The dew is still the central metaphor: "the dew doth ev'ry morning fall." The canceled stanza in the Williams manuscript describes a God without dew, who reproves rather than removes faults. But grace has nothing to do with reproof, and so the stanza vanishes. The image of reciprocal strife in the world permeates the poem, and if there is the night, there is also the sun and dew; if there are sin and death, there is also grace to cross them. The implication of this strain of duality is that if there is indeed such a bad state, there must be a good one to comfort it. The final prayer is authenticated by the notion of the dark-and-light cosmos supported by the whole poem. Herbert's confidence in the conversion of the hard heart into one "new, tender, quick" was experientially based; his fluid and mobile temperament guaranteed it.

The most eccentric of all Herbert's detailed schemes for a poem underlies *Paradise,* a poem not found in the Williams manuscript and not to be taken lightly. Palmer rightly says that anyone who studies this poem sympathetically "will discover how exquisite poetry can be when most remote from present habits of thought."[9] The conditions for the poem are really only two:

(1) Iambic tetrameter triplets (*aaa,* etc.).

(2) The rhyme words to be constructed as follows:

$$vwxyz$$
$$wxyz$$
$$xyz$$

One exception to be allowed in stanza one, where the pattern is:

$$wxyz$$
$$xyz$$
$$yz$$

Herbert used five groups of triplets:[10]

GROW	CHARM	START	SPARE	FREND
ROW	HARM	TART	PARE	REND
OW	ARM	ART	ARE	END

(Even to achieve these groups, Herbert is forced to spell "owe" as "ow," and "friend" as "frend.") These triplet groups pre-exist the poem and set the condition that lines having these endings have to be contrived so as to make sense, not to speak of making a poem. And yet *Paradise* sounds perfectly natural:

> I blesse thee, Lord, because I GROW
> Among thy trees, which in a ROW
> To thee both fruit and order OW.

What open force, or hidden CHARM
Can blast my fruit, or bring me HARM,
While the inclosure is thine ARM?

Inclose me still for fear I START.
Be to me rather sharp and TART,
Then let me want thy hand & ART.

When thou dost greater judgements SPARE,
And with thy knife but prune and PARE,
Ev'n fruitfull trees more fruitfull ARE.

Such sharpness shows the sweetest FREND.
Such cuttings rather heal then REND.
And such beginnings touch their END.

One would not at first glance take Herbert's poem for a statement about suffering, because it begins in the perfect placidity of a well-kept orchard. It suggests at first those exquisite paintings of Fra Angelico where the saints meet and embrace in gardens of the same faultless "fruit and order." In these gardens there is no Keatsian sense of process, of bursting or swelling or maturation; they are not even Spenserian gardens, where "there is perpetuall spring and harvest there/Continuall." Rather, these orchards are taken in their Platonic sense: an enclosure full of fruit-bearing trees, some of them perhaps espaliered, all of them trimmed to perfect shape, symmetrical, and fruitful.[11] Though the opening conceit is visual, the poem itself is not, unlike some other poems that share its conception, (Hopkins' "Boughs being prunèd, birds preenèd," or Howard Moss's "The Pruned Tree"). The paradox of suffering or "pruning" that underlies all these poems arises from our inability to undergo suffering voluntarily, while yet knowing that without it we would remain blank and unfinished. Even if we are thankful for it after the fact, we are not thankful for it in itself, only for its results: wisdom comes to us in our own despite. Each pruning, as Herbert's hieroglyph shows, engenders a new word; all together, the poem suggests, our prunings in life give birth to a new language expressive of suffering, composed of words that before the pruning could not have existed.

Herbert suggests in *Paradise* several modes of action that God might take toward him or, to put it another way, several apprehensions under which he might live. He might apprehend God as protection, and himself as one shielded from force and charm, enclosed by the arm of God. Or God can neglect him, and he can find himself alone in the universe, lacking God's hand and art. God can be dissatisfied with him and, with his severest "great judgement," cut him down; he will then think himself persecuted. Or God can "cultivate" him, and he can sense himself as someone pruned and pared for greater fruitfulness. Each of these possibilities offers a miniature cosmology, and some versions of religious experience emphasize one, some another. Herbert's poem expresses the middle way between a God of ultimate harshness and a God of purely benign protection. The absent God, who seems to neglect his creature, would be worse even than the God who prunes and pares. Each of these views of God is directly evolved from a view of human nature. "I . . . [am] stil'd/Thy childe" says Herbert in *Longing*, but he is only so "styled" in figurative language; he does not embrace the view that he is innocent and that God's only function toward him is a maternally protective one. Neither does he take the masochistic view that he deserves either "greater judgements" or total neglect. His own guilts and tendency to "start" suggest the need for pruning and paring; his own fruits suggest the possibility of greater fruitfulness. "Be to me rather sharp and tart," he says, but when he says this, we do not yet know whether he has experienced the sharpness he professes to be willing to undergo. However, he shows us, by his final generalizations, that he has in fact experienced that sharpness and those cuttings and has seen the healings they bring about.[12] Until now, God has been both protector and pruner; here, for the first time, he becomes the "sweetest friend," always a reconciliatory phrase for Herbert. Normally cuttings are thought of as endings, but in his "fine and wittie" conclusion, Herbert calls them "beginnings," and redefines "end" as "final cause" rather than as "cessation."[13] The "sowre-sweet" perception of suffering that closes the poem is mirrored in the paradoxical antitheses of the last triad—sharpness-sweetest, heal-rend, beginnings-end. The earlier triads often used words in twos, but always words that are synonymous— "fruit" and "order," "force" and "charm," "blast" and "harm," "sharp" and "tart," "hand" and "art," "prune" and "pare." Such pairings almost seem to say, "What is, is," while the last pairings seem to say, "What is may be something else." The recourse to the comparative ("more fruitfull") and the superlative ("sweetest"), both signs of the celestial state, are reinforced by the intimations of Alpha and Omega (in "beginnings" and "end") at the close of the poem. Such a closure is unequivocal and gives the poem its unshakable air of composure and authority.

Paradise is not, however, a paradisal poem, for all its aspirations toward that state. The tone it reflects is one of acquiescence in the preparation for paradise, even an appreciation of the advances in fruit and order so far gained; but the blessedness in the poem is envisaged, not yet possessed. Such beginnings touch their end, as the poem says, but they have not acquired it. The poem is not, after all, analogous to the achieved paradises of Fra Angelico.

Finally, as the last example of Herbert's love for order and schemata as a way toward poetic fruit, we may glance at that ethereal penultimate poem in *The Temple,* the echo verses called *Heaven.*

> O who will show me those delights on high?
>   *Echo.*   I.
> Thou Echo, thou art mortall, all men know.
>   *Echo.*   No.
> Wert thou not born among the trees and leaves?
>   *Echo.*   Leaves.
> And are there any leaves, that still abide?
>   *Echo.*   Bide.
> What leaves are they? impart the matter wholly.
>   *Echo.*   Holy.
> Are holy leaves the Echo then of blisse?
>   *Echo.*   Yes.
> Then tell me, what is that supreme delight?
>   *Echo.*   Light.
> Light to the minde: what shall the will enjoy?
>   *Echo.*   Joy.
> But are there cares and businesse with the pleasure?
>   *Echo.*   Leisure.
> Light, joy, and leisure; but shall they persever?
>   *Echo.*   Ever.

Herbert's careful arrangement of the closing poems of *The Temple,* unchanged from the Williams manuscript, shows that he approved this not once, but twice, as worthy to precede *Love* (III), no small honor for any poem. The form in this case is not unique to Herbert: echo poems pre-existed *The Temple,* both in the classical and modern languages and in English.[14] The form, however, is sufficiently difficult so that even poets of undoubted mastery faltered under the test. Sidney's echo poem in the *Arcadia* is shocking, by comparison with Herbert's, in its woodenness, its lack of invention, and its slavish repetition of identical words:

Echo, what do I gett yelding my sprite to my grieves?
                                                    Grieves.
What medecin may I finde for a paine that draw's me to death?
                                                    Death.
O poisonous medecin! what worse to me can be then it?
                                                    It.
In what state was I then, when I tooke this deadly disease?
                                                    Ease.
And what manner a mind which had to that humor a vaine?
                                                    Vaine.

Sidney may not have chosen to give his best poetry to Philisides, but other echo poems in general seem no better. The echo tends more often than not to repeat without alteration the word said by the voice, or to repeat an etymological variant of the "parent" word (the pairs in Tasso's *Eco* include *accresca—cresca, m'accieco—cieco, m'appresto—presto, dispera—spera, affida—fida*). Once in a while, the verbal invention will find something more ingenious than simple repetition or etymological identity, but such *trouvailles* are rare and so far as I can see do not form the principle of any echo poem preceding Herbert's, with the possible exception of *An Echo* from Lord Sterling's *Aurora* (1604):

Ah, will no soule give eare unto my mone?   *one.*
Who answers thus so kindly when I crie?   *I.*
What fostred thee that pities my despaire?   *aire.*
Thou blabbing guest, what know'st thou of my fall?   *all.*

What did I when I first my faire disclos'd? *los'd.*
Where was my reason, that it would not doubt? *out.*
What canst thou tell me of my ladie's will? *ill.*
Wherewith can she acquit my loyall part? *art.*
What hath she then with me to disaguise? *aguise.*
What have I done, since she gainst love repin'd? *pin'd.*
What did I when I her to life prefer'd? *er'd.*
What did mine eyes, whilst she my heart restrain'd? *rain'd.*
What did she whilst my muse her praise proclaim'd? *claim'd.*
And what? and how? this doth me most affright. *of right.*
What if I never sue to her againe? *gaine.*
And what when all my passions are represt? *rest.*
But what thing will best serve to asswage desire? *ire.*
And what will serve to mitigate my rage? *age.*
I see the sunne begins for to descend. *end.*

Clearly a strenuous effort is being made in this poem to change
the end-word between its first appearance in the voice and its second appearance in the echo, and to have the echo comment on its rhyme-word
by means of what may be called a "false" etymology: when one "re-
pines," the other "pines"; her "will" is his "ill"; to "prefer" her is to
"err"; "repressed," one can "rest"; "desire" is the obverse of "ire,"
"age" the obverse of "rage," and to "descend" is to "end." We should
like to think that such natural opposites and obverses and parallels had
a "natural" linguistic relation, and the punning rhymes make it seem
that they do. However, in *An Echo* these matchings are intermittent, and
are interspersed with rhymes that have no easily perceivable semantic
"natural relation"—"againe"–"gaine," "restrain'd"–"rain'd," "part"–
"art," "doubt"–"out."

Herbert's poem transcends not only all its native predecessors but also
all its descendants. Perhaps it triumphs first by its brevity. Instead of
trying, like Sidney, to maintain the echo-device for half-a-hundred lines,
or even, like Lord Sterling, for nearly twenty, Herbert is content with
ten. And there is a reason for, or a depth to, nearly all the rhymes. It is
impossible to know exactly how much Herbert took etymology into
account, but his frequent puns (many of them recently unearthed by
Mary Ellen Rickey in *Utmost Art*) show a mind constantly playing with

underlying significance and aware of the roots of words. Did he know that "bide" is related to the Latin *fidere,* "to trust," and the Greek *paithesthai,* "to believe"? Did he mean "bliss" to summon up "bless"? (Even though that pair are not etymologically related in fact, it is a "natural" reaction to connect them.) Such questions must remain unanswered, but there is much undeniable evidence of Herbert's intent in the rhymes he used.

As Echo echoes "on high" with her self-announcing "I," she reveals her identity with that region on high: "I" is "high." The poet's scornful denial of her immortality, voiced in the cliché "everybody knows" (always the least reliable form of knowledge), is contradicted wittily by making "know" rhyme with "No," neatly dismissing earthly popular knowledge as its own negation. "Leaves"—"leaves" echoes the "folio"—"foliage" pun possible in Latin between leaves of a book and leaves of a tree, and suggests that Scripture, being itself an echo of something greater, may, while using human locutions, mean something other by them than what we ourselves mean. All echo poems include something of the riddling speech of oracles; a principle of interpretation, usually allegorical, is almost necessarily enunciated in the course of such a poem. To know anything "wholly," Herbert continues, is to know it as "holy." The first small "movement" of the poem ends with the recapitulation: "Are holy leaves the Echo then of blisse?/Yes." This, the only imperfect rhyme in the poem, is yet the least disturbing echo, as only the sibilants of "blisse" breathe themselves softly out in "Yes."

From this repose, the poem takes on new energy, and the poet, having discovered his trustworthy source of information, can at last put his essential questions. Although one of the four questions is answered by a simple repetition ("enjoy"—"joy"), in the other three the rhyme is a pun: "delight" (*de-lacere,* "allure") is "light" (Herbert perhaps also puns on "My yoke is easy and my burden light"); "pleasure" (*placere,* "to please") is "leisure" (*licere,* "to be permitted"); and things that "persever" (*per-severus,* "severe") last for "ever" (O.E. *aefre*). The point is that if any unlettered person were asked to hazard etymologies for "delight," "persever," and "leisure," he might well make a stab at them by mentioning "light," "ever," and "pleasure." These would be "natural" etymologies, simple, unlearned. How satisfying it would be, in one sense, if they were true: leisure is pleasure, light is delight, we persever for ever. A language composed on such principles would have no hidden deceptions; to bless would be bliss, and wholeness would be holiness. In such a language, actions would be simple, as Herbert's exceptional rhyme teaches us: "What shall the will enjoy? Joy." To feel feeling, to enjoy joy, to love love—these are all ways of establishing semantically and syntactically that perfect completion of the self in which subject and object are one.

In spite of these felicities, the pathos of the poem, and its joy, depend rather on its pattern of questions than on its etymologies. The poet cannot believe in the possibility of his own happiness. Nothing else so firmly shows us the sadness of human life than the fact that it kills in us the spark of hope for something better. We literally can scarcely believe that some other fortune could be awaiting us. Whether or not we share Herbert's anticipation of another life, we sense the disappointments of this life that have created the doubting Thomas of the poem. After asking, "O who will show me" heaven's joys, and hearing reassuringly, "I," he cannot rest in the good fortune of having found a guide, but utters his first doubt: "Thou art mortall, all men know." Even after Echo's denial, he insists that genealogy is destiny, and that nature is divorced from Scripture (the pun on "leaves," though meant to disabuse him of this notion, fails, and he questions the permanence of any "leaves"). Counseled patience, he replies impatiently, "Impart the matter wholly." The patience of Echo under this harassment ("all men *know*," "wert thou *not*," "*what* leaves," "impart it *wholly*," "then *tell* me," "but *are* there," "but *shall* they") is exemplary, and acts out that patience of God with his "child" which is so frequent a theme in Herbert, or rather, that frowardness in the "child" necessitating God's patience. An unwillingness to "rest in the Lord, wait patiently for him," is the motivating force throughout *Heaven*—the restless questions undergo reprise after reprise. It is a Martha who puts these questions, and "Martha, Martha, thou art careful and troubled about many things," is the irony that underlies Echo's responses. The poet is not even satisfied with the very satisfying recapitulation that holy leaves are the echo of bliss. In one sense, this is all he can know on earth and all he needs to know. Close thy Ovid, open thy Bible. But Herbert is not content to "stay his eye" on the "thankfull glasse" of the Scriptures; he wishes to espy heaven directly. The last questions of the poet are still "flesh-bound" (as Hopkins said the human spirit was always bound to be), since the speaker still thinks in categories. What will delight the mind? What will the will enjoy? Will we still need to endure the cares and business of Martha while enjoying the delights of Mary? The anxiety and fussiness of the speaker ("Yes, that takes care of the *mind;* but what about the *will?*") receive the same calm and reassuring answers as they have all through the poem. With the second recapitulation (this time summarizing the joys of heaven—light, joy, and leisure—instead of the relation between Scripture, nature, and the supernatural—"holy leaves the Echo [are] of blisse"), there is really no other question left to ask but the yearning one of permanence: "Shall they persever?" And after the final answer—"Ever"—the restless questioner is calmed.

But even now, with the perception of human anxiety and divine reassurance as the frame of the poem, we have not reached the end of its meaning. For after all, the "divine" voice is nothing other than an echo-reflection of the human voice; it is the human voice *listening to itself.* Reflection, reflexiveness, are (says Herbert) all that is required to "correct" a faulty perspective and gain a truer one. Or at least, that is how the poem at first appears: "know" is corrected by "no," "leaves" is corrected by the punning "leaves," and "wholly" is silently emended to "holy." Nevertheless, in the second half of the poem the "divine" voice is not a "correction" of the human one: it is rather a prolongation of the human. "Delight," says the human voice—"light," says the divine; "enjoy," says the human voice—"joy," says the divine; "pleasure," says the human voice—"leisure," says the divine; "persever," says the human voice—"ever," says the divine. Listen to ourselves and we will find God, the poem says. The verses are, in this way, a radical reendorsement of the human: in our yearning, we speak God's language. When we find words of the right sort to ask about the divine—words like "delight," "enjoy," "pleasure," and "persever"—God can do nothing better than answer us in our own vocabulary. The etymological point —that if these words are not related to each other by nature, they should be—is ratified by God's responses. Surely the doctrine of final perseverance, by which transient grace turns to permanent glory, deserves to have the word "ever" embodied in it. And so the poem ends in the perfect congruence of doctrine and etymology, super-nature and nature and Scripture all at one.

One never "finishes" with a poem by Herbert, if only because when all else is said and done, its fluid music is borne in the heart "long after it is heard no more." In this poem, it would seem, at first glance, that the remarks of Echo are hypermetrical, and that the poem is written in pentameter. Such a view of the prosody makes a clear distinction between the poet and the echo, and tends to reinforce the notion of a colloquy between the human and the divine. But there is another way to regard the metrics of the poem, best shown by retranscribing the poem:

> O who will show me those delights
> On high?   I.
> Thou Echo, thou art mortall, all men
> Know.   No.
> Wert thou not born among the trees
> And leaves?   Leaves.
> And are there any leaves that still
> Abide?   Bide.
> What leaves are they? Impart the matter
> Wholly.   Holy.
> Are holy leaves the Echo then
> Of blisse?   Yes.
> Then tell me, what is that supreme
> Delight?   Light.
> Light to the mind: what shall the will
> Enjoy?   Joy.
> But are there cares and businesse with the
> Pleasure?   Leisure.
> Light, joy, and leisure; but shall they
> Persever?   Ever.

Such a retranscription, though patently artificial, takes into account the natural pauses of the voice before and after the "echo" when reading the poem. Those pauses turn the lines into isometric units, each with four "beats":

```
×   —   ×   —   ×   —   ×   —
O who will show me those delights
×   —   ×   —   ×   —   ×   —
On high            I.
×   —   ×   —   ×   — ×   —   ×
Thou Echo, thou art mortall, all men
    —   ×   —   ×   —   ×   —
Know.              No.
```

Or with a musical notation, the poem looks like this:

O	who will show me	those delights on	high?	I. Thou	Echo, thou art
mortal, all men	know.	No. Wert	thou not born a	mong the trees and
leaves?	Leaves.

The adaptation of this musical notation to the poem shows Herbert's own musical taste. It is fitting that the word to be echoed should resonate the longest, and that its echo-word should be only slightly less resonant, the first being here represented by a half-note, the other by a dotted quarter. The basic falling rhythm of the poem is better seen in the musical notation than in prosodic markings: *"who* will show me," *"are* there any," "im*part* the matter," *"light* to the minde"—these phrases in their several ways show the prosodic urgency imparted by the falling rhythm (the last by its variation from the norm). Hopkins took up this suggestion (and I believe from this poem) in turning what is here a breath of prosodic inclination into a full-dress principle: the beginning of his "The Leaden Echo and the Golden Echo" imitates the *"who* will show me" and *"are* there any" here. One would like to hear *Heaven* set to music for antiphonal voices, or better yet, for a single voice antiphonally recorded, like those duets in which famous singers are recorded singing with themselves. A musical form certainly underlies it and reinforces, paradoxically, the antiphonal nature of the poem, as well as the unexpectedly perfect identity of the antiphonal voices, in the identity of the rhyme word and its echo, each occupying more or less a bar.

The examples of substructure and superstructure in this chapter could be replaced by other instances, but the conclusions would remain the same: that Herbert was delighted by innumerable strict conditions, self-set, upon his work; that he responded with energetic ingenuity at worst, passion and invention at best, to those challenges; that he let his feelings "work and winde" themselves into the sense and the metrics; and that he felt, when he did this, like one of the stars, placed—

> That so among the rest I may
> Glitter, and curle, and winde as they:
> That winding is their fashion
> Of adoration. (*The Starre*)

The stars' fashion of adoration was also his. The "trinitie of light/Motion, and heat" possessed by the stars may be seen as the trinity of thought, art, and feeling, each indispensable, that give Herbert's most beautiful complicated poems their "celestiall quicknesse."

8

Conflicts Pictured

In this final chapter, I wish to trace some of the many ways in which Herbert's central subject, the picture of his many conflicts with God, achieved expression, complication, and resolution. Herbert's first youthful response, when he sensed such conflicts, was toward self-abnegation: God must be in the right, and he himself in the wrong. It is not unusual, in Christian religious poetry, to find some account of the disproportion between God and his creatures, but the extent of self-abasement in Herbert's early poems goes so far beyond the mean that we must take them as expressing more than a convention, and attribute their excess of feeling to Herbert himself. Though the tendency to self-condemnation never left Herbert entirely, recurring in later poems like *Sighs and Grones, Sepulchre,* or *Justice* (I), it is astonishing how conspicuously Herbert finally forsook the mode of overwrought confession.[1] The early self-abasing poems are notable for their excesses of expression as well as of feeling: in them Herbert represents himself as "full of rebellion," possessed of a "saplesse" heart full of "venom" filled with "quarries of pil'd vanities" but only "shreds of holinesse." In his "most foul transgression" his eyes see only "dust blown by wit," and his "usurping lust" has "disseized" God; he is a "wretch," a "crumme of dust," a "brittle crazie glasse"; his soul is "dark and brutish"; he weds "strange pollutions," carries "infection," loves swine, and wishes to wallow in dirt; his life is "a constant blot."[2] The central antithesis between what Herbert thought he ought to be and what, in these self-abasing moments, he believed he was, appears in the climax of *Miserie:*

Indeed at first Man was a treasure,
A box of jewels, shop of rarities,
A ring, whose posie was, *My pleasure:*
He was a garden in a Paradise:
    Glorie and grace
    Did crown his heart and face.

But sinne hath fool'd him. Now he is
A lump of flesh, without a foot or wing
To raise him to a glimpse of blisse:
A sick toss'd vessel, dashing on each thing;
    Nay, his own shelf:
    My God, I mean my self.

If the gap between creator and creature had continued to be viewed in this fashion, only continual self-reproaches, wincings, and pleas of unworthiness could have made up Herbert's verse. It is tempting to see *Love* (III) as the poem which finally gave Herbert some respite from his own scruples: we find in it the familiar protests of guilt, dust, sin, unworthiness, unkindness, ungratefulness, shame, blame, and a marring of life; but one by one these disclaimers are almost tacitly put aside by Love, and are made, through Love's responses, to seem what they are—irrelevant gestures of self-important self-reference. It is clearly more courteous not to insist on one's unfitness for the wedding feast, so Herbert is shamed into desisting from his self-attentions. Something of this sort seems to have happened in reality, to enable Herbert to cease from self-regard, to look beyond his own life and espy heaven instead, thereby widening his range both of subjects and of moods.

There is another phase in Herbert allied to the early phase of self-abasement, which might be called the phase of emulation. It follows logically after the abandon of self-disparagement, since Herbert still feels wholly unworthy of God's attention and in consequence wishes to do something remarkable to repay God's consideration in redeeming him. Many early poems record a somewhat frantic attempt to establish a footing of equality with God: *The Thanksgiving, The Reprisall, Good Friday,* and *Jordan* (II) are obvious examples, though once again *Love* (III) may be thought of as the focus wherein the problem of a contest with God suddenly becomes clarified for Herbert as a problem of self-regard, and the contest subsides in courtesy. Later, in a poem like *Artillerie,* the notion of "articling" with God is summoned again, only to be dismissed as an action Herbert can no longer take seriously. These indirections of self-abasement and combat no doubt helped Herbert to find direction out, and they were also—both the sense of unworthiness and the wish to amass achievement—genuine and persistent aspects of his character. Self-mistrust appears in several late poems, and some version of competition with God appears in the late poems *Artillerie, The Storm, Hope,* and *The Holdfast,* among others. Nevertheless, Herbert was not wrong in saying to Nicholas Ferrar that he had finally found "perfect freedom" in the service of Christ, if that phrase, borrowed from the prayer book, meant to Herbert that self-rejection and competition with God were no longer, in the end, necessary to him.

The most satisfying poems in *The Temple* describe many stages of "spiritual conflict," among them the phase, preceding that of "perfect freedom," in which it seems to Herbert that his duty is to "subject" his will to "the will of Jesus [his] Master," as he put it; but as the phrase "perfect freedom" implies, "subjection" becomes in retrospect a false label. It is difficult to picture such conflicts truthfully, neither minimizing the struggle in favor of the resolution, nor falsifying the resolution so as to terminate pain before its time. In retrospective poems, it is particularly hard to keep a balance and to remain faithful to the experience in the past as it actually occurred. With Rosemond Tuve, I believe in Herbert's fidelity to experience: "There is something unlike Herbert in the picture of a poet manipulating tensions to a predetermined end. Herbert was a great artist, perhaps because he nursed no tensions he could foreknow the resolution of; they were sins to him, keeping his Saviour on the rack. A 'picture of [a] spiritual Conflict' *is* written after not during it, yet truth to an experience which led to an end is not the same as drawing conflicting elements with steady hand towards a known end."[3]

However, it is also true that a poem is not merely a diary, and that an aesthetic victory must be won in each successful poem, whether or not a spiritual victory can be claimed. The modes of winning both victories are extremely various in Herbert, and I cannot hope to describe them fully, but some of his avenues toward each may be sketched as they appear in the most rewarding of the personal poems not already discussed. Though all of Herbert's poems are in one sense "personal"—allegories and emblems, ritual celebrations, queries, meditations, and polemics—I retain the name "personal poems" for the group of poems comprising personal colloquies, mimetic retellings of religious experience, simple first-person prayers, complaints, and laments.

In the course of his career, Herbert undertook an effort, aesthetic as well as moral, to discard the early gloomier self-judgments which had led to poems of self-abasement, an effort reflected in several of his extant revisions. Sin and sorrow, sickness and shame, debt and anxiety are deleted from *Church-musick* so that the poem can describe a state of disembodied pleasure in purely positive terms; and in the second part of *The H. Communion* Herbert suppresses the original anticlimactic ending for one more in harmony with the "lift" of the soul brought about by the sacrament. *Whitsunday* also is rethought in less gloomy terms. After recollecting the glories of the first Pentecost, Herbert originally wrote, apprehensively:

> But wee are falne from Heaven to Earth,
> And if wee can stay there, it's well.
> He y^t first fell from his great birth
> Wthout thy help, leads vs his way to Hell.

But this stanza and the two following were rejected, and though Herbert admits to his poem "the braves of conqu'ring sinne," they are present only in a brief concessive clause that does not shake Herbert's more confident later view of man's destiny. In *The Elixir,* as originally composed, the Devil, astonishing though it now seems, was permitted to make an appearance. A fourth stanza, later omitted, ran:

> He that does ought for thee,
> Marketh y^t deed for thine:
> And when the Divel shakes ye tree,
> Thou saist, this fruit is mine.

And *The Elixir* closed originally with an anticlimactic drawing-in-of-horns, as Herbert reminded himself of man's radical incapacities:

> But these are high perfections:
> Happy are they that dare
> Lett in the Light to all their actions
> And show them as they are.

Shrinking from "high perfections" was characteristic of Herbert in his fearful or gloomy moods, when he doubted his own virtue; but by the time *The Elixir* is revised, he can end in untroubled confidence:

> This is the famous stone
> That turneth all to gold:
> For that which God doth touch and own
> Cannot for lesse be told.

The emphasis has turned away from man's impaired nature and toward God's omnipotent transforming powers. It is in general a change in perspective, away from self-regard, that animates all these revisions. From this refocusing, Herbert receives unprecedented new energies, which, as he explains in *Conscience,* go both inward to cleanse the soul and outward to quell scruples:

> Peace pratler, do not lowre:
> Not a fair look, but thou dost call it foul:
> Not a sweet dish, but thou dost call it sowre:
> Musick to thee doth howl.
> By listning to thy chatting fears
> I have both lost mine eyes and eares.
>
> Pratler, no more, I say:
> My thoughts must work, but like a noiselesse sphere:
> Harmonious peace must rock them all the day:
> No room for pratlers there.
> If thou persistest, I will tell thee,
> That I have physick to expell thee.

And the receit shall be
My Saviours bloud: when ever at his board
I do but taste it, straight it cleanseth me,
        And leaves thee not a word;
    No, not a tooth or nail to scratch,
    And at my actions, carp, or catch.

        Yet if thou talkest still,
Besides my physick, know there's some for thee:
Some wood and nails to make a staffe or bill
        For those that trouble me:
    The bloudie crosse of my deare Lord
    Is both my physick and my sword.

This poem, a compound of most of the elements in Herbert, nevertheless has its components arranged not quite in order, in that it never entirely reaches its avowed aim: "My thoughts must work, but like a noise-
lesse sphere." This phrase is the quintessence of Herbert at his best, while
the final stanza of the poem, brandishing its "staffe or bill," can hardly
be thought of as a repository of noiselessness or harmonious peace. *Conscience* is one of the few poems in *The Temple* (*Jordan* [II] is another)
daring to adopt a position of some belligerence; a number display
querulousness or petulance, especially in their early stages, but true
belligerence is rare. The force necessary for the expulsion of the insidious
"pratler" and its scruples is a measure of the force those scruples exerted
on Herbert. The guilts and fears visible in the poems of self-abasement
were strong enough to provoke a real crisis of conscience when Herbert
attempted to expel them, and they redoubled their false asceticism in
response to his attack. Herbert's defense in the poem of fair looks, sweet
dishes, and music reminds us that Herbert, at his most spiritual, knew
the importance of his "eyes and eares" and other senses. When harmonious peace descended on him in *The Flower,* he would say:

        I once more smell the dew and rain,
        And relish versing.

The satisfaction given by *Conscience* arises in part from its unequivocal attitude toward fair and sweet things. We are not here confronted by

the painful irresolution of *The Rose,* with its "colour'd griefs" and "blushing woes." For a moment, caught up in a vision of the fair, the sweet, and the musical, the poem can join the celestial music of the spheres, and Herbert ascends almost to the ethereality of Vaughan; but the meddlesome conscience shows no sign of being vanquished by Herbert's commands. In a sudden turn, Herbert almost admits that he may harbor sins justifying his scruples, and so resorts to the spiritual purge of Christ's blood, but even this cleansing, leaving Herbert blameless, does not silence his carping adversary. The resort to physicality at the end of the poem is almost comic in one who so lately hoped to live in harmonious peace. No doubt we are to understand that Herbert's consciousness of having been cleansed and redeemed by Christ's death gives him the force, which by himself he could not have, to take up cudgels against himself in his scrupulous moments, but the final aggression, not in itself but because of its conjunction with the earlier hope for silent peace, seems strained, if truthful.

In spite of the defects of the final stanza of *Conscience,* it offers an instance (there are many) of Christ's being assimilated to Herbert: not to Herbert as he would like to be, but to Herbert as he is. This assimilation is to become Herbert's best solution to self-abasement. The end of the poem is a mirror image of the beginning: at the beginning, Herbert I is attacking Herbert II—the scrupulous Herbert, lowering and armed with teeth and nails, is scratching at the blameless Herbert who wishes peace. At the end, in a perfect reversal, Herbert II, armed not with teeth and nails but with bill, staff, and sword, is attacking Herbert I. Herbert II is equated, at the end, by his possession of the Cross, with Jesus—a Jesus not full of "harmonious peace," like Herbert's would-be self, but rather one sturdily armed with the means of making war, wood and nails. Herbert's initial battle with conscience, in short, sets the metaphorical terms for its own cessation, also in battle. (We may be reminded of a poem that depends (perhaps unconsciously) on *Conscience,* Hopkins' sonnet *Andromeda,* where the rescuing Christ has similarly to possess offensive equipment equal to the dragon's: Christ alights, disarming the dragon "with Gorgon's gear and barebill.")

Conscience describes a moral victory strenuous in progress, but not yet entirely happy in its results. The aesthetic interest of the poem lies in its bold truthfulness and inclusiveness (few poems could conjoin the celestial echoes of the second stanza with the "tooth and nail" scratching and catching in the third), but there is no denying that the last stanza is the weakest in the poem, and consequently the aesthetic victory, glimpsed in the "noiseless sphere," cannot be said to be fully won. Still, just as the rather testy, brisk, and enlivening language of the first *Jordan* was perhaps necessary to clear the air before Herbert could write, "There is in love a sweetnesse readie penn'd," in the second *Jordan,* so the war-like words concluding *Conscience* may have been indispensable in a final exorcism of tormenting scruples, impediments to poetry as to life. That exorcism of scruples and self-abasement made possible Herbert's best poetry, poetry of grief and love. In Herbert's finest poems, Jesus is seen as a fellow-sufferer rather than as a judge or remote deity, sighs and groans can be uttered in the confidence of ultimate relief, and Herbert can reveal his most complete self, one in which all his different aspects can meet in concord and none must suffer reprobation or denial.

Herbert's poems of grief can be seen for what they are only if placed next to his poems of self-abasement, where the abyss between Jesus and Herbert is more visible than any possible conjunction of the two. Although Herbert, it is true, expresses to Jesus in *The Thanksgiving* a wish that he may "Copie thy fair, though bloudie hand," the phrasing itself separates him from the sufferer. Herbert assimilates to Jesus—or rather Herbert assimilates Jesus to himself—in *The Bag,* which reveals not a resurrected Christ in glory but a permanently stricken one; and the same shroud of suffering remains about the image of Jesus in *The Dawning,* where the sad heart need not assume a false mirth, but can remember Christ's sufferings even while celebrating his Resurrection, since Christ left his grave-clothes as a memorial of his Passion. The phenomenon of Christ as permanent sufferer, seen also in *Conscience,* takes on more and more importance for Herbert. It is a phenomenon prefigured in *The Sacrifice,* which nonetheless, like most of the other early poems, chooses rather to oppose the suffering Christ to wicked man than to see the human self and the crucified Jesus as one.

It would be possible to consider this later assimilation of Jesus to Herbert unhealthy, a masochistic respose in suffering (and indeed there are reasons for thinking so about that uneasy poem *The Bag*), were it not for the serenity following on pain found in the two late *Affliction* poems (II and III), which in fact seem like one poem twice reworked. In these poems, with their assimiliation of Jesus to Herbert, pain is neither enjoyed nor self-prolonged; but neither is it repudiated. The second *Affliction* at first echoes *The Flower* and pines over the same paradoxes:

> Kill me not ev'ry day,
> Thou Lord of life; since thy one death for me
> Is more then all my deaths can be,
> Though I in broken pay
> Die over each houre of Methusalems stay.
>
> If all mens tears were let
> Into one common sewer, sea, and brine;
> What were they all, compar'd to thine?
> Wherein if they were set,
> They would discolour thy most bloudy sweat.
>
> Thou art my grief alone.
> Thou Lord conceal it not: and as thou art
> All my delight, so all my smart:
> Thy crosse took up in one,
> By way of imprest, all my future mone.

In the first stanza Herbert reverts to the themes of *The Thanksgiving* and *The Reprisall,* imagining that God is somehow exacting from men payment in kind for his own death. Herbert cries that he cannot possibly, even by innumerable deaths, repay Jesus for his death, and that men's tears could not hope to equal Jesus' bloody "tears" of sweat but on the contrary would only "discolour" or dilute their value. Up to this point, the poem has remained wholly in the old mode of contest between Herbert and Jesus, a mode for which there cannot be any satisfactory resolution at all. The final stanza seems to have at first very little traceable connection to the two preceding ones; the "discovery" it makes seems unmotivated by earlier details. In searching for a solution to the apparent disconnection, we must examine the difference in tone, not a specially strong one, between the first and second stanzas. In the

first, Herbert is preoccupied with his old unease: an impossible demand
seems to have been made on him for repayment, and the comparison
of "thy death" with "my deaths" is a quantitative and intellectual one.
In the second stanza, the comparison of "all mens tears" with "thine"
seems tinged with grief for Christ (as the first comparison was not), as
Herbert's mind turns from the first term of comparison, his own bitter
sufferings, to the second term, Christ's passion, which by its real presence, is seen to resemble Herbert's grief. Even so, the mysterious claim
"Thou art my grief alone" followed by the even more mysterious injunction "Thou Lord conceal it not" remains baffling, and the figure of "im-
prest" payment, though continuing the early metaphor of "broken
pay," is obscure in respect to the one who pays and the one who is paid.

The third *Affliction* seems resolved to clarify these intricacies. By
hearing himself utter "O God" in his affliction, Herbert becomes convinced that God is "in" his grief, and the last stanza of the poem defines
that indwelling:

> Thy life on earth was grief, and thou art still
> Constant unto it, making it to be
> A point of honour, now to grieve in me,
>   And in thy members suffer ill.
>   They who lament one crosse,
> Thou dying dayly, praise thee to thy losse.

Once again the ever-suffering Christ appears, enduring daily crosses in
the person of his members. This, we may say, is the theological "resolution," but the poetic one is rather different, and depends on the consistency of the divine personality. Why, asks Herbert, is Jesus' life now
one of grief? Because he chooses that it be such. And why does he so
choose? Because his life on earth was grief, and we cannot imagine him
repudiating that life and spending his time banqueting in heaven. No,
the Jesus we know is the man of sorrows acquainted with grief, and
though we in one sense "know" that his earthly life ended with his
ascent into heaven, still we really know nothing of Jesus *in propria
persona* except for his life on earth. Jesus too is faithful to his earthly
self, making it "a point of honour" not to lose contact, in his heavenly

state, with his earthly life, and in fact reliving his earthly passion daily by living in his members.

Herbert's interpretation of the theological term "members of Christ" is wholeheartedly literal, as is his invention of Christ's motives, as though he could scan Christ's mind and see his punctilious and honorable intent to suffer ill in his members, not to fail in constancy toward his earthly life. Herber's invention of constancy and honor on the part of Christ, rather than any simple invocation of the doctrine of membership in Christ, "saves" the poem in aesthetic terms, and of course Herbert's own constancy and honor in respect to his personal affliction form the basis for his invention of both qualities in Jesus and for the final assimilation of Jesus to someone grieving "in" Herbert.

In the second *Affliction* Herbert gives up, finally, on both self-abasement and repayment; in the third *Affliction* neither is even in question. When self-abasement reappears in the later poems, as it does in *Sighs and Grones*, it occurs because Herbert has chosen to address God the Father who, never having suffered, is unamenable to that identification with the suffering Herbert which Jesus can be imagined to assume. In the conflation of Jesus (whom he would imitate) with his tormented self, Herbert can combine two aspects of himself—what he is and what he would be—in a version of interior peace, but God the Father remains impossibly distant, unpropitiable, and dangerous, addressable only in self-humiliating groans:

> O do not use me
> After my sinnes! look not on my desert
> But on thy glories! then thou wilt reform
> And not refuse me: for thou onely art
> The mightie God, but I a sillie worm;
> O do not bruise me!

The imagery in the stanzas following shows that only God the Father is being addressed: he is the master for whom Herbert has been an "ill steward"; he is the deity whom Herbert has offended by covering his lust, Adam-like, with sewn fig-leaves; he is the God of "bitter wrath" whom we know from the Old Testament. However, when Herbert bethinks himself of Jesus as a means of salvation, the poem can alter its self-lacerating position. At first God and Jesus are still two separate beings: "Since *he* [Christ] di'd for my good,/O do not [*you*, God] kill me!" But in the final stanza, the Father and Jesus become one dual-natured God:

> But O reprieve me!
> For thou hast life and death at thy command;
> Thou art both *Judge* and *Saviour, feast* and *rod,*
> *Cordiall* and *Corrosive:* put not thy hand
> Into the bitter box; but O my God
> My God, relieve me!

In spite of the attitude of prayer, the stanza remains in doubt about which of his vials—justice or mercy—God will use, as we can see from the alternating ways of putting God's GOOD and *bad* choices: he can give LIFE or *death,* be *Judge or* SAVIOR, FEAST or *rod,* CORDIAL or *corrosive.* Hopkins, imitating this passage at the end of the first part of *The Wreck of the Deutschland,* made his conviction of God's benevolent intent determine the sequential position of God's attributes: the *bad* aspect is always followed by a GOOD one canceling the *bad* one out (italics and capitals mine):

> Thou art *lightning* and LOVE, I found it, a *winter* and WARM;
> *Father* and FONDLER of heart thou hast wrung,
> Hast thy *dark descending,* and most art MERCIFUL then.[4]

Sighs and Grones remains, in its concentration on God the Father, an anomaly in Herbert's later verse. A comparison with *Discipline,* which is, in subject matter, a reworking of *Sighs and Grones,* shows why *Discipline,* never omitted by anthologizers of Herbert, better represents Herbert's essential self. In *Discipline,* as in *Sighs and Grones,* we find a recognition of God's possible wrath, the plea that he will reprieve and relieve rather than bruise or destroy, and the reason for mercy (the death of Jesus), but the sense of self and of God is wholly transformed, and a new model imagined for the relation between them. Herbert's sense of self in *Discipline* includes an admission of frailty, even of recalcitrance, but he does not heap himself with abuse as he did in *Sighs and Grones,* and his God, though powerful, is one who can be addressed almost in banter:

Throw away thy rod,
Throw away thy wrath:
  O my God,
Take the gentle path.

For my hearts desire
Unto thine is bent:
  I aspire
To a full consent.

Not a word or look
I affect to own,
  But by book,
And thy book alone.

Though I fail, I weep:
Though I halt in pace,
  Yet I creep
To the throne of grace.

Then let wrath remove;
Love will do the deed:
  For with love
Stonie hearts will bleed.

Love is swift of foot;
Love's a man of warre,
  And can shoot,
And can hit from farre.

Who can scape his bow?
That which wrought on thee,
  Brought thee low,
Needs must work on me.

Throw away thy rod;
Though man frailties hath,
  Thou art God:
Throw away thy wrath.

In this poem Herbert is not afraid to urge, in his defense, his own good intentions, desires, and acts; neither does he ever really doubt that God *will* "take the gentle path."

Although *Discipline* does not become a remarkable poem until the fifth (some would say the sixth) stanza, it is immediately, from the first line, a winning poem, its appeal stemming not only from the child-like plea asking God to "throw away" his wrath as though it were an object external to himself, but also from the exceptional lilt of the metrics, in which "fast" feet ($/\smile\smile\smile$) alternate with "slow" monosyllabic ones, the latter being nevertheless isometric with the former. If the poem were set to music, the rhythm would read:

line 1	line 2	line 3	line 4
♪ ♪ ♪ ♪ | ♩	♪ ♪ ♪ ♪ | ♩	♪ ♪ | ♩	♪ ♪ ♪ ♪ | ♩

The anomalous third line calls attention to itself by slowing down the pace, and the effect of this slowness is one of taking thought: the prattle represented by the strongly accented rapid-syllabled lines is halted by the emphatic "O my God," with its widely separated syllables. The use to which Herbert puts the third line differs in each stanza, and is fairly evident in each; he may even have intended, by the "halting pace" of the third line, to show his slow progress toward grace.

As in many other poems, Herbert here composes the last stanza as a variant of the first, but though the first is conventional (as we have by now learned to expect), the last is daring in its suggestion that wrath would be a sign of frailty in God, and that gentleness is more appropriate to him: "*Man* has frailties but *thou* art God, and need not succumb to a frailty, even a godlike one like anger—therefore throw away thy wrath." In between these injunctions, first and last, stands the poem, static for several stanzas while Herbert describes his own efforts at virtue (another contest with God), but taking on momentum when he abandons the useless attempt to compel God by demonstrating his own virtue, and proposes the substitution of love for wrath. It is not clear whether Herbert is being ironical at his own expense in assuring God that "with love,/ [Even] stonie hearts will bleed," since until now no heart has been mentioned except his own, a heart whose "desire/Unto [God's will] is bent." Perhaps Herbert is only choosing to cite the extreme case, or perhaps he has by now realized the "frailty" of his own attempts at virtue. It is, in any case, in the subsequent startling descriptions of Love in stanzas six and seven that the distinction of the poem undoubtedly lies, because this Love, though both Mosaic and classical in its inspiration, is at first glance neither. Just as one might quote from the Bible, "Love is strong as death, jealousy as cruel as the grave," so Herbert says "Love is swift of foot," and we take in his meaning. But we are surprised by the small but full-dress mythologizing of Love that follows the metaphor, a mythology which is phrased more childishly than anything else in Herbert, especially in the devastating lines "And can shoot,/And can hit from farre." Herbert is lisping in numbers, and his exotic combination of the utterly infantile with the utterly sophisticated (Exodus, Cupid, and the Gospels) forms a disproportion perverse or inventive, depending on the point of view. The absurdity of preaching this sermon to God is evident, as though God did not know that Love "can shoot,/And can hit." Indeed, all these pieces of information so gravely passed on to God ("For with love/Stonie hearts will bleed") are voiced for effect rather than for information. Herbert's fanciful logic ("That which wrought on thee . . ./Needs must work on me"), along with his cajoling tone and playful intimidation ("Though *man* frailties hath,/ *Thou* art God") are the devices of a favored child, whose whimsical imitations of grown-up discourse are smiled upon by an indulgent parent. The tone sets the relation and, the children's hour over, the performance ends. The poem has been a construct of wishful fantasy: if only it were possible to talk to God like *this,* instead of in the solemn intonings of collects and invocations. The poem proposes a model of the relationship to God in which a benevolent indulgence is already presumed to be God's attitude, in which he needs no propitiation, no sighs, groans, or self-abasement. God's creature, in this model, is presupposed to be doing his best—in a halting and creeping way, perhaps, but staying nonetheless on the right path, with the right desires, prompted by the right book. In this fantasy, wrath on God's part and the suppliant self-abuse of *Sighs and Grones* on Herbert's part are simply inconceivable.

Herbert here includes neither the gravity nor the tenderness of *Love* (III) in his notion of "Love": the Love in this poem, presumably so God will find it acceptable in lieu of wrath, has a very "wrathful" appearance—he is a man of war, he shoots and hits, and he brings people low. This invention is a wonderful *jeu d'esprit,* convincing God that if he uses a Love like this, nobody will really notice that he has foregone wrath, what with all the shooting and hitting and weaponry. The symmetry of this poetic resolution readily reconciles us to a Love less beautiful than the quick-eyed and smiling Love of *Love* (III); we are in fact overwhelmingly relieved that Herbert has found an alternative to wrath, on the one hand, and to sighs and groans on the other. One who doubts Herbert's "originality" in transforming his sources has only to glance at his source here, Moses' song of triumph over Pharoah (Exod. 15:3), in which Moses said, "The Lord is a man of war." In that war song, God's wrath is shown in full: he dashes the enemy to pieces and sends forth his wrath to consume them as stubble. It is a far cry from that "man of war" to this one so marvelously giving the appearance of armed might while nevertheless wounding with the arrows of Love.

The charming parallel in *Discipline* of "thee" and "me" in the "bringing low," assuming the same mechanisms of reaction in God and man, is testimony to Herbert's intense desire for identity and reciprocity with God, most often accomplished with Jesus, but here, by the mediation of Love, with God the Father. The happiest and most fulfilled poems in *The Temple* nearly always include notions of identity or reciprocity, and the temptation to linger over such poems is strong, chiefly because we wish that Herbert had had more such moments. There are four notable poems of identity-reciprocity, besides *Love* (III). In two, *Ephes. 4.30: Grieve not the Holy Spirit* and *The Odour,* the intensity is somewhat strained; but in the other two, *The Starre* and *The Glance,* it is possible to detect nothing but trust, confidence, and love. Both *Grieve not the Holy Spirit* and *The Odour* are exercises in repetition. The first, in fact, which was set to music by both Blow and Jenkins, in its beginning almost sacrifices sense for music in its sighing repetitions (italics mine):

> And art thou *grieved,* sweet and sacred Dove,
> When I am sowre,
> And crosse thy *love?*

Grieved for me? the God of strength and power
Griev'd for a worm, which . . . I
. . . leave . . . *dead?*
Then *weep* mine eyes, *the God of love doth grieve:*
Weep foolish heart,
And *weeping* live:
For *death* is drie as dust . . .
Almighty *God doth grieve.* . . .
I sinne not to my *grief* alone
But to my *Gods* too . . .

With some diminution in intensity, repetitions of "weep," "tears,"
"grief," and "wail" continue to thread the poem, the lessening of their
occurrence arising solely from the necessity that the poem should begin
to make some sense. The thought that he has the power to make the
Holy Spirit grieve brings tears to Herbert, tears that should have arisen
earlier from his own "sowre" acts. The fantasy on tears and weeping
that follows (death is dust, tears are life, lutestrings are bowels, marble
can weep, springs unlike tears run forever) ends on the ominous, for
Herbert, note of repayment: God's crystal spring runs always for Herbert, even when he is not dry; but Herbert himself cannot conceive how
to repay God for this mercy, not being a crystal spring himself and unable, for all his "adjudging" himself "to tears and grief,/Ev'n endlesse
tears/Without relief," to go on wailing day and night. The poem makes
a hasty recovery by remembering that Jesus has already repaid God on
our behalf:

Lord, pardon, for thy Sonne makes good
My want of tears with store of bloud.

There is a confusion here in summoning Jesus as *deus ex machina,* because his sufferings, though they may indeed be thought to supplement
Herbert's tears, intrude oddly into a poem where God himself, in the
person of the Holy Spirit, has already been shown as plentifully suffering ("Almighty God doth grieve . . . he doth grone"). The final
lines pit Jesus against God, so to speak, in a suffering-contest: God's
"cleare spring" drops water, and Jesus' blood equals it in volume, with

poor Herbert's negligible store of tears almost ceasing to figure in the competition. The motif of the contest between Jesus and Herbert that began in *The Thanksgiving* has here attained a total reversal of itself, for Herbert and Jesus are now allies in attempting a "reprisall" to God for his griefs. The fiction is rather hard to admit; it is easier, for example, to accept the alliance of Herbert and Jesus in the propitiation of an angry deity in *Sighs and Grones*. The poem is nonetheless interesting, in its abandonment of the notion of a wrathful God whose anger must be satisfied: by addressing the "sweet and sacred Dove" in lieu of God the Father, Herbert, encouraged by St. Paul, can imagine this contest in the courtesy of grief, in which all participants—God, Herbert, and Jesus—end up weepers, weeping all the tears they can.

A similar contest of courtesy is envisaged in *The Odour,* a poem that aims, even more than *Grieve not the Holy Spirit,* at an almost hypnotic construction of the most lines out of the fewest words, so much so that the first and last lines of each stanza have the same rhyme word. The poem envisages Jesus and Herbert himself engaged in absolutely identical, reciprocal activities, the one breathing "My Master" and the other "My servant," the two phrases constantly circulating on errands of courtesy and love from their utterer to their hearer and back again:

> How sweetly doth *My Master* sound! *My Master!*
> As Amber-greese leaves a rich sent
>   Unto the taster:
> So do these words a sweet content,
> An orientall fragrancie, *My Master.*
>
> With these all day I do perfume my minde,
> My minde ev'n thrust into them both:
>   That I might finde
> What cordials make this curious broth,
> This broth of smells, that feeds and fats my minde.
>
> *My Master,* shall I speak? O that to thee
>   *My servant* were a little so,
>   As flesh may be;
> That these two words might creep & grow
> To some degree of spicinesse to thee!

Then should the Pomander, which was before
    A speaking sweet, mend by reflection,
        And tell me more:
    For pardon of my imperfection
Would warm and work it sweeter then before.

For when *My Master,* which alone is sweet,
    And ev'n in my unworthiness pleasing,
        Shall call and meet,
    My servant, as thee not displeasing,
That call is but the breathing of the sweet.

This breathing would with gains by sweetning me,
    (As sweet things traffick when they meet)
        Return to thee.
    And so this new commerce and sweet
Should all my life employ and busie me.

The contrast between the exclusively verbal nature of the speech-acts envisaged and the exclusively sensual nature of the imagery describing them accounts for the perceptible strain in the poem. There is no choice but to believe Herbert in his descriptions, and more than once he describes mental experience in terms of luxurious banqueting (as in *The Banquet,* a poem closely related to *The Odour*). The poetry of the banquet of sense, familiar from *The Song of Songs,* was acceptable as a transcription of religious experience, but when this luxurious language is detached from an erotic relation, mystical or not, and attached to a verbal action between servant and master, the diction sounds odd and excessive.

The Odour is valuable, however, in revealing Herbert's constant practice of inquiring into his own sources of inspiration (minimal sources, here, at that): curious about whatever "feeds and fats" his mind, he "thrusts" his mind into the words that affect it, inquiring of them what ingredients they may contain. Analysis is far more characteristic of Herbert than synthesis, but the result of the analysis is almost always a turn of the kaleidoscope, and while the same constituents or components reappear, they are rearranged into personally reconstituted shapes. Here, in the conclusion of *The Odour,* what is reconstituted is the notion of "employment" or "business," a concept that had long preoccupied Herbert. In the two early poems called *Employment,* the notion is interpreted as active service to God, and Herbert chafes at his being let languish in anterooms instead of being sent on missions:

> If as a flowre doth spread and die,
> Thou wouldst extend me to some good . . .
> The sweetness and the praise were thine . . .
>
> Let me not languish then, and spend
> A life as barren to thy praise
> As is the dust . . .

The original ending of this poem asked for the speed of light to be able to "post o'er land and ocean without rest":

> Lord that I may the sunns perfection gaine
> Give me his speed.

It is consistent with the ending of *The Odour* that Herbert later perceived, in revising *Employment* (I), that service for him lay in utterance rather than action: "Lord place me in thy consort; give one strain/ To my poore reed." In *Employment* (II), Herbert is still uncertain about the nature of his work:

> He that is weary, let him sit.
> My soul would stirre
> And trade in courtesies and wit,
> Quitting the furre
> To cold complexions needing it . . .
>
> Life is a businesse, not good cheer.

In giving an example of this "businesse," Herbert first chose bees as his representatives:

> O that I had the wing and thigh
> Of laden Bees;

> Then would I mount up instantly
>   And by degrees
> On men dropp blessings as I fly.

This energetic messenger-service is suppressed by the time Herbert revises the Williams manuscript, and a static "businesse" is substituted for it, with only the word "laden" retained:

> Oh that I were an Orenge-tree,
>   That busie plant!
> Then should I ever laden be,
>   And never want
> Some fruit for him that dressed me.

The final "employment" of *The Odour* combines both action, in its "trafficking" and "commerce," and utterance, in saying "My Master"; such service is more enterprising than motionless employment in a consort, but it retains the purely verbal nature of Herbert's offering. The poem, then, by subsuming action in speech, solves a long-standing conceptual problem of vocation for Herbert and, in its somewhat precious way, attempts a verbal texture imitative of the reciprocity it celebrates. Perhaps that is all we should ask of it, but our sense of Herbert's highest poetic capacities presses us to ask for an equilibrium never quite attained in these optative breathings, with their hothouse repetitions (seven repetitions of "sweet" and its variants in the last fifteen lines, for example).

It would seem, from both *Grieve not the Holy Spirit* and *The Odour,* that Herbert wished, at some point during the composition of the later poems in *The Temple,* to devise a style of extreme intensity, not the proliferating style of the early "sparkling poems" with their "thousands of notions" but rather a style in which a single notion would be repeated, penetrated into, elaborated upon, and fixed hypnotically in the mind. In one sense, this is a movement toward simplicity as well as toward concentration, with the subject matter confined within very narrow limits, and the diction similarly bound. But the too-visible artifice of these elaborately counterpointed stanzas made this solution a byway, not a final path toward the expression of states of reciprocity and identity with

God. That final path was toward a greater naturalness of expression, without the sacrifice of art.

In their very different ways, both *The Starre* and *The Glance* attain, not only equilibrium, but expansion, trust, and even rest. In *Artillerie* a talking star had shot into Herbert's lap, one of those "good motions" that "have the face of fire, but end in rest." In *The Starre* Herbert addresses another such shooting star (but this time a silent one), granting it briefly some of the same purgative functions as the star in *Artillerie,* but quickly passing on beyond purgation to adoration, as the "falling star" reverses nature and becomes a "rising star":

> Bright spark, shot from a brighter place,
>   Where beams surround my Saviours face,
>   Canst thou be any where
>   So well as there?
>
> Yet, if thou wilt from thence depart,
>   Take a bad lodging in my heart;
>   For thou canst make a debtor,
>   And make it better.
>
> First with thy fire-work burn to dust
>   Folly, and worse then folly, lust:
>   Then with thy light refine,
>   And make it shine:
>
> So disengag'd from sinne and sicknesse,
>   Touch it with thy celestiall quicknesse,
>   That it may hang and move
>   After thy love.
>
> Then with our trinitie of light,
>   Motion, and heat, let's take our flight
>   Unto the place where thou
>   Before didst bow.
>
> Get me a standing there, and place
>   Among the beams, which crown the face
>   Of him, who dy'd to part
>   Sinne and my heart:

That so among the rest I may
    Glitter, and curle, and winde as they:
      That winding is their fashion
        Of adoration.

Sure thou wilt joy, by gaining me
    To flie home like a laden bee
      Unto that hive of beams
        And garland-streams.

The Starre is a *jeu d'esprit* and not so moving as the greatest of Herbert's poems, but it is the sort of poetry he could have written—brilliant, animated, and gay—if his life had been less ravaged by affliction and illness. In this poem, once again, Herbert has solved a number of conceptual problems, including the ones concerning employment raised and resolved in *The Odour*. For all its "orientall fragrancie," *The Odour* adopts a minimal expressive solution (*"My Master"*) akin to those offered in *A true Hymne* (*"My joy, my life, my crown"*) or *The Forerunners* (*"Thou art still my God"*). *The Starre,* however, perhaps because of its celestial destination, can allow itself all those flamelike workings and windings, those sparkling notions and embellishments, which Herbert does not permit himself in *Jordan* (II) and *The Forerunners.* In the expressive freedom of *The Starre,* no Herbertian sadness intrudes: Herbert's natural self expands into its glorified version so easily that it is shocking to be reminded that this is a poem about dying.[5]

Because of the poem's celestial bent, the introduction is almost perfunctory; and the "folly" and "lust" of the third stanza have scarcely more than a verbal existence, since Herbert is so much in haste to arrive at his disengaged "celestiall quicknesse" (a phrase that led to Vaughan's wish, in *Quicknesse,* to leave this "false life" for the true one, "A quicknesse which my God hath kiss'd"). From this disengagement on, an unfettered flight animates the poem; with no embarrassment, Herbert thinks it no robbery to assume a form analogical to the divine, a "trinitie" of light, motion, and heat.[6] The extreme happiness with which he uses the triumphant possessive "our" in "our trinitie" and "our flight" after the procession of separate attributes belonging to the star ("thy fire-work," "thy light," "thy celestial quicknesse," "thy love") is almost in itself a sufficient "lift" to make us feel Herbert's body joining his soul in its ascent, but to reinforce the enskying of his soul, he allows the sixth stanza to rhyme in echo of the first, in order to convince us that he has indeed a "place" in the "place" where "beams surround [his] Saviours face." He then offers a startling equation of Jesus and the star: since the star "disengaged" Herbert's heart from "sinne," and since Jesus is defined as the one "who dy'd to part/Sinne and my heart," Jesus and the star become temporarily indistinguishable, and the descent of the star becomes momentarily a parable of the Incarnation. Nevertheless, as a messenger, the star remains separate, in that function at least, from Jesus, and acts at the end more like an angel. Instead of Herbert's being the laden bee of the first version of *Employment* (II), active service in God's "businesse" is reserved to the star, but the return flight shows Herbert guilty of no remissness in his acceptance of temporary passivity, since soon, in his translated state, he will join the other beams and "glitter, and curle, and winde as they." This service too is purely self-expressive: the star-beams utter themselves, and that is "their fashion/Of adoration." No transitive service is required of them, any more than it is of Hopkins' kingfishers, dragonflies, stones, and bells in *As kingfishers catch fire*:

> Each mortal thing does one thing and the same,
> Deals out that being indoors each one dwells;
> Selves, goes itself; *myself* it speaks and spells,
> Crying *What I do is me, for that I came.*

Utterances of faith ("*My Master*," "*Thou art still my God*") apparently seemed to Herbert the only final form of adoration possible within the limitations of mortal life, but in the imagined heaven of garlands, streams, and beams one could adore by self-radiation. This confidence in the "refined" and glowing heart, with its nominal trinity of light, motion, and heat, and its verbal trinity of glittering, curling, and winding, solves all conceptual difficulties about unworthiness and all verbal difficulties about "embellishments" of intentional "substance." Substance and embellishment are one in a star or sunbeam. Herbert's own self-critical worries in *Jordan* (II) about attempts to "clothe the sunne" here vanish as the sun and his attendant stars (including Herbert) in effect clothe themselves in the glittering activities of light. Nothing in the poem more becomes it than its ending, in which, after the initial separation between heart and star followed by their flight "hand in hand to heaven," a courteous disjunction is achieved. "I," says Herbert, "may glitter," and "thou," he says to the star, "wilt joy by gaining me." Although these proposals are prospective in meaning, still, coming as they do after the envisaged flight, they amount to a separate installation in heaven of Herbert and his star, a formal leavetaking by those who had briefly been twinned, allowing the poem to subside.

Much as *The Starre* pleases by the literalness of its fable, its assimilation of the glorified Herbert to the Trinity, its airy lightness, and Herbert's acceptance of his own tendencies to glitter and curl, the poem does give rather short shrift to the suffering man writing it, who is racked enough by "sinne and sicknesse" to wish to die and get a place in heaven. More quarter is given to pain in *The Glance,* and so it becomes, like *The Dawning,* a more complete poem than one attempting "mirth" alone, like *The Starre.* However, *The Glance,* though allowing misery, confines it to the middle stanza, and brackets it with past and future joy:

> When first thy sweet and gracious eye
> Vouchsaf'd ev'n in the midst of youth and night
> To look upon me, who before did lie
>   Weltring in sinne;
>   I felt a sugred strange delight,
> Passing all cordials made by any art,
> Bedew, embalme, and overunne my heart.
>   And take it in.
>
> Since that time many a bitter storm
> My soul hath felt, ev'n able to destroy,
> Had the malicious and ill-meaning harm
>   His swing and sway:
>   But still thy sweet originall joy,
> Sprung from thine eye, did work within my soul,
> And surging griefs, when they grew bold, controll,
>   And got the day.

If thy first glance so powerfull be,
A mirth but open'd and seal'd up again;
What wonders shall we feel, when we shall see
    Thy full-ey'd love!
When thou shalt look us out of pain,
And one aspect of thine spend in delight
More then a thousand sunnes disburse in light,
    In heav'n above.

There is no denying that the best line in the poem, a "splendid line" as Palmer calls it,[7] is the one in which Herbert says that God will "look us out of pain." The phrase, by being deviant from normal use, calls attention to itself, since we expect something like "God will *take* us out of pain." But it is not only the strange use of "look" that strikes us in the line; by these words we are made to realize wholly the implicit drift of the poem, which wishes as its ultimate aim to connect *feeling* with *seeing.* At the beginning, God looks, but the poet only feels ("I *felt* a sugred strange delight"), and the influence of God's eye provokes in the poet not an answering glance but a rapturous submersion as he feels his heart bedewed, embalmed, and overrun. Just as he could only "feel" God's first glance (presumably because no one can look on God and live), so he can only "feel" (submit passively to) subsequent griefs: "Many a bitter storm/My soul hath felt." At least, if Herbert is passive, God is active, and "controls" the destructive power of affliction, but there is still no evidence of the total reciprocity which alone can satisfy Herbert, a reciprocity in which God will feel and Herbert will see. That reciprocity arises at last in a wonderful conjunction of seeing and feeling both in Herbert and in God:

What wonders shall *we feel,* when *we* shall *see*
    Thy full-*eyed love!*

We might have expected:

If thy first *glance* so powerfull be . . .
What wonders shall we feel, when we shall see
    Thy love-filled *eye.*

We are accustomed to saying we *feel* love, not see it: by changing his formerly concrete phrases of aspects of God ("thy . . . eye," "thy . . . joy sprung from thine eye," "thy glance") to a phrase in which God's aspect, his eye, becomes only adjunctive to his essence ("thy full-eyed love"), Herbert can transform the experience. In a perfect reciprocity, God's *glances* are thereby said to be prompted by the *feeling* of love, and Herbert's *feeling* is prompted by *seeing* face to face. We know from *Dulnesse* that "look" and "love" were words that could conjoin themselves in Herbert's mind, and the echoes from "thy full-eyed love" hover over the phrase "look us out of pain" and turn it, almost, into "love us out of pain."

The syntax and rhetoric of *The Glance* work in favor of its assertion of confidence, since the long arc of assertion encompasses grief in what amounts to parenthetical subordination. The sentences become, for Herbert, unusually complex in order to accomplish this subordination:

When first thy . . . eye vouchsaf'd (ev'n in the midst of youth and night) to look upon me (who before did lie weltring in sinne) I felt . . . delight. Since that time my soul hath felt many a bitter storm (able to destroy had the harm his sway) but thy joy did work, and control griefs, and got the day. If thy first glance so powerful be, what wonders shall we feel when we shall see thy full-eyed love! when thou shalt look us out of pain.

In short, the syntactic form of this poem (unlike the anticlimactic form seen earlier in *Mans medley*) reinforces the assurance of ultimate bliss claimed by the poem, and the resolution (in which any one of God's aspects can spend more in delight than a thousand suns disburse in light), by paralleling the natural sun with the supernatural Sun, continues the comparison of the earthly sun-glance with the heavenly full-eyed love of "quick-eyed Love." The stroke of genius in the last stanza of the poem, however, is the one word "pain," anchoring the yearning speculations of the poem to Herbert's present case, which even in his recollections of original joy and his hope of future delight remains one of struggle between the lingering memories of first conversion and the ever-recurrent bitter storms of griefs.

In spite of Herbert's triumphant, if occasional, ability to write, even in illness, poems of security, serenity, and trust (of which *Heaven* is the purest example), he is remembered in literature chiefly for what Palmer called his "constant subject, the contradictions of love."[8] Although in Herbert's happier moments he could think one initial glance alone from God a sufficiency on which to live, in a more pained frame of mind, like that seen in *The Glimpse,* a single moment of spiritual delight seemed only a tormenting respite. This poem, staged at the threshold where Delight is taking his leave, bears a resemblance to *Love* (III) in its vying of reproach with courtesy, both feelings contesting within Herbert. Loath to be angry with Delight, his departing guest, he nonetheless finds remarkably varied ways of dissuasion, ranging from the invocation of etiquette ("Thou cam'st but now; wilt thou so soon depart?") to an implicit mockery ("Me thinks delight should have/ More skill in music, and keep better time") to an apposite fable ("Lime begg'd of old, they say,/A neighbor spring to cool his inward heat") to a proverb ("A slender thread a gentle guest will tie") to a persuasive metaphorical pun on "break" ("The droppings of the stock/ May oft break forth, and never break the lock"). In the ingenuity of these arguments, each betraying a fresh wish to delay the departing joy, Herbert pleads his case chiefly by indirection. But scattered throughout the lines, and almost obscured by the courtliness of Herbert's speech, are the words naming or suggesting the guests who, like seven devils, wait outside the door to invade the premises once delight has vanished: night, lingering pain and smart, inward heat, starvation, fear, weeping, grief, sin, and shame. All that suffering, endured in the past and apprehensively foretold for the future, is held at bay while the gentle voice goes on persuading, exemplifying, reproaching, and pleading, even in the final resignation to Delight's departure.

This mastery of the self in Herbert, reflected in the firm idea of a proper demeanor for the self even when Delight is abandoning it, makes certain of Herbert's poems of grief the more conclusive in their understatement. *The Familie* and *The Size* both show Herbert attempting to rule disorderly outcries and bring them into some sort of equilibrium. In the first, he appears at first to disavow complaints and fears ("these

wranglers") entirely, but then finally gives them houseroom so long
as they remain noiseless:

> Joyes oft are there, and griefs as oft as joyes,
> But griefs without a noise:
> Yet speak they louder than distemper'd fears.
> What is so shrill as silent tears?

The Size is even harsher on complaints about lack of joy:

> Thy Saviour sentenc'd joy,
> And in the flesh condemn'd it as unfit.

Yet in spite of such attempts at self-silencing, Herbert allowed himself poems of full complaint, among them some, like *The Collar,* representing his best work. These poems show the unhappiness of a person
not, I think, naturally melancholy; Herbert was a person meant to be
happy, one who never doubted that unhappiness is a deeply unnatural
state, so unnatural that it can only be represented by almost surrealistic
images of fragmentation and disconnection. In *Deniall,* fragmentation
is compounded by an almost wilful disorientation in time (the fragments
into which Herbert's grief has broken him are underlined):

> When *my devotions* could not pierce
> Thy silent eares;
> Then was *my heart* broken, as was *my verse:*
> *My breast* was full of fears
> And disorder:

> *My* bent *thoughts,* like a brittle bow,
> Did flie asunder:
> *Each* took his way; *some* would to pleasures go,
> *Some* to the warres and thunder
> Of alarms.

> As good go any where, *they* say,
> As to benumme
> Both *knees* and *heart,* in crying night and day,
> Come, come, my God, O come,
> But no hearing.

O that thou shouldst give *dust a tongue*
To crie to thee,
And then not heare it crying! all day long
My heart was in *my knee,*
But no hearing.

Therefore *my soul* lay out of sight,
Untun'd, unstrung:
My feeble *spirit,* unable to look right,
Like a nipt blossome, hung
Discontented.

O cheer and tune *my heartlesse breast,*
Deferre no time;
That so thy favours granting *my request,*
They and *my minde* may chime,
And mend *my ryme.*

Not only is Herbert broken into fragments,[9] but his fragments themselves can be fragmented: his thoughts (one fragment) themselves "flie asunder"; his eviscerated breast is "heartlesse"; his heart has dislocated itself to his knee; his voice is in his knees and his heart; his whole body has been reduced to its component dust—dust with a tongue. These extraordinary derangements are designedly accompanied by a sense of the past and present so intermixed that they can scarcely be disentangled. We might say, reasoning after the fact, that the poem presents three stages, of which the last is a state of envisaged happiness, when Herbert will be cheered and tuned, and can chime and rhyme. The second stage is the time in which the poem is being written, a phase in which Herbert has become capable of uttering the concluding prayer hoping for the serene stage three. But the poem tells us also about the first stage, a time of rebellion and complaint. The first two stanzas describe stage one from the viewpoint of stage two, thereby implying some self-reproach; but by the third stanza the memory of stage one has risen to such a peak that the very voice of that stage, full of revolt and despair, is heard pure and unmediated by any interference from stage two. The voice of stage one in stanza three is a raving voice, "fierce and wild" like the one in *The Collar.* Then, in the exquisite fourth stanza, Herbert attempts to mediate

between the wild despair of his earlier thoughts and his too-repressive
subsequent view of his "fears and disorder." He almost excuses the
intemperance of his previous response, pleading the taxing of mortality
beyond endurance. The beginning of this stanza rises beyond tempo-
rality into meditation, taking place neither in the past nor in the present
but in the purely mental world of reflection:

> O that thou shouldst give dust a tongue
> To crie to thee,
> And then not heare it crying!

He then returns to stage one seen from the viewpoint of stage two:

> . . . All day long
> My heart was in my knee,
> But no hearing.

In the next stanza Herbert attempts a summing up of his series of narrative episodes: "Therefore my soul and spirit drooped." This is a
description kinder to himself than the previous self-reproach implied in
"fears," "disorder," and "brittle thoughts." Now he sees himself as a
neglected instrument, untuned, even unstrung, the disorder of his heartstrings explicable by the neglect of the lutanist; he is a frail flower, frost-
nipped, not responsible for its own discontent. This self-exculpation is
what permits the final prayer; but had it not been for the almost frenzied
chase after past experience, allowed to surge up as if it again were
fully present and speaking its feelings, such a synthesis and conclusion,
combined with a vision of a possible future, would not have become
possible. Exorcism needs first to summon the devil, and Herbert's chaos
of tenses, as past and present intermingle, guarantees that the future
will not forget the past.

The fineness of construction in *Deniall* makes us almost regret that
Herbert should have attempted, so to speak, to "rewrite" such a poem,
and yet the resemblances between *Deniall* and the later *Longing* (the
latter not in the Williams manuscript) are too great to be coincidental.
Herbert's fragmentation has, in *Longing,* become even more critical.

He is a bundle of unrelated bodily parts huddled together in misery (italics mine):

> *With* sick and famisht *eyes,*
> *With* doubling *knees* and weary *bones,*
> To thee *my cries,*
> To thee *my grones,*
> To thee *my sighs, my tears* ascend:
> No end?
>
> *My throat, my soul* is hoarse;
> *My heart* is withered like a ground
> Which thou dost curse.
> *My thoughts* turn round,
> And make me giddie; Lord, I fall,
> Yet call.

In the midst of this outburst of grief, Herbert suddenly silences his cries and turns almost exactingly, as he will again later in the poem, to meditation, this time on the divine nature and its outflowing to its creatures, picturing God, as he does in both a rejected stanza of *Whitsunday* and in the rejected poem *Perseverance,* as a maternal figure:

> From thee all pitie flows.
> Mothers are kinde, because thou art,
> And dost dispose
> To them a part:
> Their infants, them; and they suck thee
> More free.

Such an interpolation into suffering may appear jarring, especially in its epigrammatic compression of statement, and even more so because its reasoned logic is followed by four more stanzas of hectic imploring even more exclamatory than the initial two. These later stanzas establish at first an absolute disjunction between Herbert and God: "my minde" versus "thine ear," "my words" versus "thy name," "my sorrows" versus "thine eare" once more. There seems no possibility that these two disjoined persons should ever join; in fact, it is the distance between them that is emphasized. Herbert's cries must "ascend" to God, and God is asked to "bow down" his ear to hear. Why should God bow? Has God ever bowed before? The answer comes to Herbert in a flash, and the poem begins its progress to a solution:

> Lord Jesus, thou didst bow
> Thy dying head upon the tree:
> O be not now
> More dead to me!
> Lord heare! *Shall he that made the eare,*
> *Not heare?*

Herbert's finding of another "bow" introduces Redemption, and the quoted words of the Psalmist introduce Creation; these are the two motives for connection between God and man. The connection once established, Herbert can begin to speak of himself and his fragments with a different possessive pronoun (italics mine):

> Behold, *thy dust* doth stirre,
> It moves, it creeps, it aims at thee:
> Wilt thou deferre
> To succour me,
> *Thy pile of dust,* wherein each crumme
> Sayes, Come?

We are wrong, however, if we think resolution is already achieved. Herbert once again gives up direct address for the metaphysics of reproachful persuasion:

> To thee help appertains.
> Hast thou left all things to their course,
> And laid the reins
> Upon the horse?
> Is all lockt? hath a sinners plea
> No key?

Indeed the world's thy book,
Where all things have their leaf assign'd:
Yet a meek look
Hath interlin'd.
Thy board is full, yet humble guests
Finde nests.

These implicit reproaches to God then burst forth in a bitter accusation, not only as though nothing had been gained by Herbert's recognition of his belonging to God as his dust, his pile of dust, but also as though a more intense pain supervened in his recognizing that he belongs to this unhearing God, or so it is said, as his *child:*

Thou tarriest, while I die,
And fall to nothing: thou dost reigne,
And rule on high,
While I remain
In bitter grief: yet am I stil'd
Thy childe.

The vertical distance is still in effect, and the earlier memory of Redemption and Creation seems to have had no visible effect. Once again, Herbert reminds himself of the Redemption, but bitterly: "Lord, didst thou leave thy throne/Not to relieve?" The act is past, and yet the relief is not present. But mercifully, Herbert thinks of one more avenue besides the Creation and the Redemption: Christ's promises yet remain, and, like Abraham in Romans 4, if Herbert believes in God's promises, and against all hope believes in hope, he will "stagger not at the promise of God through unbelief." God's promises, says Herbert, "live and bide," "speak and chide," "And in thy bosome poure my tears/ As theirs." The elusive intermediary between the exalted God and his dust-bound child has at last been found in the arc of the promise. "My soule hangs on thy promises," Herbert had said in *Perseverance.* God's promises here plead Herbert's case against God himself: self-vanquished, God must yield. Earlier, Herbert had addressed God as "Lord of my soul, love of my minde," but the relation expressed in this formula, "X of my Y," still allows of a formal disjunction in space. Now, with his own tears in Christ's bosom, and distance abolished, Herbert can cry in a new formula, "My X," "My love, my sweetnesse, heare!" His heart, he says, lies at Jesus' feet—and we may assume, abysses now abrogated, that Jesus will not find it difficult to pluck the dart from Herbert's "troubled breast which cryes,/Which dyes." This pleading ending, which preserves the anguish of the whole poem, nonetheless promises, by its rapprochement of mortal and divine, the respite it prays for. The childish repetition of "heare, heare," the repeated poignant self-descriptions, the persistence in demand in spite of all seemliness, are the qualities that make Herbert, in this vein, one of our most accurate poets of expostulation, pain, outcry, wounded hopes, and stratagems of emotion.

Few poems in English seem so uncontrolled as *Longing* or *The Collar* or *Home*—all poems in which outbursts of feeling seem allowed total expression in ways we are more accustomed to find in drama. In *Home,* Herbert cries:

> What is this weary world; this meat and drink,
>   That chains us by the teeth so fast?
> What is this woman-kinde, which I can wink
>   Into a blacknesse and distaste? . . .
>
> O loose this frame, this knot of man untie!
>   That my free soul may use her wing,
> Which now is pinion'd with mortalitie,
>   As an intangled, hamper'd thing.

These lines could perhaps not have been written unless *Hamlet* and Donne's poetry had been written first; but they still belong to the small and priceless canon in which spontaneity seems the soul of art. "My flesh and bones and joynts do pray," says Herbert in *Home,* and certainly these late cries seem like poems written by exhausted bones and joints more than by a pen full of "sparkling notions." There are, however, many late poems of sadness which are more formal, less childlike in their expression, aiming less at an appearance of spontaneity than at an appearance of cumulative consideration. They, because of their subtlety of formulation, reveal yet another facet of the "sad" Herbert to put beside the almost speechlessly expostulating Herbert of wails, cries, and tears. The best of these more deliberate poems are *The Crosse* and *The Forerunners,* the first a strange chain of warring narrative infinitives, the second a final narrative coda to *Affliction* (I). The "plot" of *The Crosse* shows God provoking Herbert, whose only hope, it would seem, is to serve him (italics mine):

> *To make me sigh,* and *seek,* and *faint,* and *die,*
> Untill I had some place, where I might sing,
>   And serve thee: and not onely I,
> But all my wealth and familie might combine
> *To set thy honour up,* as our designe.
>   And then . . .

>   . . . *to take away*
>   My power to serve thee; *to unbend*
> All my abilities, my designs *confound,*
> And *lay* my threatnings bleeding on the ground.

> Thou turnest th'edge of all things on me still,
>   Taking me up *to throw me down.*
> So that, ev'n when my hopes seem *to be sped,*
> I am to grief alive, to them as dead.

So far, the conflict is clearly marked: God occasionally acts kindly to Herbert ("taking me up") but only for purposes of torture ("to throw me down"). Herbert's infinitives are "well-meaning"—to serve God, to set his honor up. And yet, in the stanza that is clearly the best in the poem, and even one of the best in *The Temple,* God's active infinitives of torture vanish, as do Herbert's protesting ones of victimage, and only situational infinitives remain. Blame ceases to be the motivation for the stanzas, and the accusatory has given way to the disinterested as description rules over self-justification (italics mine):

> *To have* my aim, and yet *to be*
> Further from it then when I bent my bow;
> *To make* my hopes my torture, and the fee
>   Of all my woes another woe,
> Is in the midst of delicates *to need,*
> And ev'n in Paradise *to be* a weed.

This self-analysis, in which Herbert judges himself sharply and definitively as one who makes his hopes his torture, and makes the fee of all his woes another woe, is the fruit of a reflecting which has asked itself whether its own disposition to melancholy (that "ague in the soul") would not make it, wherever it was, needy in the midst of delicates. With this realization, the poem can cease to feel ill-will toward God and can call him, with some degree of truth, "my deare Father." The burden of selfhood and its contradictions are seen not as punishment but as destiny, comparable to Jesus' cross, willingly borne and not externally inflicted by a malevolent God. The identification with Jesus (replacing the former identification with the unprofitable servant) enables Herbert to appropriate Jesus' words, "Thy will be done," as his own; but still the last lines of *The Crosse,* like the last lines of *Affliction* (I), come suddenly, almost too suddenly to erase the earlier bitterness. The peculiar timelessness of infinitives, extending on into times unknown, gives this poem its suspended Tantalus-state, a verbal impression not easily effaced even by Herbert's undoubted sincerity of final resignation.

The Forerunners is on the whole a poem which defies commentary. It is perfectly clear; fully in command of its own adoration of language and its distrust of it; entirely conscious of the difference between "should" and "does" ("Beautie and beauteous words should go together"); and painfully willing to accept a "winter . . . of gross misfeature" in the mind, providing the heart "and what is lodged there" survive "livelier then before." The lingering love given to the "sparkling notions . . . sweet phrases, lovely metaphors . . . lovely enchanting language, sugar cane, hony of roses" cannot conquer Herbert's dismay at his own verbal incapacity, which produces the imagery of sexual betrayal in the third, fourth, and fifth stanzas. If we ask whether this pang is assuaged in the poem, we can only answer that it is not; Herbert's final attitude is the stoic one embodied in *"Thou art still my God."* Herbert's fidelity to this austere aesthetic has concerned some readers, who find it disturbing that he can dismiss language, finally, as "embellishment." However, he had done the same, metaphorically, in *The Quidditie,* where he says that a verse is not a gay suit, or entertainment, or news, but "that which when I use/I am with Thee"—it is, as redefined in terms of *The Forerunners,* "That which when I use/I say *Thou art still my God."* In *The*

Posie as well, the dismissal of wit, invention, and comparisons in favor of *"Lesse then the least/Of all [God's] mercies"* sets once again the essential relation of a creature to a merciful God as the center without which poetry would be, for Herbert, only an empty verbal contest of wits, scratching their epigrams on windows. (If Herbert seems Puritan in distrusting his own tendency to "deck the sense" of poems, he at least shows wisdom in that distrust, from which both Swinburne and Hopkins, to take two other exuberant poets at random, might have profited.) But it is not so much a mistrust of embellishments alone as a serious effort to determine for himself the locus of poetry that lies behind statements like those found in these poems. A conviction of "care in heaven" was for Herbert the precondition for the writing of poetry. He is no more eccentric in wanting the permanence of that precondition than Wordsworth in asking Nature to "forebode not any severing of our loves." The severing of loves is far more serious, even to a poet, than the impermanence of language. The odd aspect of *The Forerunners* is its persistent weaving of a "broider'd coat" in spite of its farewell to the birds of spring. The poem, as if in a last summoning, holds off the "bleak palenesse" of winter with one final rush of remembrance of summer. There is no reason to disbelieve Herbert's notion that "all within" could still be lively, even if the tumultuous young production of language were stilled: poems of dejection are not necessarily inferior to poems of inventive elation. Herbert died before writing a series of poems in bleak language, but his poems of deprivation of language might, had he lived to write them, have ranked with the best in English. As it is, we have only his "beauteous" intimations of a new poetry of his "winter world." Perhaps he could never have lost his fundamental gaiety nor his impetuousness in language even while living in his "dark state of tears." Certainly, however, he himself thought that he was in danger of a complete despoiling of comforts and their attendant mental delights, as he said in *The Answer:*

My comforts drop and melt away like snow:
I shake my head, and all the thoughts and ends,
Which my fierce youth did bandie, fall and flow

Like leaves about me: or like summer friends,
Flyes of estate and sunshine.

He foresaw a time of no more poetry at all, described in *Grief:*

Verses, ye are too fine a thing, too wise
For my rough sorrows: cease, be dumbe and mute . . .
And keep your measures for some lovers lute,
Whose grief allows him musick and a ryme:
For mine excludes both measure, tune, and time.
    Alas, my God!

Though the convention of telling, in beautiful verse, one's verses to
cease is in evidence here, Herbert's grief is also clear in these poems, and
it is possible that he might have ceased to write entirely, justifying those
readers who see in this aesthetic of the minimal word a dangerous route
to the abolition of art, the final victory of "silent tears" in the conviction that "Thou shalt answer, Lord, for me."[10] However, I do not think
the deduction a necessary one, since the poetry of the "vertuous soul"
in Herbert seems more powerful than the poetry of "sweet spring, full of
sweet dayes and roses." The quintessential poem of "the vertuous soul"
—as Herbert himself knew in placing it just before the final rededication
of his poems (*A Wreath,* matching *The Dedication*) preceding the
poems on the Last Things—is *The Elixir:*

Teach me, my God and King,
    In all things thee to see,
And what I do in any thing,
    To do it as for thee:

Not rudely, as a beast,
    To runne into an action;
But still to make thee prepossest,
    And give it his perfection.

A man that looks on glasse,
    On it may stay his eye;
Or if he pleaseth, through it passe,
    And then the heav'n espie.

All may of thee partake:
Nothing can be so mean,
Which with his tincture (for thy sake)
Will not grow bright and clean.

A servant with this clause
Makes drudgerie divine:
Who sweeps a room, as for thy laws,
Makes that and th'action fine.

This is the famous stone
That turneth all to gold:
For that which God doth touch and own
Cannot for lesse be told.

The Elixir is a forbidding poem. "What is this strange and uncouth thing?" we might ask, reading it, especially since it aims at representing perfection (its first title) or the quintessence or elixir that gave it its second name. How could a poet so decorative, fanciful, and fertile as Herbert write a poem so obdurately heavy-footed and choppy? With one exception the quatrains, as Stein has noted, proceed in two-line clumps,[11] and the kindest word for the meter would be "sturdy." I cannot think of any beginning of a great poem in English so unpromising as the first stanza of *The Elixir,* which is pure versified catechism, with banal rhymes, an awkward repetition of "things—thing," and an infantile vocabulary. Once again, Herbert is beginning with recalcitrant materials —here, the clichés of hymn singing—and "thrusting his mind" into them to see what they can be made to yield.

To "see" God in all things means at first, to Herbert, to make some special effort to see in a way different from the usual: with a complacent tonal echo of the Pharisee, he says that certain men see only as far as the nearest window, so to speak, but that the true observer of God's ordinances will look further, and thereby see heaven. The level of consciousness implied is high: the man must "please" to keep his eye from making a stay at the window-pane. A similarly high degree of consciousness is implied in Herbert's formulation by which one "does" something "as for God": this requires that we suspend natural impulse, forbear to run like a beast into an action, but rather take thought before the action, and make God "pre-possest" of that action. The vocabulary of the second stanza, and its comparison, have rapidly left behind the diction and simple reference of catechetical hymn-singing, and Herbert's two instances (acting and looking) are highly intellectualized and reflective rather than emotional and affective. The effort of perfection is wholly internal and dependent on taking thought before or during an action, that it may duly be prepossessed by God or directed toward heaven. There is an absence of simplicity and naturalness in all this, and Herbert must have realized his own over-intellectuality in response to the "given" of the first stanza, because he searches for another formulation for perfection. (He had earlier, in the unrevised version in the Williams manuscript, tried the formulations of "referring" all things he did to God and "doing" things "for" God before adopting the formula in stanza one of "seeing" God in all things and "doing" things "as for God.")

Now the metaphor changes to a mixed Eucharistic/alchemical one: "All may of thee partake." Partaking is not intellectual: all things partake of the quintessence by being infused with its tincture, just as men partake of the Eucharist. Neither of these participatory activities invokes consciousness in the way that making God prepossessed or casting one's eye further on does. A "mean" thing which grows "bright and clean" is renewed from within by the tincture, not by taking thought and trying to add a cubit to its stature. From the elitism of the first referrals ("I can be better than a beast and better than the shortsighted"), Herbert descends to a new humility: "I am a mean thing which may be made bright and clean ('new, tender, quick') by partaking of a better thing than I." The new formulation "for thy sake," shortly to be followed by another, "for thy laws," implies not a superior level of consciousness but a different level of love and obedience, self-submission rather than self-exaltation. Instead of being a "high" thing (not rude like a beast, not earthbound like the myopic man), Herbert becomes a "low" thing, a servant, in what Stein has called the "transforming" stanza.[12] But there are really two "transforming" stanzas, the fourth and fifth, and both of these, in which mean things grow bright and fine, differ from the intellectual stanzas of willed self-change that precede them. Nothing is accomplished in the *outside* world in the two self-conscious stanzas of prepossession and espial of heaven; Herbert speaks there as though perfection were a wholly self-contained activity. However, in his self-correction in stanzas four and five, perfection, which consists not in self-examination but in submission to God's laws and in doing things for his sake, results in a remarkable burnishing of one's surroundings: things grow bright and clean, and the room is made fine, as well as the action. The intellectual problem is solved, at least for Herbert, by turning away from X-ray vision to the servant sweeping, and his obvious poetic pleasure in the solution is reflected in his, for once, obtrusive "poetic" effect—the alliteration making "drudgerie divine" and the zeugma making "that and th'action fine."

What is still missing is an acknowledgment of the original wish *not* to be rude or earth-bound, not bestial or shortsighted; the image of a servant engaged in drudgery does not, however bright and clean, quite satisfy Herbert's necessarily aristocratic appetite for something radiantly quintessential. Besides, the effort, even though changed from an effort of consciousness to an effort of will, is still all on man's part: he partakes, he sweeps. However, the passage from self-consciousness to service guarantees a divine response, if only in terms of the reader's immediate echoing, as soon as the word "servant" is used in a Christian context, of "Well done, thou good and faithful servant." God bends, in that reciprocity Herbert cannot do without, and "touches" and "owns" his servant, turning all to gold—servant, sweeping, drudgery, and all. The double puns in "touch" and "own," so much less noticeable than the alliteration and zeugma preceding them, represent a far more Herbertian resolution than the earlier "embellishments." The exceptionally static nature of the closing stanza recalls strongly the seasoned timber of *Vertue,* just as the muted last two lines recall the equilibrium voiced in "then *chiefly* lives." Herbert could have ended in the realm of transfiguration:

> When God doth touch and own,
> Such wealth cannot be told;
> The power of his famous stone
> Can turn all things to gold.

But rather than close with the alchemizing of nature into nobility, Herbert "buries" his transformation in the second line of the stanza, and ends with a notable understatement. The poem has in fact come close, earlier on, to a sustained, if quiet, hyperbole: after the intellectualizing of the second and third stanzas, Herbert, through his own invented metaphor, espies heaven and announces, expansively and generously, "*All* may of thee partake:/*Nothing* can be so mean/ . . . A *servant* with this clause/Makes *drudgerie* divine." All—nothing; *even* a servant —*even* drudgery. These stretched claims are reinforced by the stone's turning *all* to gold, but then the poem subsides almost in modesty, as if it were audacious to claim perfection too boldly.

It takes a long acquaintance with Herbert—his delights, his temptations, and his gifts—to see *The Elixir* for what it is, the most implicit possible repudiation of both religious cliché and intellectual self-absorption, a poem infinitely restricted in means and surely spoken by the virtuous soul who has either lost or put away his "lovely enchanting language, sugar cane, hony of roses." In this poem there is no decking of the sense as if it were to sell. And yet the poem has long been a favorite in anthologies: somehow readers have sensed that one version of the essential Herbert lies here.[13] It is only by knowing the multiple inventions of Herbert's poetic powers—in emblems, in pattern poems, in autobiographical *récits,* in numberless stanza forms, in the reinvention of tradition—that we sense what this spareness means and how antithetical, in one sense, it was to Herbert's nature, and yet how, in another sense, it was the bedrock in which all the luxuriant foliage of his more elaborate poetry was rooted. We may be forgiven if, frightened almost by this stoic sparseness, we return for reassurance to the Herbert of lilt and impetuousness, as in *Easter:*

> I got me flowers to straw thy way;
> I got me boughs off many a tree:
> But thou wast up by break of day,
> And brought'st thy sweets along with thee.

That is the simplest Herbert and by no means the least beautiful. But before Herbert could pass beyond the "contesting" with Jesus' arising that forms the subject of this little poem and arrive at the reconciliation with God the Father so evident in *The Elixir* in its final version, there was a long pilgrimage full of disappointments, checks, and brackish waters. The continual sense of journey and trial in Herbert perhaps explains why his readers return most often to the closing poem in *The Temple* as the touchstone for all the rest. It is the end of the journey, and it resumes so many of Herbert's themes that each time it is read it offers a different facet of itself to the mind.

Love (III), like so many of Herbert's poems, is a contest in which the abashed poet feels unequal to the contest of love with God; as in other poems, the contest is prolonged; and as in *The Collar* and *Dialogue,* God's speech is gently reproachful, but with a light irony and comedy recalling *Love unknown:*

> Love bade me welcome: yet my soul drew back,
>   Guiltie of dust and sinne.
> But quick-ey'd Love, observing me grow slack
>   From my first entrance in,
> Drew nearer to me, sweetly questioning,
>   If I lack'd any thing.
>
> A guest, I answer'd, worthy to be here:
>   Love said, You shall be he.
> I the unkinde, ungratefull? Ah my deare,
>   I cannot look on thee.
> Love took my hand, and smiling did reply,
>   Who made the eyes but I?
>
> Truth Lord, but I have marr'd them: let my shame
>   Go where it doth deserve.
> And know you not, sayes Love, who bore the blame?
>   My deare, then I will serve.
> You must sit down, sayes Love, and taste my meat:
>   So I did sit and eat.

The distance between God and the soul, so distressing in many poems in *The Temple,* here shrinks, during the actual progress of the poem, to nothing: "Love . . . drew nearer . . ./Love took my hand." The painful distinction, often evident in *The Temple,* between God the Father-Judge and God the Son-Redeemer vanishes here. Both are simply "Love," who can say as Creator, "Who made the eyes but I?" and as

Redeemer, "Know you not who bore the blame?" The whole question of blame and shame—God's power to punish and man's to suffer—which resonates throughout Herbert's work is here dismissed as an unprofitable query in the realm of love, and the smaller question debating the guilt of dusty mortality and the guilt of sin in causing the fall from perfection is answered by Love's gentle remark about worthiness. Worthiness is not a condition here but hereafter: "You *shall be* he."

The observant, "quick-ey'd," courteous, conversational, and smiling Love is himself at first a mysterious creation, quite unlike any other literary version of God. Gradually we realize that as we follow the "chronological" progress of the poem, which shows the gradual domestication, so to speak, of a hesitant guest, we are at the same time following an allegorical progression which reveals the nature of the host at this feast. By his actions, we deduce the nature of Love: Love is welcoming, Love is observant, Love is solicitous, Love is kind, Love is long-suffering, Love is not easily provoked, Love is not vainglorious, Love never fails. The source is clearly St. Paul's definition of Charity. But we may also conclude that this is the God Herbert created in his own best self-image—light, graceful, witty, not above a turn of phrase, and yet considerate, careful for the comfort of his guests, affectionate, firm, and above all generous.

But the allegorical structure alone, defining the nature of Love, does not by itself sustain the poem: it is coupled with the awkward hesitation of the speaker, who is speaking to us after he has gone through the gaucherie he describes; the voice is that of one of the blessed in heaven, an extraordinarily daring choice of verbal impersonation. Equally daring is the ordinariness of the conversation in its give-and-take, in view of the awe natural to the subject. The social comedy between the dusty guest and the gentle host casts a glimmer of lightness and irony even on this highest encounter: the dismayed, rather glum, and ashamed guest is countered with delicate wit—"You *shall be* he"—and with the lightest of reproaches, until he himself, in sitting down in silent grateful acquiescence, attains at last the perfect simplicity that Love has displayed throughout the poem. Together with all the beauty of the substance of *Love*, its finely managed rhythm contributes to its convincing power. Like some decorous minuet, the poem leads its characters through steps in a delicate hovering: a pace forward, a hanging back, a slackening, a drawing nearer, a lack, a fullness, a dropping of the eyes, a glance, a touch, a reluctance, a proffer, a refusal, a demurrer, an insistence—and then the final seating at the feast. No prosody is adequate to describe Herbert's subtleties in the hesitancies of encounter, of which the famous monosyllables composing the poem represent only one part.[14] To think that such a poem could be constructed on a "source" of only nine words—"He shall . . . make them to sit down to meat" (Luke 12:37) —is to stand astonished at Herbert's powers. And to realize that the poem reworks its source, leaving us to imagine the end, convinces us of Herbert's preference for implication. The Bible verse in full runs: "Blessed are those servants, whom the lord when he cometh shall find watching: verily I say unto you, that he shall gird himself, and make them to sit down to meat, and will come forth and serve them." In Herbert, it is the soul who comes, not the Lord; it is the Lord who is watching, not the servants, in every case making the Lord more attentive and caring; but Herbert, expecting us to know the verse, lets us imagine who will "serve," after the soul's offer to do so is declined. The final definition of Love is a silent one. Sublime as *Heaven* is, with its ethereal evocation of "light, joy, and leisure," we conclude by preferring to it, as Herbert himself did, the heaven in which a welcome, a smile, a colloquy, a taking by the hand, and a seat at a table stand for all the heart can wish.

Notes

Index

Notes

INTRODUCTION

1. *Shelburne Essays, Fourth Series* (New York: G. P. Putnam's, 1906), p. 74.

2. Herbert J. C. Grierson, *Metaphysical Lyrics and Poems of the Seventeenth Century* (Oxford: Clarendon Press, 1921), p. xliv.

3. George Herbert Palmer, ed., *The English Works of George Herbert,* 3 vols. (Boston and New York: Houghton Mifflin, 1905), I, xii.

4. T. S. Eliot, "George Herbert," *The Spectator* 148 (Mar. 12, 1932): 360.

5. The most comprehensive account of Herbert's work is still to be found in the essays and annotations of George Herbert Palmer. However, his critical presuppositions and especially his chronological rearrangement of the poems have made his account more questionable today than it was when first published.

6. Even a critic so sensitive to Herbert's general nature as Helen White, for instance, seems in her long discussion of *The Elixir* to miss most signs of variation in feeling and attitude in the final version of the poem. See her *Metaphysical Poets* (New York: Macmillan, 1956), pp. 189–194.

7. Eliot, "George Herbert," p. 361.

8. Quoted from *Coleridge's Miscellaneous Criticism,* ed. Thomas Middleton Raysor (Cambridge: Harvard University Press, 1936), p. 244.

9. A. E. Housman, *The Name and Nature of Poetry* (New York: Macmillan, 1933), p. 33.

10. These rankings, especially against Donne, continue to be made, but they are made on the basis of incomplete and glancing descriptions of Herbert. A. S. P. Woodhouse, for instance, in his 1965 Weil lectures published as *The Poet and His Faith* (Chicago: University of Chicago Press, 1965), remarks that "Herbert had nothing of Donne's strong animal nature . . . It is perhaps a deficiency in such energy as much as anything else that prevents Herbert's poetry from rising to sustained flights" (p. 66). He also speaks of Herbert's "simple evangelical conception that he is God's" (p. 69), calls *The Temple* "a manual of devotion," and says that "it is the seventeenth century's *Christian Year"* (p. 73). I might have been reassured by Auden's remark about Donne versus Herbert—

"Great as [Donne] is, I find [him] an insufferable prima donna; give me George Herbert every time" (*New York Review of Books* 18 [Apr. 20, 1972]: 3)—were it not for his other opinions on Herbert: that "since all of Herbert's poems are concerned with the religious life, they cannot be judged by aesthetic standards alone" (*Poet to Poet: George Herbert Selected by W. H. Auden* [Harmondsworth: Penguin Books, 1973], p. 9); and that *The Sacrifice* is Herbert's greatest poem ("A Kind of Poetic Justice," *The Observer Review*, Oct. 29, 1972, p. 38).

11. William Empson, *Seven Types of Ambiguity* (New York: New Directions, 1947, rev. from British 1930 edition), p. 210.

12. George Herbert, *Works*, ed. F. E. Hutchinson (Oxford: Clarendon Press, 1941), p. 233. Hereafter cited as *Works*.

13. Helen Gardner. "Introduction," *The Poems of George Herbert* (London: Oxford University Press, 1961), p. xix.

14. Eliot, "George Herbert," p. 361.

15. No small part of Herbert's strength and lightness is due to his prosodic mastery. He is the Schubert of English poetry, with a new ripple in every invention. A cascade of forms flashes through *The Temple*, like one of Schubert's brooks, delighting in turns and reversals, now modest, now glittering. Our prosody is inadequate as yet to a proper representation of this genius, and each attempt, including the lengthiest and most recent, Arnold Stein's in *George Herbert's Lyrics* (Baltimore: Johns Hopkins Press, 1968), founders on its own notational inadequacy.

Coburn Freer, in *Music for a King: George Herbert's Style and the Metrical Psalms* (Baltimore: Johns Hopkins Press, 1972), attempts a prosodic description based on certain of Herbert's models, the metrical versions of the Psalms. But he bends Herbert's infinitely flexible rhythms to the Procrustean bed of Psalm prosody, and in fact seems to find a great many of Herbert's poems prosodically displeasing, a conclusion few will share. Of Herbert's imitators, many of whom imitated exactly the cruder aspects (feet, lines, stanzas, rhymes, and "counterpoint") of his prosody, only Vaughan achieves some of the same effortless rhythm. The uselessness of discussing those cruder aspects is made evident by the study of those imitators, while the subtleties distinguishing Herbert from them, even if one invokes such elements as pitch and juncture, elude exact description. If an exact description were attempted, it would be both exhausting and ponderous, and so I leave prosody to one side, except to remark from time to time particular effects.

1. A READING OF *VERTUE*

1. This text, like all subsequent ones, is cited from *Works*, the edition most complete and most accessible to the reader. It contains all of Herbert's poetry and prose. The posthumously published volume *The Temple* (1633) contains most of Herbert's English poetry. I quote on occasion from the poems found in a manuscript ("the Williams manuscript," which Hutchinson abbreviates as *W*) now in

Dr. Williams's Library, Gordon Square, London (MS. Jones B 62). This manuscript, in the hand of an amanuensis but with corrections in Herbert's hand, contains both English and Latin poems. Since, as Palmer first noted, none of these
poems contains references to Herbert as a priest, the poems in the manuscript are
thought to have been composed before Herbert's ordination to the priesthood
in 1630. Most of the poems in the Williams manuscript appear in *The Temple,*
often in revised form. The Williams manuscript therefore represents, as Hutchinson says, an earlier stage of Herbert's work. All the Williams manuscript variants, as well as the poems therein contained which do not appear in *The
Temple,* are printed in Hutchinson's edition. Following Hutchinson's practice,
I distinguish different poems bearing the same title (such as the five poems all
entitled *Affliction*) by Roman numerals according to their position in *The
Temple.*

Max Patrick recently argued in *The Editor as Critic and the Critic as Editor*
(Los Angeles: William Andrews Clark Memorial Library, University of California, 1973) that the proper copytext for *The Temple* is not the Bodleian manuscript used by Hutchinson but the printed edition of 1633, as emended in the
second edition, also of 1633. The slight difference in text would not in any case,
even if Patrick's conjectures are correct, affect my interpretations here. The
printed variants are recorded in Hutchinson and are available to inspection.

2. Robert Ellrodt, *Les Poètes Métaphysiques Anglais* (Paris: Corti, 1960),
I, 283.

3. In *The Poetical Works of John and Charles Wesley,* collected by G. Osborn
(London, 1868, 1869), I, 10 (first published in 1739):

VIRTUE

Altered from Herbert

Sweet Day, so cool, so calm, so bright,
    The bridal of the earth and sky:
The dew shall weep thy fall tonight,
    For thou with all thy sweets must die!

Sweet Rose, so fragrant and so brave,
    Dazzling the rash beholder's eye:
Thy root is ever in its grave,
    And thou with all thy sweets must die!

Sweet Spring, so beauteous and so gay,
    Storehouse, where sweets unnumber'd lie:
Not long thy fading glories stay,
    But thou with all thy sweets must die!

Only a sweet and virtuous mind,
    When Nature all in ruins lies,
When earth and heaven a period find,
    Begins a life that never dies.

A version depending on Wesley's (the first two stanzas are identical) was printed in *The Charmer: A Choice Collection of Songs, Scots and English*, 2nd ed. (Edinburgh, 1752). Its extraordinary last stanza offers sufficient evidence why Herbert, as he stood, was not congenial to eighteenth century taste. Here are the last two stanzas:

> Sweet spring, full of sweet days and roses,
> A box, where sweets compacted lie,
> Not long ere all thy fragrant posies,
> With all their sweets, must fade and die.
>
> Sweet love alone, sweet wedded love,
> To thee no period is assign'd;
> Thy tender joys by time improve,
> In death itself the most refin'd.

4. Rosemond Tuve, *Elizabethan and Metaphysical Imagery* (Chicago: University of Chicago Press, 1947), ch. 9 *passim*.

5. Stein, *Herbert*, p. 176. Stein justifies the use of "season'd timber" by saying that it "achieves its purpose after death—not as a tree but as wood," and adds that the soul "is, in the traditional metaphor, 'dead' to the distracting influences of the world" (pp. 180–181). But Herbert's soul loves the world, in the best sense. And the unyielding, never-giving function of the soul is useful only *before* death (its function after death is pure sweetness), so that to make us think of the previous "death" of the tree that produced the timber seems no part of Herbert's intention.

6. Joseph H. Summers, *George Herbert: His Religion and Art* (Cambridge: Harvard University Press, 1954), p. 117.

7. Mary Ellen Rickey, *Utmost Art* (Lexington: University of Kentucky Press, 1968), p. 21. Rickey adds that "the introduction of the soul upsets the entire well-realized effect of the foregoing lines" (p. 22). On the contrary, the soul has been "present" from the beginning, by implication, in attitude and tone.

8. A. Davenport, "George Herbert and Ovid," *Notes and Queries*, n.s. 2 (1955): 98.

9. Ellrodt says in *Poètes Métaphysiques*, I, 283, "Ce ciel est le ciel de la nature, le ciel paien ('sky' et non 'heaven')." Herbert, to my knowledge, never uses "heaven" as a word of landscape, so it would be out of the question for him to choose to use it here. To suggest the quasi-spiritual nature of the day, Herbert shows it linking earth to the region of air, and since a bridal by its nature joins two *different* things, we may assume that the sky here is precisely *not* "earthly."

10. It is significant that Wesley felt obliged to introduce "fragrant" in rewriting the stanza. He altered the emphatic rhyhm of the first and second lines as well.

11. See Stein, *Herbert*, p. 179.

12. See, e.g., the absurd ending in the version from *The Charmer*, reproduced above in note 3.

13. Rickey, *Utmost Art*, p. 93.

14. Stein, *Herbert,* p. 182.

15. Palmer, *Herbert,* III, 334.

16. I except the *carpe diem* poems that represent nature as cyclical, since they are irrelevant to Herbert's poem, which represents nature as mortal.

17. The late M. Jacques Teyssier of the University of Bordeaux defined for me this distinction between the definite and indefinite article. A mother will say, e.g., to a disobedient child, "A good child doesn't do that," and not, "The good child doesn't do that." The indefinite article makes it possible to have in mind a potential particular application: "A cow needs grass, so I am buying land to pasture my cow in." "The cow is herbivorous," however, is a statement of essence and does not imply my possible ownership of a cow. "A sweet and virtuous soul never gives, and so if my soul is sweet and virtuous, I shall remain staunch."

18. Tuve, *Elizabethan and Metaphysical Imagery,* p. 303.

19. The verb "lives," which closes the poem, is a hypothetical one, grammatically speaking, since it follows on the hypothetical case *"Though* the whole world *turn* to coal." However, it rhymes with "gives," which is in the present tense of habit (denied habitude, in this case). Consequently, we tend to take the final "lives" as also a present tense. The effect of this "deceptive" syntax—"The soul lives now but chiefly lives then"—is to confer immortality on the soul as it preserves its "present tense" through the Last Day. A future tense, to match the "must die" (envisaging the future) of the other verses, would be wholly out of place predicated about a spiritual substance that cannot be subject to time, or to changes in time.

20. Elsie Leach, "John Wesley's Use of George Herbert," *Huntington Library Quarterly* 16 (1953) : 199.

2. ALTERNATIVES: THE REINVENTED POEM

1. Valentina Poggi, *George Herbert* (Bologna: Casa Editrice Prof. Riccardo Pàtron, 1967), pp. 203 ff.

2. Stein, *Herbert,* pp. 150, 151.

3. I do not agree with Stanley Fish, in *Self-Consuming Artifacts* (Los Angeles: University of California Press, 1972), p. 201, that in the ending of this poem, "At first we tend to read 'Loved' as 'you are loved by me,' but the immediate context . . . demands an alternate reading: 'I decree that I am loved by you.' "

4. It could be argued that each stanza is addressed, not to all sinners, but rather to a special subclass of sinners, some less "sinful" than others. Yet it would still be necessary to explain the order (from more revulsion to less) in Herbert's responses to the sinners.

5. When John Wesley rewrote *The Invitation* for hymn singing, he did far more than adapt the meter. An adaptation faithful to Herbert's meaning had been made in 1697, reprinted in *Select Hymns Taken out of Mr. Herbert's Temple* (1697), intro. William E. Stephenson, Augustan Reprint Society no. 98 (Los Angeles: William Andrews Clark Memorial Library, University of California, 1962), pp. 31–32. Wesley's adaptation in *Wesley,* I, 111–113, insists on

the wickedness and carnality of the sinners, intensifying in every case Herbert's description, and showing none of Herbert's changes of attitude.

6. Herbert's commentator, George Ryley (who wrote in 1715), was in fact untroubled by Herbert's invention here, saying, "All fiction is built upon some prior Truth; And this bears so near an Analogy to the Scripture of Truth, that I need not grate the Ears of my Reader, if (for Brevity Sake) I Look thro' it, as tho' it were a *plain true History.*" See his *Mr. Herbert's Temple and Church Militant Explained and Improved by a Discourse upon Each Poem Critical and Practical,* ed. John Martin Heissler (Ann Arbor: University Microfilms, 1961), pp. 539, 541. Ryley's naïve delight in emblems may account for his willingness to read fiction as fact: "There is certainly something," he says of *The Pulley* (calling it "one of the most gratefull Poems in the whole book"), "in this fictitious, Allusive, way of writing, that has allways Charmed the Ears, and suited the Genii of all ages . . . And I can't but think our Author (Mr. Herbert) has, in more places than one, and here particularly, Carried his tho't to as great, and high a pitch of heroic Invention as most poets of Any day" (p. 539).

7. My colleague Gerald Fitzgerald has shown me two charming examples from Renaissance Latin poetry. One, from the *Basia* of Johannes Secundus, asks why roses are red as well as white, and explains that it is because Venus kissed some petals and they burned from the ardor of her lips. One of Mantuan's elegies asks why so many men are farmers, and explains that it is because Eve, when God visited her, hid most of her children out of shame, fearing to be reproached for the sexual appetite which had engendered so many. God decreed high estate for the visible children, but when he unearthed the ones hidden away in the barn, he condemned them to be farmers, since they reeked of soil. The appeal of such topics—a riddle and an answer—resides in the wit and grace of the hyperbolic story invented, as well as in the informal presentation of deities.

8. *Select Hymns,* p. 13.

9. It may seem that to enumerate the literal fancies underlying Herbert's descriptions of God's actions were to consider too curiously. Yet when we look for precedent, we find even the theatrical Donne remaining strangely cautious in his attribution of actions to God. Though he may *ask* God to batter his heart, to overthrow him, and to break, blow, burn and make him new, such language is clearly the hyperbolic rhetoric of a recalcitrant heart. The only actions Donne actually predicates of God are kind ones: God is said to knock, breathe, shine, and seek to mend. The strong rhetoric returns at the end of the sonnet ("imprison me"), yet Donne retires into *puns* of force ("enthrall" and "ravish") rather than using words having only a forceful sense, finding it impossible to attribute to God actions carrying only a pejorative meaning. Besides, Donne is careful to attach to every forceful action an intended result: "That I may rise and stand, o'erthrow me"; "Except you enthrall me [I] never shall be free." Herbert can offer no such immediate causal motives for God's inflictions: they seem to respond to no unworthiness in himself. He is the same faithful servant, and only God is capricious.

10. Palmer, *Herbert,* I, 144.

11. James Montgomery, *The Christian Poet* (Glasgow, 1827), pp. 243–244.

12. Summers, *Herbert*, p. 89.

13. This chapter was written before the appearance of Stanley Fish's provocative account of Herbert in *Self-Consuming Artifacts*, pp. 156–223. I am glad to see that Fish's sense of Herbert's poetic procedure agrees very much in one respect with the view expressed here, that a poem by Herbert is a constantly evolving object. But where Fish sees an ever-more-complete self-effacement at work, "a surrender not only of a way of seeing, but of initiative, will, and finally of being" (p. 158), I see a progressive discarding of the "other"—the received idea, the cliché, the devotional triteness—yielding, finally, a picture of a self wholly itself, individual, unique, and original. Fish's description approximates more closely to what has normally been regarded as mystical experience; Herbert's commentators, almost unanimously, distinguish his devotion from mystical experience.

Fish's initial argument, that the surrender of the soul to God "requires the silencing of [Herbert's] voice and the relinquishing of the claims of authorship" (p. 158), is based on his taking as Herbert's final opinion the lines from *The Flower:* "We say amisse,/This or that is:/Thy word is all, if we could spell." However, I find these lines to be uttered by the rebellious soul, bent on calling God's actions arbitrary. Later, the repentant soul discovers that God's actions are intelligible and just. The opinion in these lines is refuted by the rest of the poem and is not an opinion finally endorsed by Herbert at all. Yet Fish draws a long skein of deduction from these lines, all of it mistaken, and attributes to Herbert ideas which I am confident he never had, e.g., that "to stop saying amiss is not only to stop distinguishing 'this' from 'that,' but to stop distinguishing oneself from God, and finally to stop, to cease to be" (p. 157). I cannot imagine Herbert subscribing to such ideas. It is perhaps worthwhile to notice that these lines, quoted by Fish as Herbertian orthodoxy, troubled Wesley by their petulance and their accusatory nature. When he was rewriting *The Flower,* he changed them to reflect a more orthodox view, the one Herbert arrives at later in the poem: that God's actions, especially his wrathful ones, are directly proportionate to our sins (in the case of Herbert, the sin of presumption). Wesley wishes a blameless poem for church singing, and so he also omits the final warning against pride which closes the poem. The relevant lines, in *Wesley*, I, 44, are:

> Thy will supreme disposes all;
> We prove Thy justice in our fall,
> Thy mercy in our rise we feel . . .

> These are Thy wonders, Lord of love,
> Thy mercy thus delights to prove
> We are but flowers that bloom and die!
> Soon as this saving truth we see,
> Within Thy garden placed by Thee,
> Time we survive, and death defy.

3. BEAUTY IN DISCOVERY: EMBLEMS AND ALLEGORIES

1. Rosemond Tuve, *Allegorical Imagery* (Princeton: Princeton University Press, 1966), p. 197.

2. Rosemary Freeman, in *English Emblem Books* (London: Chatto and Windus, 1948), p. 156, says very truly that "the moral of Herbert's poetry, unlike that of the emblem books, is a highly complex thing, but like that of the emblem books it is built up through images. Yet the function (and hence the quality) of these images is different: for Herbert they are the focus of ideas, for Quarles merely the source of ideas." Freeman's topic, however, constrains her to the examination of discrete lines and images for the most part; she does not show how the complex moral of a whole poem emerges.

3. Jesus' "wit" in the Gospels ("Render to Caesar," "Let him who is without sin cast the first stone") is never bantering or intimate.

4. Fish, in *Self-Consuming Artifacts,* pp. 207–215, considers *The Altar* at length and finds it a considerably more complicated poem than I do.

5. The poem *The Church-floore* resembles *The Altar* in wishing to construct in itself a physical object corresponding to its subject. Coburn Freer, in *Music for a King,* p. 121, "solves" the relation of form to subject in this poem, explaining why four stanzas are necessary to complete the rhyme scheme, each stanza serving as one triangle in an alternately black-and-speckled tiled floor, four triangles being needed to complete two squares, one colored and one speckled:

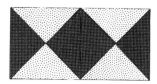

The oddness of the invention is striking, but the poem, as a poem, is not remarkable.

6. *Works* p. 520. The same urgent wish to clarify the poem (which stubbornly refuses clarification on these terms) appears in the exchange in *Notes and Queries,* 1st ser. 9:54; 10:18, reported by the Rev. Alexander B. Grosart in his Fuller Worthies' edition of Herbert (Printed for Private Circulation, 1874), pp. 299–301. One Dr. Husenbeth of Norwich, writing as F.C.H., not only suggested an interpretation but indeed rewrote the poem so as to "expand" the poet's "ideas." His version, which perhaps more properly belongs in my chapter on imitators and adapters, follows his interpretation: "The short poem of this author [George Herbert] entitled *Hope* turns evidently upon matrimonial speculation; though it may well serve to show the vanity of human expectation in many more things. The watch was given apparently to remind Hope that the time for the wedding was fairly come; but Hope, by returning an anchor, intimated that the petitioner must hope on for an indefinite time. The next present, of a prayer-book, was a broad hint that the matrimonial service was ardently looked for. The

optic glass given in return showed that the lover must be content to look to a prospect still distant. It was natural then that tears of disappointment should flow, and be sent to propitiate unfeeling Hope. Still the sender was mocked with only a few green ears of corn, which might yet be blighted, and never arrive at maturity. Well might the poor lover, who had been so long expecting a ring as a token of the fulfillment of her anxious wish, resolve in her despair to have done with Hope. After writing the above the thought occurred to me that the poet's ideas might be so expanded as to supply at once the answer to each part of the enigma. I send the results of the experiment:

> "I gave to Hope a watch of mine; but he,
>   Regardless of my just and plain request,
> An anchor, as a warning, gave to me,
>   That on futurity I still must rest.
> Then an old prayer-book I did present,
>   Still for the marriage service fit to use;
> And he in mockery an optic sent,
>   My patience yet to try with distant views.
> With that I gave a phial full of tears,
>   My wounded spirit could no more endure;
> But he return'd me just a few green ears,
>   Which blight might soon forbid to grow mature.
> Ah, loiterer! I'll no more, no more I'll bring,
>   Nor trust again to thy deceiving tale;
> I did expect ere now the nuptial ring
>   To crown my hopes, but all my prospects fail."

These plodding alternate lines of emblem and gloss, coupled with the prose explanation, provoked more prose from the original querist; nobody seemed to wish the poem to remain suggestive rather than explicit. Even Palmer, who was rarely so tempted, rewrote *Hope* ("translating into abstract terms Herbert's imagery of things") as follows (Palmer, *Herbert*, III, 201):

> To Love I said, "Hast thou forgotten Time?"
>   "Time counts for naught with Love, for Love is Hope."
> But I prayed still the prayer I ever prayed.
>   "Look far away," said Love, "Not on things near."
> I wept.
>   "Nay, here and now is fruit," he said. "Unripe indeed."
> "Why such delay?" cried I. "Give all or none!"

The result of these tinkerings is so bad, in both cases, that we can only be thankful Herbert felt no obligation to gloss or "translate" his emblems himself. Such adaptations convince us even more strongly that Herbert's art does not reside in his subject matter.

7. *Coloss. 3.3* is considered, in all its complexity, in Fish, *Self-Consuming Artifacts*, pp. 203–206.

8. Rosemond Tuve, in *A Reading of George Herbert* (Chicago: University of Chicago Press, 1952), pp. 132–135), thinks that Herbert "quite probably did see Christ the Grape-bunch in an actual old window." That may be so, though we have no way of knowing; it is at least equally probable that Herbert invented the sort of stained-glass window that he would have liked to see, posing the kind of verbal riddle his mind enjoyed. It would not be the first time he rewrote tradition.

9. Tuve, in *Herbert,* pp. 164–168, describes the traditions drawn on for the imagery.

10. The echo of Richard II's pitiable speech to Bolingbroke, noted by Hutchinson (*Works,* p. 527n), may have arisen in Herbert by simple contrast. Richard says he is the bucket which is down in the "deepe Well": "That Bucket downe, and full of Teares am I,/Drinking my Griefes, whil'st you mount up on high" (IV.ii.184–189 [in Hutchinson's citation]). Herbert is being lifted up from the well of tears to heaven, but the image serves in either case. And Herbert *has* been down in the well of tears, full of self-regard. When he is down there, the view looks terrifying; but when he looks up, through "Christ's pure veil," the way is clear to heaven.

11. There are many passages in *A Priest to the Temple* that treat of preaching and are relevant to *The Windows* (as well as to other poems in *The Temple*). In Chapter IV (*The Parsons Knowledg*) Herbert says that for the understanding of Scripture the means the Parson uses are, "first, a holy Life, remembering what his Master saith, that *if any do Gods will, he shall know of the Doctrine, John 7.* and assuring himself, that wicked men, however learned, do not know the Scriptures, because they feel them not, and because they are not understood but with the same Spirit that writ them." In Chapter VII (*The Parson preaching*), which should be read in conjunction with *The Windows,* Herbert gives detailed rhetorical instructions to the preacher who, when he preaches, "procures attention by all possible art." But, Herbert continues, "By these and other means the Parson procures attention; but the character of his Sermon is Holiness; he is not witty, or learned, or eloquent, but Holy. A Character, that *Hermogenes* never dream'd of, and therefore he could give no precepts thereof. But it is gained, first, by choosing texts of Devotion, not Controversie, moving and ravishing texts, whereof the Scriptures are full. Secondly, by dipping, and seasoning all our words and sentences in our hearts, before they come into our mouths, truly affecting, and cordially expressing all that we say; so that the auditors may plainly perceive that every word is hart-deep." Herbert, more than the ordinary churchgoer indifferent to language, would be exquisitely sensitive to any insincerity of diction and to any cliché or fatigue in expression. The Parson, Herbert adds in Chapter XXI (*The Parson Catechizing*), "is first a Sermon to himself, and then to others." The passage closest to *The Windows* comes at the close of *A Priest to the Temple,* in "The Authour's Prayer before Sermon," a prayer that closes: "Lord Jesu! teach thou me, that I may teach them: Sanctifie, and

inable all my powers, that in their full strength they may deliver thy message reverently, readily, faithfully, & fruitfully. O make thy word a swift word, passing from the ear to the heart, from the heart to the life and conversation: that as the rain returns not empty, so neither may thy word, but accomplish that for which it is given."

12. Cf. Tuve, *Allegorical Imagery*, pp. 16, 19.

13. Although the rose has a long emblematic history, as D. C. Allen says in *Image and Meaning* (Baltimore: Johns Hopkins Press, 1960), his reading of Herbert's poem is not convincing. He suggests that "there are two flowers, an earthly one and a heavenly one . . . The literal rose that [the speaker] removes from his bosom and displays is at once Christian and Christ" (pp. 78–79). There is no evidence in the poem that the proffered and returned rose is anything but a natural rose, which by its innate qualities alone (of beauty and purgative effect) both displays and "sentences" worldly joys.

14. Quoted from *Biographia Literaria*, p. xix, in *Works*, p. 522.

15. I cannot, as Coburn Freer does in *Music for a King*, p. 140, see humor in *The Pilgrimage*. Freer calls the second stanza "deliberately whimsical" and "jesting," and suggests that the "wild wold" is "parody in the vein of William Carlos Williams' *phlegm/ahem* although the foul journey that *The Pilgrimage* describes is not entirely humorous." To me, the journey is not humorous at all. Often Herbert's puns are not humorous; they are simply means of compactness. Freer differs from Empson, who in *Seven Types of Ambiguity*, 2nd ed. (New York: New Directions, 1947), p. 129, finds the tone of the passage on Passion "prosaic, arid, without momentum." I too find the stanza dry, with the dryness of recollection, which does not aim at the imitative reconstruction of passion; riddling epigram ("A wasted place, but sometimes rich") is Herbert's mode here. These differences of opinion show how difficult Herbert still is.

16. Summers, *Herbert*, pp. 173–175.

17. Ryley, *Mr. Herbert's Temple*, p. 478.

4. IMITATORS AND ADAPTERS

1. " 'Poem to the Author,' by R. Langford of Grayes-Inn, Counsellour-of-Law," in Christopher Harvey, *The Synagogue* (Roycroft, 1679), p. 2. The first edition of *The Synagogue* was printed in London in 1640.

2. See Harold Bloom, *The Anxiety of Influence* (New York: Oxford University Press, 1972).

3. *Select Hymns*, "Introduction," p. iv. Stephenson cites "six main ideas" that the poems chosen by this adapter express, and though there is some coherence in the negative side of his choice ("He was determined, it seems, to root out Herbert's association of his poems with dates in the calendar of the Church of England," p. iv), a different choice could be made of thirty-two poems, equally well expressing the "six main ideas." The "ideas," after all, are such large notions as "man's ever-shifting nature," "the worthlessness of the individual," "a celebration of whatever in man may be united with redemptive deity." These "ideas" are everywhere in Herbert, and it seems that the adapter, with some

negative exclusions, chose the poems he preferred *tout court*. All poems cited in my text come from the reprinted collection.

4. Stephenson's remarks about the work of the adapter, however, are not entirely reliable. This chapter will show the deletions and transpositions of the adapter and may cast doubt on Stephenson's statement that the adapter "did not undertake to destroy by modification the "conceited" complexity of the chosen poems, or to make wholesale alterations of Herbert's diction" (p. v).

5. Not, as Hutchinson would have it (*Works*, p. 534) "a new world," since "fabrick" is the antecedent of "their" in the last line. God, molding his new fabric, has left the old fabric unto their sins.

6. Palmer, *Herbert*, III, 10.

7. Rickey, *Utmost Art*, pp. 138–139.

8. Summers, *Herbert*, p. 137.

9. Ryley, *Mr. Herbert's Temple*, p. 598.

10. Summers, *Herbert*, p. 137.

11. Summers, *Herbert*, p. 138.

12. For *Vertue* and *The Invitation* see Wesley, *Poetical Works* I, 10, 111–113; for *Anacreontick*, Wesley's adaptation of *The Rose*, see John Wesley, *A Collection of Moral and Sacred Poems* (Bristol, 1744), III, 139.

13. Leach, "Wesley's Herbert," pp. 119, 201, 202.

14. Stein, *Herbert*, pp. 124–125.

15. Wesley, *A Collection of Moral and Sacred Poems*, III, 86, 139.

16. Stein, *Herbert*, pp. 170–177.

17. Palmer, *Herbert*, III, 320.

18. See Summers, *Herbert*, p. 92.

19. Ryley points out, in *Mr. Herbert's Temple*, p. 516, that although Herbert has represented his relation to God as one of slave to cruel master, when God speaks, "God claims *my child*, not *my Slave*," thereby impugning the reliability of Herbert's vision of his status and preparing for Herbert's reversal of attitude in the face of God's articulating the true nature of the relation.

5. "MY GOD, I MEAN MYSELF": LITURGICAL AND HOMILETIC POEMS

1. Rickey, *Utmost Art*, ch. 4, gives the most careful analysis available of Herbert's development between the time of composition of *W* and of the later poems. She notes how much of the early poetry "deals with objects and festivals of the church" (p. 130).

2. See, e.g., the letter to Sir John Danvers of March 18, 1617/18, *Works*, p. 365: "Now this *Lent* I am forbid utterly to eat any Fish."

3. The same observation may be made of the poems *Sunday* and *The Priesthood*. In the former, there is a visible vacillation between the intellectually allegorical and the personally symbolic. Others may find different terms for these appearances, but anyone commenting on the poem has to search for ways to distinguish the figurative language in the first stanza and the last lines from the very different figure comparing the days of the week to a man's body. The fail-

ure of the latter seems not to be explicable by any method attributing our dislike to a change in the history of ideas. Nearly all of Herbert's "ideas" represent vanished ways of thinking: we must still explain why some figures succeed aesthetically and others not. In *The Priesthood* there is an uneasy ceremony of address ("Blest Order, which in power dost so excell . . ./Fain would I draw nigh,/Fain put thee on"), which sits ill with both sudden self-abasement ("I throw me at his feet") and with a detached epigrammatic vein ("The poore do by submission/What pride by opposition"). The same strain between feeling and form is felt in the closing lines of *The Flower.*

4. Fish, *Self-Consuming Artifacts,* ch. 3 *passim.* However, when I say that "the self is indistinguishable from God," I intend a diametrically opposite view from Fish's. He thinks Herbert's individuality is obliterated. I, on the contrary, think that God, who may earlier have seemed alien, remote, and judgmental, now seems *identical to Herbert,* in personality, response, and desire. God becomes Herbert; Herbert does not lose himself in God. The imagined movement is often downward, as grace "drops from above" or God "touches" and "owns" ("acknowledges") Herbert. But even when Herbert ascends to God (by a sunbeam or a silk twist), it is never to merge in mystical union. Herbert simply becomes a glorified version of his usual self, able to "glitter, and curle, and winde" better than before, till the sun's beams sing and his music shines. He does not become a sun and stop being a musician. If he is modified, so is the sun. The precious voice of the individual self may be joined in a consort, but it is never annihilated.

5. Fish, in *Self-Consuming Artifacts,* p. 209, remarks the assimilation of day and night, but attributes it to Herbert's wish to eliminate the distinction in order to *show* that God is "all love." Yet that was the proposition to be proved, rather than the fact being demonstrated. To understand the original violent distinction between day and night, we must invoke Herbert's self-hatred. Stein, in *Herbert,* p. 104, rightly sees the "frigidity" of the opening lines of the poem, but quite fails to understand the beauty of the rest, except for the last four lines, regarding stanzas two and three as "some standard motions of praise-and-lament" while serenely calling the opening of the last stanza "leisured triviality" summarizing "the general lack of concentration in the poem." I find the poem entirely beautiful, nowhere more so than in the contrast, in stanzas two and three, between the hectic diction of self-reproach and the gentle finality of God's reassuring words. As for Herbert's "musing" in the last stanza, it appears trivial only when its symbolic reference is not felt.

6. Such lines, though they seem unsuccessful to us, may have pleased some readers. Ryley, who in *Mr. Herbert's Temple* seems to admire all of Herbert, singles out these lines for special commendation: "She wipt his feet (after she had washed them with her tears) with her hair. here the Poet very Elegantly fancys this Action was Attended with 1. the feet of Christ Entangled, as Jewells, in her hair: & 2nly after Resolution to follow his Steps" (p. 592). Herbert himself may have found these lines an "elegant fancy," but it was the sort of fancy he disapproved of in his more sober moments.

7. In Donne's sonnet on Mary Magdalene, intended as a courtly tribute to Herbert's mother Magdalen Herbert, no mention is made of Mary Magdalene's "filth" (naturally). Donne, conflating Mary Magdalene with Mary the sister of Martha, dwells on how greatly she was graced in being once allowed to know "more than the Church did know,/The *Resurrection*" and in being allowed to "harbour *Christ* himself, a Guest." The courtesy of Donne's sonnet makes Herbert's dwelling on his mother's patron saint's "filth" the more disturbing. For Donne's sonnet, see *The Divine Poems,* ed. Helen Gardner (Oxford: Clarendon Press, 1952), p. 1.

8. Some of the same ambiguities of feeling occur in the very peculiar *Church rents and schismes,* with its equally incoherent combinations of a trampled rose, a worm with "many feet and hair," bitten shreds of rose petals, blood-letting, and eyes that lick up dew and then pour it out. Female symbols, even when used of the Church itself, were unmanageable for Herbert.

9. Rickey, *Utmost Art,* pp. 124-152.

10. Jonathan Cross, in an unpublished paper on Herbert's homiletic poetry written for a seminar in George Herbert at Boston University, pointed out this mimetic style.

11. Tuve, *Herbert,* pp. 159-160.

12. Tuve, in *Herbert,* p. 160, finds a parallel to the week-man in the Sarum Primer.

13. Stein, *Herbert,* pp. 156-169.

14. Robert Graves, *Poetic Unreason* (London: Cecil Palmer, 1925), pp. 57-63. Graves sees the poem, once the story proper begins in line 9, as a thinly disguised sexual fantasy of an essentially female Christ, who comes "undressing all the way," is attacked by "one/That ran upon him with a spear," and then displays the entered wound as "a bag" to receive what anyone may care to thrust inside. Herbert's tendency is certainly to see God, in any benevolent aspect, as more female than male; the usual female aspect is maternal, but Graves is probably right in seeing the female aspect here as sexual.

15. I am indebted in my discussion of *The Bag* to an unpublished paper on the poem written by my student Jonathan Cross at Boston University, which drew my attention to the mythological explanation as a generic base for the middle of the poem, and to the generally naïve Sunday-school formulation of the life of Jesus contained in the poem, including the suppression of any real pain in the death of Jesus.

16. Christ's ultimate generosity issues in the final pun on "any thing": in the penultimate stanza "any thing" is equivalent to the French "quelque chose," while in the last stanza it means "n'importe quoi."

6. CONFIGURATIONS AND CONSTELLATIONS: ETHICAL, DISCURSIVE, AND SPECULATIVE LYRICS

1. George Herbert Palmer, though his divisions of the poems into topical groups may be questioned, nevertheless chose two groups of such poems and

called them *Meditation* and *Bemerton Study,* respectively, in his two volumes. "The poems of these two Groups," says Palmer (*Herbert,* II, 207), "have an abstract and impersonal character distinguishing them from the rest of the work of this singularly personal writer. In them Herbert's favorite pronoun, *I,* rarely appears."

2. See, e.g., a poem by an imitator of Herbert, Nathaniel Wanley (1634–1680), called *The Invitation:* Wanley creates the same nostalgia for Mosaic familiarity with God and describes God's present estrangement from his creatures, but ends in a Herbertian "either-or" plea which if granted will restore the desired union:

> Lord, what unvalued pleasures crowned
> The times of old!
> When thou wert so familiar found,
> Those days were gold.
>
> When Abram wished, thou couldst afford
> With him to feast;
> When Lot but said, "Turn in, my Lord,"
> Thou wert his guest . . .
>
> O thou great ALPHA, King of Kings,
> Or bow to me,
> Or lend my soul seraphic wings
> To get to thee.

Nathaniel Wanley, *Poems,* ed. L. C. Martin (Oxford: Clarendon Press, 1928), pp. 9–10. Most of Wanley's poems do not resemble Herbert's so closely as Vaughan's, and a good number are written in iambic closed couplets.

3. *Affliction* (V), about the stability in storms of Noah's ark, I except from this "Mosaic" group because it was written earlier (unlike the others, it appears in *W*), and because it is far more willing than they, being written when Herbert was younger, to accept affliction, thinking it perhaps temporary: "Affliction then is ours;/We are the trees, whom shaking fastens more." The later poems in the group are written with more exhaustion and less bravado.

4. Tuve, in *Herbert,* pp. 175–180, argues that "Joyes coat" is, as the commentators find Joseph's coat to be, "humanitas Christi." She wishes to dismiss Hutchinson's interpretation of the "joy" and the "relief" as the capacity to sing in grief. Yet one interpretation does not exclude the other. Agreeing as I do with Tuve that a resolution based solely on verse-making is unlikely in a poet so religious as Herbert, I accept her criticism of Hutchinson's superficiality. Nevertheless, if the *reason* that Herbert can sing is that Christ shared our anguish, that joy nevertheless issues in song, which gives "relief."

5. Summers, *Herbert,* pp. 129–135.

6. Yvor Winters, *Primitivism and Decadence: A Study of American Experimental Poetry* (New York: Arrow Editions, 1937), p. 10.

7. Stein, *Herbert*, pp. 37–43, in a careful analysis of Herbert's time and time-lessness, identification and detachment, exerted imaginativeness and quiet insight, shows Herbert's art throughout the poem. I am here more concerned with it as a bridge between entirely conventional speculative or intellectual poems and the later poems of personal restatement of religious truths.

7. FRUIT AND ORDER: FORMAL PATTERNS

1. Stein, *Herbert*, p. 154.
2. Stein, *Herbert*, pp. 148–149.
3. I do not treat here certain poems (e.g., *Sinne's round, The Wreath, Trinitie Sunday, Clasping of hands,* or *Aaron*) which either have received adequate commentary in respect to their formal patterning or which sufficiently demonstrate their own form. *Coloss. 3.3* is admirably treated in Fish, *Self-Consuming Artifacts,* pp. 203–206. Although Fish's concern is with Herbert's manipulation of the reader, his exposition of the structural patterns in the poem demonstrates Herbert's care for all elements of his form.
4. Stein, *Herbert*, p. 146.
5. Palmer, *Herbert*, II, 106.
6. Rickey, *Utmost Art*, p. 137.
7. Palmer, in *Herbert*, II, 310, writing on the word "grasse," asks: "Can Herbert have intended this word to take the place of the *grace* which appears in the third line of all the other stanzas except the last?" The speculation is justified, and we may conjecture that Herbert's first plan *was* to put "grace" in line 3 throughout. His willingness to jettison "plan" when it interfered with truth or with consistency of imagery (as here) is one of his most attractive qualities, since we know how dear the element of "plan" was to him. Wesley, in adapting this poem (*Poetical Works,* I, 40), seems not to have perceived the plan by which "grasse" substitutes for "grace," and writes instead, "The dew for which my spirit calls." Cf. the similar discarding of the plan for continued rhymes in "-ose" in Herbert's poem *The Rose*.
8. Herbert may also have had in mind Zechariah 9:11: "As for thee also, by the blood of thy covenant I have sent forth thy prisoners out of the pit wherein is no water."
9. Palmer, *Herbert*, I, 148.
10. Samuel Speed, in *Prison-Pietie* (1677) used in his poem *The Petition* the triplets "stare," "tare," "are"; "brought," "rought" (for "wrought"), "ought"; and "chill," "hill," "ill."
11. Tuve, in *Allegorical Imagery,* pp. 108–109, quotes the sort of passage which, in various medieval forms, underlies a poem like *Paradise:* "The good man or woman [is figured] as a 'fair garden full of grene and of faire trees and of good fruyt,' planted by the great gardener. The 'graffes' in it are . . . vertues . . . 'Goddes sone, that is the verrey sunne bi his vertue and brigtnesse,' makes them grow; this 'paradis rigt delitable' in 'the herte' is the image of the other: '. . . rigt as God sett ertheli paradis ful of goode trees and fruygt, and in the

myddel sett the tree of lif . . . Rigt so doth gostly to the herte the goode gardyner, that is God the fadre, for he sett the tree of vertue and in the myddel the tree of lif, that is Ihesu Crist.' (Quoted from the fourth tractate of the *Somme le roi,* printed in EETS, vol. 217 as *The Book of Vices and Virtues*)."

12. Psychoanalytic interpretation might see this poem as a masochistic acquiescence in castration: to accept castration is to be reconciled with the father by no longer possessing a potential rival masculine member. The masochistic element in Herbert's character is scarcely to be doubted. However, the larger issue of suffering as a means to wisdom (even if based on an unconscious castration imagery) contradicts a restrictedly masochistic interpretation. Because suffering (of whatever species, including castration) involves mutilation of the self, we cannot consciously will it. We can only will its effects, as Herbert does here, and thus after the fact accept what has occurred to enlighten us.

13. Summers, in *Herbert,* also makes this point and adds, rightly, that "the cutting away of the fruitless branches images the final 'cutting away' of the body and the release of the soul at death" (p. 139).

14. The examples of echo poems and echo rhymes quoted are taken *passim* from Elbridge Colby, *The Echo-Device in Literature* (New York: New York Public Library, 1920).

8. CONFLICTS PICTURED

1. Thus, Rosemond Tuve is entirely right in saying in "George Herbert and *Caritas," Journal of the Warburg and Courtauld Institute* 22 (1959): 303–331, that "self-abasement is not the note of his poetry" (p. 317). But since Tuve's concern is chiefly with Herbert's best poetry, she does not need to point out Herbert's false starts, of which self-abasement was one.

2. See the poems *Nature, The Sinner, Repentance, Love* (II), *The Temper* (I), *The Windows, Christmas,* and *Miserie.*

3. Tuve, "George Herbert and *Caritas,"* p. 313n.

4. Hopkins may have learned this technique too from Herbert, who uses it in *Bitter-sweet* for his own actions. Gods' actions in the poem are incomprehensible and go from *bad to* GOOD or the reverse with no consistency, while Herbert's own actions go without deviation from *bad to* GOOD (italics and capitals mine):

> Ah my DEARE *angrie* Lord,
> Since thou dost LOVE, yet *strike;*
> *Cast down,* yet HELP afford;
> Sure I will do the like.

> I will *complain,* yet PRAISE;
> I will *bewail,* APPROVE:
> And all my *sowre*-SWEET dayes
> I will *lament,* and LOVE.

Even the graphic representations I use here are too coarse for Herbert's intent. "Complain" implies some criticism of God, perhaps, while "bewail" does not; as for "lament," it is so often used of one's own faults, as is "bewail," that by the end Herbert's actions do not, like God's, seem contrastive, but rather associative, an impression reinforced by the alliteration of "lament" and "love" (as Hopkins too alliterated his contrastive elements—"lightning and love," "winter and warm" —to insist on their fundamental identity).

5. Ryley (Mr. Herbert's Temple, pp. 217–220), with whom I tend to agree, views the star as a "good motion" (Artillerie) or, as he puts it, "grace," and he regards the passage of the poem as one from grace to glory, where the soul finds its final resting place. Palmer, however (Herbert, II, 364), says that "this strange poem . . . discusses [Herbert's] divine call," an interpretation resting in part on what seems to be Palmer's gratuitous introduction of Isaiah's coal of fire and in part on his failure to realize that Herbert's "Saviour" is here visualized as the Sun (Son) surrounded by sunbeams. The star here is, one might say, a condensed sunbeam by which Herbert can "climbe to [God]" (Mattens).

6. The wish to represent the Trinity by the combination of light, motion, and heat may account for Herbert's conversion of a sunbeam (static, and warm rather than fiery) into a shooting star.

7. Palmer, Herbert, III, 330.

8. Palmer, Herbert, III, 201.

9. Herbert is so fragmented in this poem that he could not decide, literally, which portion of himself was having the experience described in it. He wrote the penultimate line three times:

> O cheer and tune my heartlesse breast,
> Deferre no time;
> That so thy favours granting my request,
> They and my heart (W)
> soul (W)
> minde may chime,
> And mend my ryme.

10. Rosalie Colie links this "aspiration to muteness" (a phrase borrowed from D. G. James) to Herbert's wish to be a child, in-fans, speechless. See her Paradoxia Epidemica (Princeton University Press, 1966), p. 201.

11. Stein, Herbert, p. 141 n.

12. Stein, Herber*, p. 140.

13. Helen Gardner, in her recent anthologies The Oxford Book of English Verse and A Book of Religious Verse (Oxford: Clarendon Press, 1973), omits The Elixir from both and Vertue from the latter. Her preference seems to be for the more overtly Donne-like passionate poetry. Helen White, however, says categorically in The Metaphysical Poets, p. 189, that The Elixir is "one of the most beautiful and meaningful of all Herbert's poems," adding that "most people asked to pick out a typical Herbert poem would probably choose this one.

Certainly it could not be left out of any list of the half dozen universal favorites."

14. One charm in these lines is Herbert's persistent transformation of the pentameter into a four-beat two-step:

> Lóve bade me wélcome: but my sóul drew báck.
>
> But quíck-ey'd Lóve, obsérving me grow sláck
>
> A guést, I ánswer'd, wórthy to be hére
>
> Lóve took my hánd, and smíling did replý.

As Douglas Bush says in *English Poetry* (New York: Oxford University Press, 1952), p. 62: "Bountiful love on the one side, guilty reluctance on the other, are conveyed not only in words and implications but in quick and positive, hovering and broken rhythms."

Index of Titles

Index of First Lines